Of Wilderness and Wolves

A BUR OAK BOOK

Holly Carver, series editor

Of Wilderness and
WOLVES

by Paul L. Errington

EDITED AND WITH AN INTRODUCTION BY
MATTHEW WYNN SIVILS

ILLUSTRATIONS BY
CHARLES W. SCHWARTZ

University of Iowa Press, Iowa City

© University of Iowa Press, Iowa City 52242
Copyright © 2015 by the University of Iowa Press
www.uiowapress.org
Printed in the United States of America

Design by Erin Kirk New

The University of Iowa Press is a member of Green Press
Initiative and is committed to preserving natural resources.

Printed on acid-free paper

ISBN 978-1-60938-365-7 (pbk)
ISBN 978-1-60938-366-4 (ebk)

Library of Congress Cataloging-in-Publication Data
is on file at the Library of Congress

Contents

Acknowledgments

I must first thank the late Carolyn Storm Errington, who edited her husband's manuscripts during his life, who shepherded many of those manuscripts into print after his death, and who—before her own passing—provided for the continuation of Paul L. Errington's intellectual legacy. Without her foresight, this book would not exist. Paul and Carolyn's sons, Peter and Frederick Errington, along with Frederick's wife, Deborah Gewertz, have each played an important part in the creation of this volume, and I am deeply grateful for their help.

For their support of this project, as well as for their often sage advice, I thank the staff of the University of Iowa Press, particularly Holly Carver and James McCoy, who, in publishing this book, have aided in the promotion and preservation of Errington's work. I also owe a great debt to the librarians and archivists of the Iowa State University Library Department of Special Collections and to the staff of the State Historical Society of Missouri, especially Anne E. Cox, who helped me navigate their Charles W. Schwartz collection. I likewise thank my former graduate students, John Linstrom and Lance Sacknoff, for their help transcribing the text, and I thank Iowa State University's College of Liberal Arts and Sciences for supplying the grant that allowed me to pay them for their work.

Lastly, for their patience and encouragement, I thank my wife, Alisa, and our children, Allston and Freya.

Introduction

MATTHEW WYNN SIVILS

Born on June 14, 1902, Paul Lester Errington grew up in rural Brookings County in east-central South Dakota. His mother's family owned a farm bordering Lake Tetonkaha, and the wetland environment proved ideal for the development of the fledgling naturalist. As Errington chronicles in his autobiography, *The Red Gods Call*, he spent much of his youth enjoying the outdoors, but at age eight he was stricken with polio. The disease damaged his legs and seriously hindered his ability to walk. Rather than resigning himself to the effects of the disease, Errington displayed the self-discipline and strong will that served him well throughout his life. Deciding to overcome the effects of polio and improve his marksmanship at the same time, he began an exhausting regimen of long walks with a tireless friend named Kirk Mears. The older Mears was already an excellent shot, and the two boys, who often took their rifles along, would travel as much as thirty miles a day, stopping only to conduct shooting contests before moving on. "Gradually," wrote Errington, "I found I had less and less fatigue to hide," and "Gradually, too, I gained on him in the shooting."[1]

With most of his mobility restored, Errington continued his project of becoming an expert outdoorsman. He found inspiration not only in his rural South Dakota surroundings, but also at the Brookings County Library, where, as he writes, "I spent almost every evening . . . and usually took home a book. My favorite subjects were prehistoric man and ancient history, Spartan ways of physical training, exploits of the Vikings and other sea rovers, Indian fighting and pioneering, and the rawest of raw Nature that I could find." He was predictably fond of books by writers such as Ernest Thompson Seton, Jack London, and Charles G.D. Roberts, who regaled their readers with tales of wilderness adventures and wild animals. These stories fired his will to, as he put it, "live in the wilderness as a wild creature myself, as a predator along with the mink, the lynx, the bear, and the wolf." By the time he had turned thirteen he had firmly decided to become a professional trapper, even if he initially kept the news from his mother and stepfather, both of whom hoped he would "go to college and study to become a professor."[2] While his family put an end to his plan of quitting school to live in the wilderness, they were otherwise supportive. They regularly allowed him to go on hunting and trapping trips, even letting him spend an entire December on a trapping excursion on their land near Lake Tetonkaha, with the agreement that he clear his absence with his teachers and make up his homework. For Errington, these often-solitary forays into the wild were another kind of education. As arduous as these trips were, he saw them as practice for far more demanding expeditions to come.

Upon finishing high school, Errington felt he was finally ready to test himself against a wilderness more challenging, more unforgiving, than anything he had experienced before. Throughout his formative years of reading adventure tales and camping under rural South Dakota skies, he had wanted to trap professionally in the northern wilds. Now he had the ability and the freedom to do so, and he knew just the place to go: the Big Bog wilderness in northern Minnesota. Even now, this area remains one of the harshest in the continental United States, but in 1920 when Errington was there, it was a remarkably wild place, with scarcely touched white cedar swamps and a proliferation of wildlife. It was an expanse of natural majesty beyond anything he had yet known, and the seven months he stayed there—living off the land, surviving the extreme cold (sometimes 40 to 50 below), and running lengthy trap lines along a frozen Tamarack River—amounted to one of his most foundational experiences, one that stayed with him for the rest of his life. Decades later, Errington would write, "For the most part, memories are what the Big Bog paid off in: memories of northern terrain, of cold, of deep-snow traplines, of wilderness wild creatures—whether of squalling lynx or a white-footed mouse that cached prune pits in my footwear."[3] He wrote about his experiences in the Big Bog many times, and one of his best accounts is found in chapter 7 of this book, in which he recalls, "At night, the ice might boom and the tree trunks pop; a wolf howl carried well in the brittle air."

For the next few years, Errington continued trapping, but mostly stayed close to home to help with the family farm. In 1924, he enrolled at South Dakota State College (now South Dakota State University), where he began to develop as a biologist and as a writer. He proved a promising student, and four years later—having secured a three-year fellowship funded jointly by the Sporting Arms and Ammunition Manufacturer's Institute and the U.S. Biological Survey—he began his graduate studies at the University of Wisconsin. Bolstered by his lifetime as a serious outdoorsman, Errington found in the academic study of biology a calling worthy of his talents, and he made a strong impression on his professors. One of them, A.W. Schorger, would later write, "Only a brief acquaintance with Paul was necessary to reveal his singleness of purpose and intense interest in his investigations."[4]

Early in his doctoral program, Errington struck up a friendship with a soon-to-be hired faculty member named Aldo Leopold. It was the start of a lifelong professional friendship. Years later, in 1948, Errington would be asked to write the legendary ecologist's obituary for the *Journal of Wildlife Management*, in which he offers a window into their early relationship: "I was never formally his student. Informally, I moved in on him, his home, and his library for hours at a stretch, talking 'shop' or anything else. I wasn't a restful satellite and sometimes argued in an evening until neither of us could sleep long after going to bed, but he was gracious toward me and patient with my ex-trapper's social deficiencies."[5] Leopold thought highly of Errington as well. In Leopold's landmark book on wildlife ecology, *Game Management*, he would cite young Errington's research no fewer than thirty times. And Errington's research was already making an impact on the field in many other venues. During his graduate studies, he published twenty single-authored articles in both scientific and popular wildlife magazines, a remarkable amount even by today's standards.

After graduating in 1932, Errington joined the research faculty of Iowa State College (now Iowa State University), the institution where he would work for the rest of his life. He quickly became a major force in the development of the emerging discipline of wildlife ecology, spending decades conducting research upon the very marshland ecosystems he loved as a young trapper. Errington was particularly interested in the intricacies of predation as it played out upon the marshland stage, especially in the population dynamics of the muskrat. Errington's experience as a trapper told him that the conventional understanding of predation—one in which predators sometimes overhunt their prey—was misguided. Drawing upon his research on the interactions between muskrats and minks, he revolutionized our understanding of predator/prey dynamics, arguing that a predator could harvest its prey only to a certain point before the expense of energy became too high for it to bother with an increasingly elusive catch. He called this idea "the theory of the threshold of security," and it refuted the old belief that predators should be eliminated because they threatened the extinction of game animals such as deer. Errington, the trapper turned wildlife biologist, had reshaped the way ecologists thought about one of the major problems in wildlife ecology.[6]

By the end of the 1940s, Errington had become one of the most influential biologists of the twentieth century, but he also wanted to reach a popular audience. As a younger man, he had written several short stories with the aim of becoming a fiction writer. "I wrote and wrote—sometimes late into an evening—sitting on the side of a bed, with lantern or lamp on one wooden shotgun shell case in front of me and the manuscript on another."[7] Despite his early ambitions, he eventually recognized that his stories were the work of a beginner: "When I ultimately realized that my manuscripts were awful, I destroyed them with a greater feeling of accomplishment than their creation had given me."[8] Decades later, in the early 1950s, the man who had started out as a trapper only to become an internationally famous wildlife biologist returned to his goal of writing for a readership beyond that of the academic journals. He was particularly impressed with how Aldo Leopold's nature writing, especially *A Sand County Almanac* (1947), had resonated with the general public. Errington set out to write a similar book based upon his deep love and knowledge of the oft-misunderstood marshland ecosystem. The timing was right for Errington to return to the task of writing for popular consumption. He had a model in Leopold's book, he had become a much more sophisticated writer, and—above all—he had the help of his wife, Carolyn, who served as the perfect sounding board and editor. The resulting book, *Of Men and Marshes*, was published by Macmillan in 1957, and while it apparently did not sell well, it was met with strong critical praise. A review in *The New Yorker* states, "He speaks to us here . . . not as a scientist but as a man and a human—his method is to show us a marsh as a home, to escort us through it in the different seasons of the year, and let us see for ourselves the beauty and wonder that are there. A telling and moving experience."[9] While writing *Of Men and Marshes*, Errington also began work on other manuscripts, including one about his experience with another misunderstood denizen of the natural world, the wolf.

On August 30, 1961, he sent his manuscript of *Of Wilderness and Wolves* to Cecil Scott, a senior editor at Macmillan. Errington had worked on this manuscript for at least the better part of a decade, and it was—as had been *Of Men and Marshes*—unapologetically inspired by Aldo Leopold's *A Sand County Almanac*. It was also, true to most of Errington's professional efforts, a decidedly ambitious undertaking. Errington strove to share both his considerable scientific knowledge and his more philosophical ideas about nature with a wide audience, one that he believed was in need of a strong dose of ecological reality. In his cover letter to Scott, Errington shared some of his hopes for the book: "Although I wrote it as a possible companion piece to *Of Men and Marshes*, I did have in mind a wider group of readers than those primarily interested in outdoor subjects. It was intended to be an outdoor book, but I hoped that it also would have a literary and philosophical appeal for discriminating readers rather generally."[10]

In *Of Wilderness and Wolves*, Errington has much to say, and no particular wish to sugar coat matters, about humanity's dysfunctional relationship with the natural world, particularly with large predators like the wolf: "Man needs to do some growing up. This need is manifested, among other ways, by the emotional unreason he tends to show toward the behavior of wild creatures. The immoderations and inconsistencies in his attitude toward wolves or other predatory or competing species are particularly revealing of lack of maturity." He goes on to isolate several lessons he hopes to impress upon his readership:

I shall simply express my misgivings concerning man's continued wastage of the natural values of which we have little left to waste, his continued misappraisals of biological relationships that should no longer be subject to so much misappraisal, his continued imputation of moral evil where moral evil does not exist, and his continued punishment of wild animals for being what they are, for being wild and for living in the only ways that they could be expected to live.

It is a deservedly critical take on mankind's abusive and ignorant mismanagement of our natural resources. But, overall, his book does not scold. Rather, it presents a level-headed argument that relates the results of his own research and that of his colleagues. Keeping his layperson audience in mind, he also shares anecdotes drawn from his lifetime of experience in the wilderness, as well as comparable accounts from others. Weaving these sources of wilderness knowledge together, Errington offers a series of instructive and at times profound insights about how humanity should rethink, revalue, and preserve our increasingly threatened natural world.

But for whatever reason, Macmillan seemed reluctant to publish Errington's manuscript. Between August 30, 1961 and July 9, 1962, Macmillan editor Cecil Scott sent Errington at least eight letters about the manuscript, often nearly sending him a publishing contract, only to back away from or delay that decision, and usually without any clear reason for his misgivings. Matters had started out well enough, but soon became stalled. On October 4, 1961, Scott sent a letter that boded well for the manuscript's future at Macmillan. He states that he and his assistant read the manuscript and they "were much impressed with it." Scott writes "To confirm our feelings, we have approached our best outside reader with a request that he, too, read and report on the manuscript. Unfortunately, he was about to depart for a month abroad, and asked that we hold it here for him until the end of October."[11] Scott contacted Errington again on December 28, 1961, with the good news that "the report is now in (incidentally, it is a good one) and I should be writing to you about our final decision within the next ten days to two weeks."[12] The next known letter in their exchange appeared two months later on

March 1, 1962, when Scott wrote to say he had reread the manuscript and wanted a justification for the inclusion of chapter 10 and to ask if Errington might include something in the epilogue "about yourself, the author, who you are, why you wrote the book, and what you hope it will accomplish."[13] The letter does not mention a contract, and Scott seems to have backed away from his earlier enthusiasm.

Given the supposedly positive reviewer report, Macmillan's, or at least Scott's, reluctance to proceed with a contract is perplexing. His request that Errington include in his epilogue some discussion of himself makes even less sense because his manuscript contains considerable biographical detail (especially in chapters 1, 7, 8, 11, and 12). Plus, in the months since he first submitted the manuscript, Errington had become even more of a celebrity, and not just among the scientific crowd. In the December 22, 1961, special double issue of *Life Magazine* devoted to "Our Splendid Outdoors," Errington was featured as one of the top ten naturalists of his day. The brief article, entitled "A New Elite of American Naturalists: Heirs of a Great Tradition," lists Errington first. Along with a picture of him paddling his canoe in an Iowa marsh (a photo taken by the famed Alfred Eisenstaedt), the article conveys him as "A gentle outdoorsman with the eyes of an eagle, Errington specializes in the fauna and flora of marshes. He has studied muskrats so closely that his knuckles are scarred from their teeth. Once he almost died from a muskrat disease."[14] Following him in the list are Edwin Way Teale; Roger Tory Peterson; Richard H. Pough; Sigurd Olson; Rachel Carson; H. Albert Hochbaum; the Murie brothers, Adolph and Olaus; and Joseph Wood Krutch. The *Life* article had indeed placed Errington in esteemed company, and he was fairly well acquainted with at least three of the members of the group. The multitalented H. Albert Hochbaum was Errington's friend and had even illustrated *Of Men and Marshes*, Sigurd Olson's work is mentioned a couple of times in the *Of Wilderness and Wolves* text, and Adolph Murie's work with wolves features several times throughout the text. (In fact, Errington expressly thanks Murie in the preface for his input on the manuscript.) Thus Errington was not only one of *Life Magazine*'s "elite," he was well connected to those within that group. From a publishing point of view, it would have made good sense to capitalize on the timely popularity of Errington and the work of American naturalists in general, which the *Life* article had furthered, but there is no indication in their correspondence that Scott was even aware of this article, as unlikely as that would seem. Yet, even after he had addressed Scott's concern about biographical details and provided a solid case for the inclusion of the Scandinavian-focused tenth chapter ("because I thought that it added some global balance to the treatment of man-wolf-wilderness relationships over the northern hemisphere"), Macmillan did not issue a contract.[15]

On May 10, 1962, Scott wrote to Errington to say that he now agreed that chapter 10 should be retained, and that while he now was unsure about the value of chapters 6 and 12, he would leave it to Errington's judgment whether they should be included or not. Scott ends by writing, "I have recommended a contract offer to our Contract Committee and I should be sending you the details (if they pass it as I fully expect they will) in the course of the next few days. You have been most patient with me. My excuse is that I like to be absolutely sure before going ahead. As I have written earlier in this letter, I like your book extremely. In my opinion, it will be a most honorable addition to our list." While ostensibly waiting for Macmillan to process the contract request, Scott also asked that Errington supply at least sixteen photographs "of wolf tracks, of wolves, etc., etc."[16] Errington, however, really wanted the talented wildlife artist, Charles W. Schwartz, to illustrate the book. After speaking with Errington about the project, Schwartz was keen on the idea and had even begun some provisional work on the illustrations.[17] Errington mentioned Schwartz's work to Scott, including the fact that Schwartz—who by that point had made a name for himself as a naturalist, wildlife documentary filmmaker, and wildlife artist—had illustrated both Aldo Leopold's *A Sand County Almanac* and *Round River*.[18]

Strangely for an editor in charge of Macmillan's outdoor books, Scott responded that he did not know Schwartz's work and asked Errington to send him some samples of his drawings. Scott admitted that he was reluctant to use anything other than photographs because he felt "almost all successful books on animals today seem to be illustrated by photographs, the reason being, I suppose that the reader feels that he gains a truer picture of the animals discussed."[19] Errington asked Schwartz for some samples of his artwork to show Scott, and Schwartz sent an impressive portfolio of drawings, including dozens of sketches from his copiously illustrated *The Wild Mammals of Missouri*, as well as copies of illustrations placed in other publications. He even sent a pair of drawings he had already made expressly for *Of Wilderness and Wolves* (which could not be located). For payment, Schwartz asked only $40 per image, which Scott admitted was "very reasonable,"[20] but in the end Macmillan's editor insisted he wanted photographs, stating that "in today's market the reader of a book such as yours prefers first rate photography to any other kind of illustration."[21] Scott even suggested that Hochbaum's *Of Men and Marshes* illustrations had contributed to the book's lackluster sales: "if we had used in your OF MEN AND MARSHES photographs rather than these sensitive drawings, we would have been considerably more successful."[22]

Errington, who was anxious to receive a contract, told Scott he would be happy to use photographs of wolves instead of drawings, and could obtain them easily. By July 2, he mailed Scott a new draft of chapter 12, as well as a sample of wolf photographs taken by Douglas Pimlott and Adolph Stebler.[23] On that same day, Errington sent a letter to Charles W. Schwartz bemoaning the fact that Macmillan had rejected his drawings in favor of photographs. But Errington was still keen to work with Schwartz in the future, and wrote that once he had secured a publisher for his other manuscript in progress, *Of Predation and Life*, he would recommend that Schwartz illustrate the book.[24]

Seven days later, Cecil Scott wrote apparently his last letter to Paul Errington. In it he promised to read the newly revised chapter 12, to think more about Errington's request for further suggestions for revision, and to get back with him "around the middle of the month."[25] Weeks and then months passed. Still Errington heard nothing from Macmillan. Finally, on October 13, he sent Scott a letter filled with thinly veiled frustration: "I have been reluctant to press you for a decision on *Of Wilderness and Wolves*, for I think I am coming to learn something of the problems of publishers and the delays and interruptions that seem always to be complicating plans." He went on to explain that a couple of the manuscript's chapters had attracted "prepublication prospects" with editors, including one at a "national magazine." He writes, "I really need to know where the manuscript stands with you before I can go ahead with inquiries" about publishing chapters individually in those magazines. He ends the letter by holding out hope that they will "come to a favorable agreement on the manuscript."[26] It was not to be. Some time later, Carolyn Errington wrote a note to her literary agent and friend, Carol H. Woodward (who had worked at Macmillan and had helped with the publication of *Of Men and Marshes*): "Carol: There was no response to this letter from Macmillan. C.S.E."[27] It would seem that Scott, who on May 10 of that year had high praise for the manuscript ("I like your book extremely. In my opinion, it will be a most honorable addition to our list"), had backed away from his earlier endorsement.[28]

Three weeks later, on November 5, 1962, after undergoing a surgical procedure related to his ongoing battle with cancer, Paul Errington suffered an embolism and died. While dealing with the loss of her husband, Carolyn resolved to see his work published. She was still hopeful that Macmillan would pick up the book. She wanted to see it in print because of its own merits, but also because it would be a reminder of her meaningful relationship with Paul. In a December 18 letter to her family, Carolyn wrote, "You will discover when *Of Wilderness and Wolves* is published that the dedication is to me. When Paul first told me of his intention to dedicate this book to me I urged him not to on the ground that I did not need any public recognition of this sort; it was enough for me to know his feelings."[29] On the same day, she sent another letter to Carol H. Woodward: "I hope that Macmillan will publish Paul's literary and philosophic book, *Of Wilderness and Wolves*. It was submitted over a year ago and negotiations were well along toward acceptance of it when we last (last summer) heard from Mr. Cecil Scott."[30] But there were no letters from Macmillan, and a month later she wrote to Scott informing him of her husband's death, saying that "Concerning *Of Wilderness and Wolves*: I wonder if I may please have either an acceptance or a rejection from your company very soon."[31] Scott's assistant replied with condolences and told Carolyn that Scott was "in Europe at the moment, on business" and would return "early in February."[32]

Finally, on February 20, Scott wrote to Carolyn. He apologized for not getting back to her sooner, and expressed his sympathies for her loss: "I am very sad indeed to hear of Dr. Errington's death. . . . I do know both from his writing and from his correspondence with me that Dr. Errington was a man of good will, a man with things to say which were important and lasting. . . ." In closing he asked for another "week or ten days" to consider the manuscript before making his final decision.[33] Any eventual rejection letter from Scott is absent from the Errington archives, but years later, in a 1967 cover letter to the editor of Iowa State University Press, Carolyn summarized Macmillan's apparent rationale for rejecting the book: "Mr. Scott liked the manuscript and had all but offered a publishing contract when Paul died in November 1962; then, several months later he rejected the manuscript because he would not have Paul to work with on some revision he thought necessary."[34]

With the manuscript no longer under consideration at Macmillan, Carolyn decided to employ the services of Carol H. Woodward, who spent the next five years submitting the manuscript to top publishers, including Dutton, the University of California Press, Harper and Row, Knopf, and Houghton Mifflin, but they all demurred, often praising the manuscript as they declined. In 1967, Woodward returned the manuscript for *Of Wilderness and Wolves* to Carolyn Errington with a kind letter saying that, despite much interest on the part of various publishers, she had been unable to place the book. Woodward suggested that Carolyn, as she had done with *Of Predation and Life* (which had required polish after Errington's death), revise the *Of Wilderness and Wolves* manuscript and try again. "Perhaps," writes Woodward, "after you have gone over it with your competent pencil, it will be easier to place it. . . . Whatever is done with it (and I feel strongly that it is worth publishing), I do hope to keep in touch with you."[35] Carolyn did not, however, engage in any extensive revisions. Instead—perhaps hoping that the press's recent publication of *Of Predation and Life* would bode well for the wolf book—she sent it to Iowa State University Press in December of 1967, but they too declined to see it through. By that point it had been over five years since Errington's death, and over six since he had first submitted the manuscript to Macmillan. Carolyn—in an effort finally to have Paul's ideas about wolves and conservation placed before the public—submitted portions of the manuscript for magazine publication. She placed chapter 12 "Of Man and Modernity" in the winter 1968 issue of *Atlantic Naturalist*. The titular ninth chapter, "Of Wilderness and Wolves," was published in two parts in the autumn 1969 and winter 1970–1971 issues of *The Living Wilderness*.[36] After that, Carolyn placed the well-traveled manuscript into her files and moved on. Over twenty years later, in her 1987 collection of Errington's work, entitled *A Question of Values* (Iowa State University Press, 1987), she reprinted those two chapters, along with a much shortened version of the eleventh chapter: "Of Modernity and Wolves and A Wolf Named Dagwood." The rest of Errington's manuscript, one of the most progressive works of nature writing of the twentieth century, would not see print until this edition.

The trouble Paul and Carolyn Errington had in placing this book raises the question of how a manuscript by one of the nation's foremost wildlife ecologists—on the exciting topic of wolves no less—could fare so poorly when submitted for publication. This reluctance on the part of various presses to publish *Of Wilderness and Wolves* probably stemmed from several factors related to the book's subject matter and to its presentation of that information. While books sympathetic to the plight of wolves have since become common, in the early 1960s, when Errington submitted his manuscript to Macmillan, he was in relatively uncharted territory. Sympathetic nonfiction portrayals of wolves had appeared from time to time, notably in Adolph Murie's landmark study of wolves in Alaska, *The Wolves of Mount McKinley* (1944), and in Leopold's famous chapter, "Thinking Like a Mountain," from *A Sand County Almanac* (in which he describes his conservationist epiphany after killing a wolf). But no one had written a book-length work of environmental philosophy, backed by scientific study and individual experience, aimed at a general readership. Errington asks his readers to reappraise our culturally ingrained hatred of the wolf, while also offering some harsh (if deserved) criticism of our wasteful and shortsighted environmental practices. The combination might have seemed, at least to editors, as something of a bitter pill. The lackluster sales of Errington's *Of Men and Marshes* probably also contributed to the reluctance editors felt at taking on what Errington saw as something of a sequel to that book.

In the end, however, *Of Wilderness and Wolves* was mostly a victim of multiple instances of bad timing. In June of 1962, about a month after Cecil Scott wrote to Errington to say, "I like your book extremely . . . it will be a most honorable addition to our list," *The New Yorker* published the first of three prepublication installments of Rachel Carson's *Silent Spring*. These installments ignited a firestorm of controversy sparked by the chemical industry, which threatened lawsuits against *The New Yorker* and Houghton Mifflin, which published the book in its entirety in September of 1962. Far less incendiary than Carson's masterpiece, Errington's book is nonetheless highly critical of what he viewed as our backward view of the natural world. One such moment occurs in chapter 4 (entitled "Of Wolves, Reindeer, Caribou, and Human Mistakes"), where he writes that humanity "has acquired modern weapons and transportation to implement a Stone-Age psychology, I do not think that the resulting combination of power and irresponsibility has survival value." With the Carson controversy heating up at the time Errington's manuscript was under consideration at Macmillan, Scott may have wanted a rosier celebration of the natural world, one that did not irritate people with unpleasant realities, or possibly raise the ire of some powerful and litigious corporate entity. The relationship between the publication of Carson's *Silent Spring* with Macmillan's seeming loss of interest in the Errington manuscript may be coincidental, but the fact remains that Scott would never again praise the manuscript as highly as he had in May of 1962, a month before the start of the Carson controversy.

On the surface, Errington's death may seem to have most doomed publication of *Of Wilderness and Wolves*, and as Carolyn noted, Scott apparently claimed to have rejected the book "because he would not have Paul to work with on some revision he thought necessary."[37] Macmillan had, however, repeatedly delayed making any decision on the manuscript well before his untimely death, and Errington, as his final letter to Scott indicates, had grown frustrated with Macmillan's prevarication. As Carolyn would prove again and again in bringing to fruition the less polished manuscripts as *Of Predation and Life* and *The Red Gods Call* (as well as placing some of his shorter pieces in magazines), she was a fully capable editor and literary champion.

Yet there was still another development that hampered Carolyn's efforts to publish *Of Wilderness and Wolves*: the 1963 publication of Farley Mowat's bestselling book *Never Cry Wolf*. In a September 17, 1963, rejection letter sent to Carolyn's agent Carol H. Woodward, Houghton Mifflin's editor Paul Brooks (who had served as Rachel Carson's editor and who was an acclaimed nature writer himself) wrote:

> I wish I could say that I thought we could publish it successfully. Personally, I was enormously interested in it. . . . I know something of the criminal and misunderstood persecution of wolves that is still going on, and I am in favor of the greatest possible circulation of Dr. Errington's views.
>
> Unfortunately, we find ourselves faced with two almost insurmountable hurdles. The first of which is the fact that this is a group of essays rather than a continuous narrative, and I don't think the literary quality is quite high enough to make such a collection successful in book form. The second is the immanent publication of an enormously readable book dealing at first hand with the same subject, Farley Mowat's NEVER CRY WOLF, which is about to appear—or maybe has just appeared—on the Atlantic-Little, Brown list."[38]

Brooks's concerns about the marketability of a book of essays seem odd given that so many of the best works of mid-twentieth-century nature writing are collections of essays, including Leopold's *A Sand County Almanac* and much of Carson's work. And, while Errington's writing is sometimes less than polished, it is more than redeemed by passages of beautiful and insightful prose. Rather, it would seem—as Brooks indicates—that the publication of Mowat's *Never Cry Wolf* scared publishers away from any book resembling that bestseller. That Mowat's book would undermine the fate of Errington's is particularly unfortunate because the books are so very different. As is now well known among environmental literary critics, *Never Cry Wolf* is anything but credible, and it has in recent years become known as largely a work of fiction, one that has arguably done a disservice to wolves by presenting them in an unrealistic and anthropomorphized manner.[39]

Errington, on the other hand, never substituted sensationalism for veracity. He always adhered to fact. He was truthful in presenting his own experiences and in portraying wolves, even when that presentation rejects the incredible for the everyday. And while Errington, especially as a youth, was fond of the exciting stories of the so-called nature-fakers, such as Ernest Thomas Seton and Jack London, he realized that such stories could lead to false assumptions about the true nature of wolves. Thus, in *Of Wilderness and Wolves*, his main goal was not to spin tall tales but to establish the value and grandeur of wolves for a general readership. As he writes, "Let us regard the wolves as but the species of wild dogs that they are, no more the vehicles of perversions than any other wild animals that live, where, how, and because they can. It should be possible to regard wolves for what they are, without mythology and sensationalism." It is as much a testament to our shortsightedness as it is to Errington's vision that the wisdom of this book, so long delayed, still speaks so directly to our environmental crises. Now, over half a century late, we finally have the chance to learn from this lost masterpiece.

A Note on the Text and Illustrations

The source for this book is the typescript Paul L. Errington completed in the days before his death on November 5, 1962. That typescript, given to me by Errington's sons, Frederick and Peter, bears minor revisions in both Paul Errington's and his wife Carolyn Storm Errington's handwriting. Stylistic in nature, these revisions are in keeping with Errington's usual practice of working closely with Carolyn to produce a polished manuscript. As such, they almost certainly represent his creative wishes and have been retained. Aside from silently correcting a very limited number of obvious typographical errors, I have made no changes to the text.

The cover and other illustrations in this book are by the renowned Charles W. Schwartz (1914–1991). An accomplished biologist, wildlife artist, wildlife photographer, documentary maker, and writer, Schwartz illustrated, among many other books, Aldo Leopold's *A Sand County Almanac*. With his wife, Elizabeth "Libby" Schwartz (also an accomplished zoologist), he wrote and illustrated *The Wild Mammals of Missouri*, which is regarded as one of the most ambitious and visually stunning works of twentieth-century natural history. As is discussed in the introduction, when his friend Paul Errington invited him to illustrate *Of Wilderness and Wolves*, Schwartz readily agreed, going so far as to create a couple of drawings (which have not been located) even before receiving a contract. Unfortunately, an editor who wanted photographs instead of drawings ended their planned collaboration. In an attempt to at least partially realize Errington's and Schwartz's original wishes, I include in this edition seven illustrations now housed in the Charles W. Schwartz Collection at the State Historical Society of Missouri.

NOTES

1. P.L. Errington, *Red Gods Call*, 18.
2. P.L. Errington, *Red Gods Call*, 27.
3. P.L. Errington, *Red Gods Call*, 97.
4. Schorger, "In Memoriam," 54–55.
5. P.L. Errington, *A Question of Values*, 173–174.
6. For a more detailed look at Errington's theories on predation see Kohler, "Paul Errington, Aldo Leopold, and Wildlife Ecology" and Pritchard et al., "The Landscape of Paul Errington's Work."
7. P.L. Errington, *Red Gods Call*, 138.
8. P.L. Errington, *Red Gods Call*, 137.
9. Review of *Of Men and Marshes*, 119.
10. P.L. Errington, Letter to Cecil Scott, 30 August 1961.
11. Scott, Letter to Paul. L. Errington, 4 October 1961.
12. Scott, Letter to Paul L. Errington, 28 December 1961.
13. Scott, Letter to Paul L. Errington, 1 March 1962.
14. "A New Elite of American Naturalists: Heirs of a Great Tradition."
15. P.L. Errington, Letter to Cecil Scott, 8 March 1962.
16. Scott, Letter to Paul L. Errington, 10 May 1962.
17. Schwartz, Letter to Paul L. Errington, 26 May 1962.
18. P.L. Errington, Letter to Cecil Scott, 15 May 1962.
19. Scott, Letter to Paul L. Errington, 23 May 1962.

20. Schwartz, Letter to Paul L. Errington, 26 May 1962; Scott, Letter to Paul L. Errington, 21 June 1962.

21. Scott, Letter to Paul L. Errington, 21 June 1962.

22. Scott, Letter to Paul L. Errington, 21 June 1962.

23. P.L. Errington, Letter to Cecil Scott, 2 July 1962.

24. P.L. Errington, Letter to Charles Schwartz, 2 July 1962.

25. Scott, Letter to Paul L. Errington, 9 July 1962.

26. P.L. Errington, Letter to Cecil Scott, 13 October 1962.

27. This note from Carolyn Errington to Carol H. Woodward is handwritten at the top of her copy of P.L. Errington, Letter to Cecil Scott, 13 October 1962.

28. Scott, Letter to Paul L. Errington, 10 May 1962.

29. C.S. Errington, Letter to Auntie and A.G., 18 December 1962.

30. C.S. Errington, Letter to Carol H. Woodward, 18 December 1962.

31. C.S. Errington, Letter to Cecil Scott, 14 January 1963.

32. Holstein, Letter to Carolyn Storm Errington, 15 January 1963.

33. Cecil Scott to Carolyn Storm Errington, 20 February 1963.

34. C.S. Errington, Letter to Merritt Bailey, 26 December 1967.

35. Woodward, Letter to Carolyn Storm Errington, 12 October 1967.

36. P.L. Errington, "Of Man and Maturity"; P.L. Errington, "Of Wilderness and Wolves."

37. C.S. Errington, Letter to Merritt Bailey, 26 December 1967.

38. Brooks, Letter to Carol H. Woodward, 17 September 1963.

39. For a full discussion of the controversy surrounding Mowat's *Never Cry Wolf*, as well as a useful survey of wolf books in general, see S.K. Robisch's *Wolves and the Wolf Myth in American Literature*, especially 28–57.

BIBLIOGRAPHY AND SUGGESTED READING

Brooks, Paul. Letter to Carole H. Woodward. 17 September 1963. Box 32/1. Iowa State University Special Collections, Paul L. Errington Papers.

Errington, Carolyn Storm. Letter to Auntie and A.G. 18 December 1962. Box 32/1. Iowa State University Special Collections, Paul L. Errington Papers.

———. Letter to Carol H. Woodward. 18 December 1962. Box 32/1. Iowa State University Special Collections, Paul L. Errington Papers.

———. Letter to Cecil Scott. 14 January 1963. Box 32/1. Iowa State University Special Collections, Paul L. Errington Papers.

———. Letter to Merritt Bailey. 26 December 1967. Box 32/1. Iowa State University Special Collections, Paul L. Errington Papers.

Errington, Paul L. Letter to Cecil Scott. 30 August 1961. Box 32/1. Iowa State University Special Collections, Paul L. Errington Papers.

———. Letter to Cecil Scott. 8 March 1962. Box 32/1. Iowa State University Special Collections, Paul L. Errington Papers.

———. Letter to Cecil Scott. 15 May 1962. Box 32/1. Iowa State University Special Collections, Paul L. Errington Papers.

———. Letter to Cecil Scott. 2 July 1962. Box 32/1. Iowa State University Special Collections, Paul L. Errington Papers.

———. Letter to Cecil Scott. 13 October 1962. Box 32/1. Iowa State University Special Collections, Paul L. Errington Papers.

———. Letter to Charles Schwartz. 2 July 1962. Box 32/1. Iowa State University Special Collections, Paul L. Errington Papers.

———. *Muskrat Populations*. Ames: Iowa State University Press, 1963.

———. *Muskrats and Marsh Management*. Harrisburg, PA: Stackpole, 1961.

———. "The Northern Bobwhite: Environmental Factors Influencing Its Status." Diss. University of Wisconsin, 1932.

———. "Of Man and Maturity." *Atlantic Naturalist* 23.4 (1968): 195–203.

———. *Of Men and Marshes*. New York: Macmillan, 1957. Rpt. Iowa City: University of Iowa Press, 2012.

———. *Of Predation and Life*. Ames: Iowa State University Press, 1967.

———. "Of Wilderness and Wolves." *Living Wilderness* 33 (1969): 3–7.

———. *A Question of Values*. Ed. Carolyn Errington. Ames: Iowa State University Press, 1987.

———. *The Red Gods Call*. Ames: Iowa State University Press, 1973.

Hostein, Marcy. Letter to Carolyn Storm Errington. 15 January 1963. Box 32/1. Iowa State University Special Collections, Paul L. Errington Papers.

Kohler, Robert E. "Paul Errington, Aldo Leopold, and Wildlife Ecology: Residential Science." *Historical Studies in the Natural Sciences* 41.2 (2011): 216–254.

Meine, Curt. *Aldo Leopold: His Life and Work*. Madison: University of Wisconsin Press, 1988.

"A New Elite of American Naturalists: Heirs of a Great Tradition." *Life Magazine*. 22 December 1961: 105–110.

Newton, Julianne Lutz. *Aldo Leopold's Odyssey*. Washington, D.C.: Island Press, 2006.

Pritchard, James A., Diane M. Debinski, Brian Olechnowski, and Ron Vannimwegen. "The Landscape of Paul Errington's Work." *Wildlife Society Bulletin* 34.5 (2006): 1411–1416.

Review of *Of Men and Marshes*. *New Yorker*. 25 January 1958: 119.

Robisch, S.K. *Wolves and the Wolf Myth in American Literature*. Reno: University of Nevada Press, 2009.

Schorger, A.W. "In Memoriam: Paul Lester Errington." *The Auk* 83.1 (1966): 52–65.

Schwartz, Charles. Letter to Paul L. Errington. 26 May 1962. Box 32/1. Iowa State University Special Collections, Paul L. Errington Papers.

Scott, Cecil. Letter to Carolyn Storm Errington. 20 February 1963. Box 32/1. Iowa State University Special Collections, Paul L. Errington Papers.

————. Letter to Paul L. Errington. 4 October 1961. Box 32/1. Iowa State University Special Collections, Paul L. Errington Papers.

————. Letter to Paul L. Errington. 28 December 1961. Box 32/1. Iowa State University Special Collections, Paul L. Errington Papers.

————. Letter to Paul L. Errington. 1 March 1962. Box 32/1. Iowa State University Special Collections, Paul L. Errington Papers.

————. Letter to Paul L. Errington. 10 May 1962. Box 32/1. Iowa State University Special Collections, Paul L. Errington Papers.

————. Letter to Paul L. Errington. 23 May 1962. Box 32/1. Iowa State University Special Collections, Paul L. Errington Papers.

————. Letter to Paul L. Errington. 21 June 1962. Box 32/1. Iowa State University Special Collections, Paul L. Errington Papers.

————. Letter to Paul L. Errington. 9 July 1962. Box 32/1. Iowa State University Special Collections, Paul L. Errington Papers.

Scott, Thomas G. "Obituary: Paul L. Errington." *The Journal of Wildlife Management* 27.2 (1963): 321–324.

Sivils, Matthew Wynn. "Carolyn Errington's Role in the Publication of Paul L. Errington's *Of Predation and Life*." *Notes on Contemporary Literature* 40.4 (2010): 8–10.

————. "Ernest Thompson Seton, the Pathetic Fallacy, and Paul L. Errington's *Of Predation and Life*." *Notes on Contemporary Literature* 40.2 (2010): 2–4.

Woodward, Carol H. Letter to Carolyn Storm Errington. 12 October 1967. Box 32/1. Iowa State University Special Collections, Paul L. Errington Papers.

Of Wilderness and
WOLVES

To Carolyn, my wife and friend, mother of my sons,

and critic of my manuscripts, I dedicate this book with thanks.

— P. L. E.

Preface

This book is intended to be an essay on values, especially the hard-to-define and hard-to-maintain values that tend to be lost with increasing human domination of the earth. They are the distinctive values of wilderness.

Although I recognize that wilderness anywhere may have distinctive values, I am largely restricting the scope of the book to northern regions of types with which I am familiar from firsthand experience. I chose the wolves as the central characters of this writing partly because I really could not help it, because an intense interest in wolves has grown on me throughout my life and because the wolves, themselves, are so much creatures of wilderness—also because there are few other wild animals about which the public has more traditionally fallacious ideas.

*

This book is an outgrowth of technical specialties as well as personal interests, and of the specialties and interests of many people other than myself. So many people are in its background that I cannot feasibly list the names of all those who have directly or indirectly, knowingly or unknowingly, contributed to it. Many of them will be cited in appropriate places in the chapters to follow, but I do wish to acknowledge the particular help and encouragement given me by Ira N. Gabrielson, of the Wildlife Management Institute.

Writing this book on Nature and man and predators and prey has entailed much drafting and revising. For critical reading of various manuscript versions and chapters, I am grateful to, besides Gabrielson and my wife, Carolyn:

Margaret Bonine Fox of Yachats, Oregon and Richard J. Lowther of Ames, Iowa; Adolph Murie, Adolph Stebler, and Stanley P. Young of the U.S. Department of the Interior; James Ayars, Harlow B. Mills, and Thomas G. Scott of the Illinois Natural History Survey; A. Starker Leopold and Emlen T. Littell of the University of California; C.H. Douglas Clarke and Douglas H. Pimlott of the Ontario Department of Lands and Forests; John Paul Scott of the Jackson Memorial Laboratory, Bar Harbor, Maine; Mrs. Lois Crisler, Lake George, Colorado; Ian McTaggart Cowan of the University of British Columbia; Milton Stenlund of the Minnesota Department of Conservation; Yngvar Hagen of the Norwegian State Game Research; Kai Curry-Lindahl of Stockholm's Northern Museum; Gunnar Markgren of Boda Research Station, Sweden; Bo Österlöf of Uddeholm, Sweden.

In the background of this book is the diverse natural history of fur trappers, wolfers, ranchers, backwoods and wilderness men and camp companions, of zoo and museum personnel, of scholars and naturalists. Were its origin to be traced far enough, undoubtedly there would be persons whose names have become faceless, whose faces have become nameless, or whose identities have become completely lost to me with the passage of years. Whether or not they would now endorse my views, or I theirs, I am glad to acknowledge their influence for what it was.

I also acknowledge the advantage of having access to a first-class science library, such as that of Iowa State University at Ames, my home city. In connection with the extensive reading necessitated by this undertaking, it was always gratifying to be able to draw on virtually any pertinent literature as needed.

Finally, I wish to express gratitude for a John Simon Guggenheim Memorial Fellowship, which afforded me an opportune freedom for following up scientific interests in natural interrelationships, including those involving wolves and wolf prey.

*

Extending back are my own memories of long winters, of northern lights and sinking frost lines, of drifting snow over plains and ice, of stillness of spruce and cedar swamps, of snare wire and Newhouse traps, of weariness, loneliness, and beauty. Much of my life up to graduate training was that of a professional hunter and trapper. I was a predator, myself, and lived close to the land.

PART I

Some Small Beginnings
in Experience

CHAPTER I

Of Wolves and Boyhood Fear and Fascination

My family's farm next to the Oakwood–Tetonkaha lake chain of east-central South Dakota was right in the midst of some first-of-the-century wolf country. It could be that I there acquired the beginning of a great childhood fear of wolves, though my parents had moved to the county seat of Brookings before my recognized memories began. At any rate, I remember fearing wolves about as far back as I remember anything. However, I am sure that my early fear of wolves was never based upon any actual danger from them.

Most of what the public called wolves were, even in those days, only the abundant coyotes, but there were still the buffalo wolves—the real lobos—and much wild land in east-central South Dakota. At the time of my birth, South Dakota had been a state for twelve years.

*

My home, as a five-year-old, was a Brookings rooming house. In the winter evenings, as we sat around the supper table in the lamplight, the conversation of the adults frequently got around to wolves. It seemed awfully close to home for me to hear of the wolves up by the farm or still nearer than that to Brookings. Mostly, the wolves were said to kill sheep but occasionally something bigger, and there were tales and conjectures as to how dangerous they could be to humans. There was talk about the howling of wolves and the terror of livestock in a farmyard when creatures with shining eyes prowled outside; talk about how much of a victim the wolves would devour at a feeding and about what it was like to know that you were being followed by wolves. I listened to all of it and tried to keep in the lamplight as much as possible and to keep quiet and close to whatever men looked strongest and bravest.

I asked whether wolves came into houses in town and was told that they did not come even near towns. I never felt reassured.

I thought that I had been hearing a wolf padding in the hallway and in the dark corners out of sight, and the time came when I thought I got a good look at it. It was in the kitchen, standing in front of the stove, its great dark body fully outlined in the evening dusk and looking exactly like pictures that I had seen of wolves. It stood facing me but made no overt movement. I backed away and went into another room to tell the grown-ups about it. When I prevailed upon one of the men to come out in the kitchen with me and to see for himself, the wolf had gone. It had been there, I knew, and no amount of grown-up disbelief and soothing words to the effect that I had been dreaming could change my conviction that I had seen a wolf in the house.

*

Despite my boyhood in town, I did much prowling about the family farm whenever I could get there. Sometimes, somewhere I would see a dead sheep that something BIG was eating upon. Crumbly Indian bones lay exposed outside of a hillside hole, as if they might once have been dug out by wolves. The thought of Indians had somewhat the same frightening appeal to me as the thought of wolves. I was often reminded of both in the course of my walking along the lakeshore, for flint arrowheads could lie washing among the pebbles, and the stretches of sandy beaches could have tracks that might have been left by either tame dogs or something else. When off by myself, I tried to think that those tracks must have been dog tracks. I do not recall that I ever asked for any adult opinion about further possibilities.

When I was eight, one of the neighbor teenagers chased a pack of eight buffalo wolves on horseback through a large sheep pasture, hoping to get near enough to shoot, but the wolves met the problem satisfactorily from their standpoint; even so, the incident proved, if anyone needed proof, that there were more than coyotes about.

The following summer, I accompanied a crayfish-catching party to a creek that ran through a rough and wild tract of land near the farm. Real work was involved in the filling of wash boilers with pinching crayfishes, and the hilltops had a greater attraction for me.

I did not have to climb up many hilltops before finding everything that I then wanted to find. There were holes that I could have crawled into without difficulty, but I was not tempted to crawl into them. Within the holes, darkness extended way, way down. The heaped earth outside had dog-like tracks, the vegetation was flattened, and scattered around were bits of wool. I stood outside with my goose pimples, shivering and hardly able to breathe, and I looked at the crayfishing grown-ups to make sure that they could see if something came out and grabbed me, but I had to stay a while longer and peer into the holes. I felt better after withdrawing from the vicinity of the den but continued to walk the hilltops until time to go home.

In the fall of my eleventh year, I was taken on a weekend camping trip to Lake Albert, which was then known for its wonderful abundance of game. My memory did not register in that one trip everything that there was to know about the land that we traveled through—not even a trip that required walking beside a two-cylinder, chain-drive Reo as it strained through the deeper ruts in mud and sand—but I am sure that the land was as wild as I recall. It was wild, years afterward, when I knew it much better, when solid blocks, miles across, had only an occasional cultivated field or set of buildings. For long, the rougher moraines were used by the settlers mainly for grazing and haying. Grasslands and marshes were fringed with plum thickets and poison ivy and buckbrush and hardwoods. Wooded ravines were dominated by shrubs and bur oaks.

There were bobwhite quail about our campsite beside Lake Albert, and we had some of them to eat along with the more common prairie chickens. As dusk came, we sat at the campfire, under more sky than I think I had ever seen before. It was late when supper was cooked, and I ate my share of the fried quail and prairie chicken without noticing much what any of it tasted like. I was too preoccupied with some howling that seemed to come from rather near by.

The howling may have been coyote, but I thought it was wolf. As memory brings it to me, it had a long, authoritative oo-sound, and while I heard that I was aware of no other sounds.

Wolf Howling, by Charles W. Schwartz. Charles W. Schwartz Collection,
the State Historical Society of Missouri.

The night air was chilly close to the fire, it was chilly in the tent, and,
until I went to sleep, I was chilly under all of my bedding. I was not sure
how much I was enjoying the camping trip.

✻

For a period of months, still as an eleven-year-old, I spent almost every
evening at the Brookings public library and usually took home a book. My
favorite subjects were prehistoric man and ancient history, Spartan ways
of physical training, exploits of the Vikings and other sea rovers, Indian
fighting and pioneering, and the rawest of raw Nature that I could find.

Ernest Thompson Seton's books were on the library shelves, and I read
about woodcraft, about Indian life, about trappers, and about Canadian
wildernesses. One memorable picture showed a wolf approaching to
attack in the night, and, for a time, I dreamed of this wolf. I discovered
more wolves to dream about in Jack London's *The Call of the Wild*.

The Call of the Wild was the most fascinating and disturbing book that I ever read as a youngster. I responded to just about everything in it, from the title to the final paragraph with its wolves running under the Arctic lights. Emotionally, it turned me inside out.

A picture in *The Call of the Wild* showed a primitive man huddled at a fire. Beyond the fire, eyes shone in the darkness. Then, in the late hours of nights, the shining eyes would become transferred to a circle around my bed. I had a whole wolf pack in the room, off and on all winter and sometimes for several nights in succession. At times, I could recognize and sweat out the nightmare and go back to sleep readily, even if I might go right back to the wolves. At other times, when everything was so dark and silent and the encircling wolf pack drew closer to my bed until the eyes and muzzles and teeth and lolling tongues were within reach if I dared to reach out for them, I would throw off the bedding and rush screaming from the room.

Not all of my mental images of wolves were fearsome, and I began losing my fear of wolves so imperceptibly that I did not know just when it happened. I began to realize that there might be places where wolves belonged—not too close to home but off in the wilderness, somewhere. I longed to hunt wolves, to meet the charge of a pack with a thirty-thirty rifle, but I still wanted to have my wolves awaiting me in the remote places, always available for the hunting. Mine was not, however, entirely a hunting-preserve viewpoint. I felt that there was something very right about London's dog, Buck, and his wild brethren ranging naturally through the forest, taking their prey as they could get it and responding to the passage of the seasons as wolfish creatures had done before them.

The lonely valley at the close of *The Call of the Wild* took definite form in my mind. Whenever I thought of it, or of anything like it, I visualized wolves. They might be solitary wolves or groups of wolves. They might be running or walking or standing. They might cause my skin to prickle, just imagining them.

In the course of my survey of the library shelves, I found a series of books written by Charles G.D. Roberts and illustrated by Charles Livingston Bull. Throughout them all, wild creatures peered from coniferous boughs or withdrew into shadows or hunted in the moonlight or ate or were eaten. I remember a title, *The Watchers of the Trails*, that elicited in me a sensation of being watched—but without fear on my part—as I walked home after the library closed for the night. Another, *The Haunters of the Silences*, really haunted me, still in a pleasurable way. I longed to walk the wilds with a rifle on my arm. I had no special desire to kill anything but I wanted to live in the wilderness as a wild creature myself, as a predator along with the mink, the lynx, the bear, and the wolf.

✻

During sixth and seventh grades, I continued to spend much time in the public library. On weeknight evenings, in particular, I would head for my favorite shelves, to read and reread.

I still liked to read about the Viking Age, about cavemen and saber-toothed tigers and mammoths and the coming of the glacial ice. I still read Seton and Roberts and studied pictures of northern scenes and northern wildlife: pictures of conifers with boughs weighted by snow, pictures of wolf and lynx and moose and caribou, of marten and fisher and mink and weasel, of rabbits in thickets, of grouse in trees, of goshawks and falcons and owls in the air, and of trails in the snow.

One winter night as I left the library steps, I saw before me a sky shimmering with green and red of northern lights. I visualized myself on snowshoes in a wilderness, with traps on my back and the thirty-thirty on my arm.

That made up my mind for me as to what I wanted to do for a living, and I began making some daring plans that were not always well received at home.

✻

It would be several years before I got up to the North Woods, but, at age fifteen or when a freshman in high school, I did have a satisfying trapping venture, a short professional apprenticeship on the marshes about the old home farm. I had been given permission to stay out of school for the month of December.

That first winter camp was a tent heated by a sheet-iron stove on a small wooded island surrounded by lake ice and hilly shores. The only visitor that I had was our tenant at the farm, who wanted to make sure that I was not having trouble. He was a veteran hunter and trapper, himself, and soon our conversation got around to wolves and coyotes.

What about the coyotes that howled from the hilltops at night? About how many were there, anyway? I had not seen many tracks in any one place, but did not think that so much howling could have come from only a few. I was told that maybe there were two or three or a couple more around, that these could make a lot of noise.

I did not mention to my visitor the fright that the coyotes had given me on one cold, still night, when they had seemed everywhere and closing in on the camp. I had sat up in bed with a twenty-two repeating rifle in my hands. It was reassuring to know that the whole orchestral effect of howls and whines was due to such a small number of wary coyotes attending to their own business of living. This, I could actually enjoy for what it was, whether the coyote song graded off toward the sounds of chimes in one pitch or toward the bawling of a wolf in another.

The call of a lobo remained a possibility on a South Dakota winter night, but it had been years since any big wolves had been known in the neighborhood of our farm. I had enough carryover from childhood fears to be relieved that anything as formidable as lobo wolves were not likely to be around to sniff and appraise the sleeping contents of that flimsy tent.

Those first weeks of winter camping had their beauty. It was not the beauty of wilderness conifers weighted down with snow, but, in Brookings County hills, I could find views of wild lands without signs of man in them. I remember marsh and lake edges and hills and gullies with new snow marked only by my own tracks and those of wild creatures.

This installment of my professional training was sufficient after two weeks. I was glad to go home, to clean up, warm up, and feed up, to make up my school work, and to enjoy the feeling of having taken care of myself, of having made out reasonably well in the trapping.

*

During the rest of my early and middle teens, my hunting and trapping was chiefly restricted to the vicinity of Brookings. These were years of a pronounced decline of even the coyotes of the hilly wild lands about the old home farm in the Oakwood–Tetonkaha area—a decline in which, despite my efforts, I had no part. Consequently, any relations that I then had with the wolves and coyotes had to be through the media of reading and daydreams.

From the library books (and a small personal book collection of uneven merit that I had been building up), I learned where the best wolf country could be found in different regions of North America, especially in the Canadian North. The daydreams took me there so easily, set up the most attractive and adventurous situations so easily, and always supplied their own easy answers to all problems. In these daydreams, the wolf packs would be charging me with savage persistence, so that I had to shoot fast, dropping a wolf with each bullet, from the first wolf at which I could get good aim up to the last wolf falling practically at my feet. The daydreams had a built-in adjustment mechanism to take me effortlessly through the problems of skinning large numbers of wolves out in the wilderness bush in Far North winter weather, but they still permitted calculations as to profits from such killings on the basis of bounties and the pelt values quoted in the price lists of the fur companies.

The daydreams further convinced me that a wilderness wolf hunter would need a repeating rifle having a large magazine capacity for cartridges. Since my boyhood reading, I always had had a romantic attachment for a thirty-thirty, that gun for the he-man of the lonely wilds, although I never had had the gun in my hands. But, in studying the gun catalogs in anticipation of the time when I would be buy-ing a wolf gun, I began thinking less of having a thirty-thirty, with its magazine capacity of only six cartridges for a carbine. The forty-four-forty was another gun with he-man associations and a magazine capacity of up to fourteen cartridges; and, in the daydream testing, it dropped more charging wolves and just as efficaciously as did the thirty-thirty.

I did get some early experience with the forty-four-forty's smaller-cal-iber relative, the thirty-two-twenty, of equally large magazine capacity. Despite its being an obsolete model, of worn and slightly uncertain mechanical action and worn and pitted barrel, it shot well with the cartridges that I cheaply hand loaded in the family kitchen.

Out in some spacious hay lands near Brookings, I could put bricks on top of a row of fence posts, sit down on dry pieces of ground at distances up to two hundred paces, wrap elbows around knees, and, thus steadied, smash the bricks with sufficient regularity to assure me that I could kill a wolf or coyote if I ever got a good chance. So with a feeling that the old thirty-two-twenty and I were made for each other, I carried it with magazine full far into the countryside. My walking hunts took me as far away as ten miles or more from Brookings and into the hills and sheep pastures about Lake Campbell off to the south and equally far to the north, about Bruce. (Still farther northward from Bruce, up toward Estelline, lay some of the best sheep and wolf country in east-central South Dakota.)

That teenage wolf hunting gave me healthful exercise, familiarity with certain parts of South Dakota, and expertness in shooting from the practice associated with it. It gave me no wolves, nor coyotes, nor anything else of predatory big game.

(Along about this time or somewhat later, a youthful rabbit hunter whom I then considered of rather doubtful proficiency jumped a coyote outside of Brookings. He killed it with one load of number six shot at thirty yards, sold the skin for an advantageous price, and got favorable publicity for his feat.)

My final choice of a rifle for wolf hunting was a two-fifty-three-thousand. Its magazine held only five cartridges, but the gun itself was extremely accurate and had such a flat trajectory that one did not raise the sights—merely aimed a few inches high—for shooting at three hundred yards. I realized that if I ever succeeded in shooting wolves in daylight, it would most likely be with a rifle that could reach out after them.

Somewhere past my mid-teens, I had outgrown the daydreams of the charging wolf packs.

*

In time, I outgrew more misconceptions and acquired a better background for distinguishing between wolves of fiction and wolves of reality. This better background emerged gradually both from the life that I did lead for some years as a trapper and from the later scientific training, reading, and experience that made up my professional career as a biologist working with wild animals living in natural ways.

PART II

Toward Understanding Wolves, What They Are, and What They Do—A Factual Background

CHAPTER 2

Of the Nature of Wolves

Technical classifications of the dog family, Canidae, reflect human interpretations of natural relationships. From the Latin word for dogs comes the genus *Canis*. Most of our modern large wolves belong to the species, *Canis lupus*, in which the *lupus* part is Latin for wolf. The smaller North American coyote or prairie wolf is *Canis latrans*, meaning barking dog. Our third modern North American wolf, a native of southeastern United States, is intermediate in size between *Canis lupus* and *Canis latrans* and is known as *Canis niger*, literally meaning black dog, although its common name is red wolf. (The contradiction in the red wolf's names resulted from the original scientific description having been made from a black-phase specimen rather than from one of the more typical red phase.)

Back in Pleistocene time, a large, widely distributed, wolfish contemporary of the saber-toothed tiger may have been quite an animal. Its scientific name is *Canis diris*, a fearful, dreadful, terrible dog. How fearful, dreadful, and terrible it actually was remains uncertain; some modern wolves exceed it in size, and tar pit bone deposits suggest that it may have been a ready scavenger.

There are more members of the genus *Canis*, past and present. The Old World jackal is *Canis aureus* or golden dog. *Canis dingo* is the Australian wild dog, the dingo, believed to have been originally introduced on that isolated continent by man from an unknown but suspected Asiatic stock.

Our domesticated dogs are collectively designated as *Canis familiaris*, the dog we all know. Reputable scientists may hold widely divergent views regarding the origin or origins of domestic dogs, and I have no wish to plunge into any such controversies as may exist. The consensus seems to be that *Canis lupus* has been the main source. Insofar as many if not

Red Wolf, by Charles W. Schwartz. Charles W. Schwartz Collection,
the State Historical Society of Missouri.

most species of *Canis* are interfertile, other species besides *lupus* may have contributed at different times and places but probably not very much. J.P. Scott favors the theory of a single domestication of dogs from *Canis lupus* followed by a period of very rapid adaptive radiation all over the human-inhabited world.

But, however little inclined one may be to make too-positive statements as to how much *lupus* or something else that is canine may be in the makeup of a particular member of the genus *Canis*, it should still not be misleading to regard them all as dogs. Dogs they are, whether called dogs or wolves or coyotes or jackals or dingoes.

*

In view of the original wild sources of domestic dogs, it should not be remarkable that some domestic dogs may show inclinations toward wildness; in view of the taming if not partial domestication of wild dogs that has repeatedly occurred during historical times, it should not be remarkable that some of the wild dogs should continue to show inclinations toward tameness.

Somewhere I read—but have since been unable to rediscover the account—a description of early plainsmen finding buffalo wolves lounging around like so many camp dogs in a North American Indian village, with children walking among them unafraid. Such observers as George Bird Grinnell have recorded many scarcely less extreme instances of mutual fearlessness in man-wolf relations. Within the past century, wolves have regularly followed plainsmen's hunting parties or awaited about the outskirts of camps in expectation of feeding upon game killed by the human hunters. Wolves were then often attracted by the sound of shooting. Sometimes, the human hunters were apprehensive about the wolves but mostly they seemed unconcerned as long as the wolves did not make serious nuisances of themselves.

Even at the present time, wild individuals of the genus *Canis* may be friendly with man if their fear of him be lost.

Mrs. Lila Lofberg's account of the taming of a group of grown coyotes illustrates astounding potentialities. The Lofbergs lived in the mountains, where their home was snowbound for eight months of the year, and their intimate experiences with coyotes began when a starving animal came into their yard. They so much won the confidence of this and several other animals that the coyotes continued living in close association with them after they were no longer dependent upon them for food. A coyote mother brought pups to the house, and free-living coyotes otherwise showed confidence in them. When one of the coyotes mangled a foot, apparently in escaping from a steel trap left set and unattended by an irresponsible trapper, it went home to the Lofbergs.

I know of no exact parallel in relationships of present-day man and large wolves, and maybe there are not any. Nevertheless, even though tame wolves raised from puppyhood do not experience such an exceptional change in attitude toward man as the Lofberg coyotes showed, it is not unknown for hand-raised wolves to live free predatory lives and still continue associations with human friends.

Lois Crisler has written of the young wolves that she and her husband kept in their Alaskan camps. These wolves had their freedom. They accompanied the Crislers on travels over the tundra, romping like exuberant companions. They killed their own prey, came back to camp when they wished. Sometimes, they slept in the same tent or in the same room as the Crislers—sometimes after returning bloody from a hunt. Sometimes, the Crislers were awakened by the muzzles of friendly wolves next to their faces.

That sort of friendliness toward human friends is consistent with what long has been known of canine nature. Konrad Lorenz described the ghastly sight of a roe deer that his three dogs had killed and dismembered in his garden—also the absolute confidence with which he entrusted the dogs with his child, a creature so much more helpless than the roe deer had been.

There remains the question of how fundamental may be the unevenly manifested tendency of *Canis* to associate with man. It cannot be wholly for food or protection or anything so simple or patent. For lack of a better expression, may we say that something special in canine nature allows much of the uniqueness that can exist in relationships between man and *Canis*?

In the case of friendships between man and the less-domesticated types or individuals among the dog family, man may be treated not so much as a master but as a comrade. The comradeship I have known between man and wolves seemed to be mutual, without the wolves showing the subservience that man so often expects of domestic dogs over which he claims mastery.

(The observations of Konrad Lorenz concerning his tame dingo further illustrate this kind of independence. At the age of a year and a half, the dingo accepted punishment for misdeeds—killing the Lorenz ducks—without protest or resentment, but the punishment did not deter it from trying anew to kill more ducks. Although it would with good humor tolerate much from a human friend, it was not being made over into anything incompatible with its nature as a dingo.)

What might be called friendships between man and wolves have their ways of ultimately breaking up—often because of divided loyalties. If man does not expect too much of the wolf, there is unlikely to be unpleasantness over the breakup other than regret on the part of a person who has come to be as fond of a wolf companion as he would be of a beloved domestic dog. After more or less vacillation, the tamed wolf joins wild wolves, and that is that. The Lofberg coyotes provided something of an exception, inasmuch as the tamed coyotes brought still-wild coyotes into their comfortable association with man.

I am unsure of myself when attempting to generalize on the subject of *Canis* respecting man's person. Of course, individual dogs even of old domestic breeds may be savage toward man, whether as a result of their heredity or the circumstances of their upbringing. I once experienced an unprovoked attack by a couple of strange dogs in my backyard and had to keep sweeping at them with a hat while retreating to the safety of an enclosed porch. Not long ago, a German shepherd dog earned space in a scientific journal by the killing and eating of a lady who had been taking it for a walk. Or a team of abused sledge dogs might turn on a hated driver.

In considering the evidence of which I know, I have gotten a pronounced impression that some of the common races of domestic dogs can be more dangerous to man than wolves—quite apart from any danger resulting from the crazed behavior of rabies or other special cases. Douglas Clarke has suggested that the notorious beasts of Gévaudan, which terrorized and disrupted the life of a French province for nearly four years, may not have been true wolves at all but rather wolf-dog hybrids. This might explain their extraordinary size, peculiar coloration, and lack of respect toward man. In some places, street dogs are said to be highly dangerous. Reports of dogs killing miserable or helpless Asiatic people at times of famine or epidemics surely have truth in them.

Most of the actual records that I have seen of wolves preying upon man in Europe relate to the actions of a few individual wolves, and the wolf victims were mainly children. The issue is not whether wolves *could* kill a human adult. A grown man with a strong physique would probably be a pushover in unarmed combat with an ordinary self-hunting, large wolf—that is, if the wolf were fighting to kill him. A trapped wolf has been known to snap off tree limbs two inches in diameter and to scar a modern rifle barrel with tooth marks. But, with a club in his hands, man gains greatly in formidability, and man has had like or better implements for longer than anyone can accurately say.

I think of a phenomenon noted in my studies of predatory behavior: Irrespective of the fighting prowess that a given hawk, raccoon, mink, or fox may demonstrate when committed to a fight, it does not follow that even an animal capable of a ferocious attack is disposed to fight its utmost and risk severe injuries as a routine part of living. One need not ascribe human motivations to any intelligent predator for not wanting to pay overmuch for a meal when it can eat something else more cheaply. We can assume that hunting and killing can be fun for many predators—such as members of the dog family—up to a certain point, but encounters of wolves with man undoubtedly went past the point of a pleasant adventure often enough to be discouraging to the wolves even where wolf populations have had prospective sources of human prey as relatively defenseless as the children of the European peasantry that drew so much of the recorded wolf predation upon man.

From a predator's standpoint, children should be incomparably the easier prey, but why have not greatly more children been killed by wolves during the centuries of historic time when wolves were abundant in both European and North American countrysides? Can we merely dismiss this by saying that man is not natural prey? Does man's peculiar status as a potential companion animal for wild dogs have any underlying relation to the respect that they rather generally show for his living body in Europe and North America? (This respect does not seem transferable very much to his dead body—unless based upon great fear—for domestic and wild dogs alike have fed upon cadavers as far back as literature goes.)

We have only to consider the remarkably easy relationships that often existed between North American Indians and wolves before the complications introduced by the white man to see that there must have been more than fear of man's weapons involved. Granted, that some of the tameness of wolves may have been due to their fraternizing with camp dogs, in combination with the attractions of the meat supply made available through the hunting activities of the Indians. Granted, also, that Indians, for their own reasons, sometimes killed wolves and that relations between Indians and wolves may not have been exactly idyllic. Still, the normal relations between many Indians and wolves seemed to go somewhat beyond mere mutual toleration. In at least some places, Indians could regard the wolves as brothers. George Bird Grinnell gave the example of an Indian hunter cheerily calling out a greeting as he passed a wolf barking from a hilltop.

The white man changed all that when he earnestly began to persecute wolves—about the time when big game became scarce and the wolves were turning to domestic stock. Nevertheless, the wolves took a lot of shooting, trapping, and poisoning before their survivors learned how dangerous their new adversary could be.

Meanwhile, North American wolves followed and frightened many people, especially those walking long distances in sparsely settled country on winter nights. I shall not say that some of these people may not have been justified in climbing trees or spending a night in the protection of an open fire. But, so often, nobody knows what the wolves may have intended. Perhaps they were hungry or curious or only enjoying the entertainment. Unfrightened wild wolves may be attracted by what is novel to them.

Douglas Clarke—unarmed at the time—had huge Yukon wolves running ahead, behind, and on all sides of him at night, yet, on the basis of his experience with wolves, he had no fear of them. Adolph Murie, another man of much experience with wolves of the American Far North, did become sufficiently uneasy as a group of wolves approached to make sure that he could reach a pistol if he had need of it; the wolves turned aside with no threatening actions, although they barked and howled at distances of a hundred to two hundred yards, and one kept abreast of him for a half mile.

The Crislers howled too, and thus called to themselves, a pack of ten strange wild wolves. The pack spread out in a loose semicircle, watching. As soon as the wolves learned that they had been called by human beings and not by other wolves, they trotted off in a desultory way, without evidences of fear. Douglas Pimlott and his colleagues regularly howled to wild wolves as part of their study techniques and sometimes have called the wild ones very close to them.

The question often comes up as to when the desperation of hunger may outweigh the natural respect or the peculiarly doggish responsiveness that many kinds of wild dogs are capable of showing toward man. The hungry coyotes that came to the Lofbergs were not vicious—rather, they were starving with what might be interpreted as resignation. That wolves hungry to the point of ferocity might forget their ordinary rules of behavior would seem entirely possible. Even so, recklessness from hunger is still unlikely to be an absolute thing on the part of intelligent animals.

Defensive behavior of trapped, wounded, or cornered wolves against human attackers is well known (though not invariably nor perhaps even usually shown). No one should confuse this special category with the normal behavior of free-living wolves. The Lapps had an old custom of overtaking on skis and killing (sometimes torturing) with spears wolves handicapped by deep snow; and this could result in people getting severely bitten in close-quarters action. Lorenz described the behavior of a captive wolf, an animal that showed the greatest of friendliness toward him during their usual relationships but which became dangerous from fright as soon as anything happened to cause it to lose its feeling of security.

But it is remarkable what wolves may not do, even in self-defense. Stanley Young wrote of a Colorado hunter who sent his small son into wolf dens after young wolves. The boy often found a young wolf extremely difficult to handle down there in the hole, and occasionally took hold of an adult female, but never suffered any disastrous results.

In trying to sum up the basic psychological responsiveness of wolves and other dogs toward man, I should say that it is all characterized by variability. Considering the complexities of wolf psychology, it should not be surprising that wolves have, on occasion, departed from their usual behavior patterns by making or attempting to make prey of human beings. What surprises me is that wolves have not preyed upon man much more often. There does seem to be an innate tendency of members of the dog family to regard man as a special animal. The manifestations thereof may not be of either fear or tameness, but of a peculiar disinclination to attack living people as prey animals.

Racial memory? How can anyone know what may have been imprinted on canine psychology at the time of Stone Age campfires or before? Is there anything about the odor of a human being (or posture or movements or anything else) to remind wild wolves that here was something ineligible or undesirable as wolf prey?

*

Members of the dog family mark their property rights and home ranges with scent stations. Domestic dogs anoint trees and hydrants and advertise their personalities on automobile tires; wild dogs may use for scenting many movable as well as stationary objects, such as miscellaneous dried or fragmentary carcasses. They may bury them, dig them up again, carry them from place to place. In these ways, individuals keep informed about much of what goes on in local dogdom.

When the scent of a strange individual appears, resident animals may show decided interest. Stanley Young wrote that placing urine from a strange wolf on a wolf runway caused excitement among the wolves frequenting that runway. The social order of all of the wild dogs I know exerts a fundamental influence on what individuals and numbers are tolerated in a particular area. It can be strict and complex, and animals that fail to conform may be in trouble.

Far from going about or establishing themselves just anywhere, wild dogs as well as domestic dogs tend to have more or less definite home ranges, some parts of which they actively defend. Familiarity with the lay of the land can be highly important to them both in routine daily life and at times of crisis. The wild dogs know where they have the best chances of finding and capturing prey and the best escape routes in the event that they themselves meet with danger.

Not all members of a wild canine population are equally well situated. Some may wander about the outskirts of occupied home ranges or territories, or occasionally pass through occupied home ranges of others, but this for them may not be even a relatively secure or happy way of life. Homeless individuals can find much difficulty in fitting into places where their presence is resented by their dominant fellows. If the homeless are normal animals that live under a handicap chiefly because of their youth and their temporary lack of opportunity in a dog-filled dog's world, they may ultimately find a social opening for themselves—if they stay alive and psychologically undamaged. If aged, ailing, or with inferiority complexes, the wanderers may be lucky if they can avoid the worst troubles and live out their years in some kind of peace somewhere.

It is not well to make overly sweeping statements as to social relations among any canine populations. Individualistic members of the dog family may be rule-breakers in addition to being conformers. Sometimes, it appears that one individual hates another because it hates him and likes another for no more distinguishable reason. Within their psychological limits and the rigidities of their social codes, they can be free agents. Certainly, much of what they do can be what they want to do.

Some of the most interesting of Adolph Murie's observations of free-living Alaskan wolves were of a group of five that reacted toward each other like trusted old friends. They had their individualities, their customs, their attachments to each other, and their recognition of the social proprieties. One member became the mother of a litter that fitted into the group without friction. A strange wolf was unsuccessful in joining the group, though Murie thought at first that it might be accepted; but the others suddenly turned against it, driving it away drastically punished. Clearly, the wolves chose their own friends. One member of the group showed enough signs of age that Murie nicknamed him "Grandpa," yet his age seemed to be no social handicap to him; he belonged.

There can be no doubt that the intolerance of wolves to crowding by their own kind must tend to limit their populations in a given area. This is not inconsistent with the fact that the existing wolf populations of North America are everywhere sparse compared with the tremendous numbers formerly occurring on the western plains. North American wolves are believed to have reached peak numbers during the years when the hide hunters were slaughtering the bison herds. Higher tolerance of crowding could thus occur at times of lush living. The wolves could well concentrate on a temporary scale when and where attracted by large quantities of meat at camps or butchering sites. Nevertheless, many of the old accounts often refer to smaller groups of wolves and to concentrations of wolves dispersing after they had fed, so that no one should think that the wolves then lacked a social order. Still, we do not know to what extent the early wolf concentrations may have meant overlapping or shifting of home ranges or to what extent the wolves—well-fed or hungry—may have become conditioned to tolerate high densities of their own kind.

Free-living wolves may both restrict their movements and maintain large home ranges. Adolph Stebler concluded that a wolf he studied in northern Michigan had spent at least ten days or two weeks in the vicinity of a deer carcass, during which time it probably had not ranged over as much as a square mile. He also estimated that a group of four wolves on one study area used two hundred and sixty-five square miles of winter range in 1938, and twelve years later a group of three used seventy-five square miles. In another area, a pack of six wolves had a winter range of forty-eight square miles, which seemed mainly determined by the location of deeryards. Pimlott found that major drainages were likely to form boundaries for ranges of Ontario wolves. Daniel Q. Thompson considered the range of a northern Wisconsin group to be about one hundred and fifty square miles.

Ian McTaggart Cowan gave an example of a small group of relatively sedentary wolves having a normal year-round range apparently not exceeding fifty square miles. Resident animals in another of Cowan's study areas roamed over about fifty-five square miles. The same author referred to one pack circuit that must have been at least seventy miles in length. He described the summer range of one group as fairly small and located some sixty to seventy miles away from the winter range.

Summer is a season when wolves may hunt singly or in pairs in circumscribed areas. What seem to be packs may also remain together in spring and summer, as shown not only by Murie's observations in Alaska but also by those of Pimlott on many wolf groups in Algonquin Provincial Park, Ontario. Even so, certain wolves may remain highly mobile during the summer months. Stebler's wolf work in the Upper Peninsula of Michigan suggests that the summer range may be larger than the winter range, after dispersal of the yarded deer. Cowan mentioned a summer instance of wolves having preceded him down a trail for a total distance of twenty-two miles. Murie's wolves traveled twenty miles nightly from a den to take advantage of a caribou calving area.

Milton Stenlund wrote of wolves' inherent desire to travel. Some covered thirty to sixty miles in a night without stopping to hunt. One specific instance related to a pack that traveled thirty-five miles one night almost entirely on lake ice.

Although the old view that wolves follow definite circuits or make rounds at regular intervals has been challenged in recent years, wolves may use the same trails or crossings again and again, year after year. Stenlund noted that wolves in winter often followed the routes and portages of summer canoe parties—along lakes, and streams, in the lowest valleys between lakes and rivers. Generally, the easiest routes between hunting grounds would be followed, but the wolves at times would travel directly cross-country or over some of the steepest hills to hunt or—seemingly—to satisfy some whim. Certain parts of a pack range might be visited regularly; other parts, only once or twice during a winter.

Intolerance of wolves to other wolves may be expected to function without any great precision as a mechanism in population control. Apart from socially acceptable visits by old acquaintances, a certain amount of at least transitory encroachment should be inevitable in well-populated wolf country. Some wolf or group may just move around in ways that the regular occupants of the range do not care about or can do nothing about.

An overall tendency toward stability in numbers and social relations still persists in the wolves, despite the variation in their needs and behavior. Wolves do partly what they want to and partly what they can, as relates to their fellows, their food, their hunting and denning terrain, and the season of the year.

*

The Crislers obtained a remarkable insight into the moods and fundamental social behavior of wolves by rearing seven young, which were members of two litters. These wolves could be psychologically deep as well as transparent. They were sensitive animals having many personalities—loving, jealous, playful, moody, generous—and they were strongly conscious of property rights. One wolf was regarded as almost mysterious because it seemed to have no peculiarities; it was an unjealous, affectionate, undemanding, big, hearty wolf. (The latter may also be said of some of the wolves that Pimlott reared from puppyhood in connection with his studies.)

The Crislers found their wolves essentially non-fighting, but there could be fighting—mostly in the form of brief spats because of transgressions. An attack by a dog upon a litter of wolf pups precipitated a crazed battle among the pups themselves. Mrs. Crisler wrote in a letter that this "going berserk is a mysterious thing to me" and cited an instance of a litter of wolf pups behaving in a similar manner after one of their number returned to the pen with mercurochrome on its forehead. That melee could not be calmed for hours. A Crisler wolf was upset the first time it witnessed a dogfight; it acted as if it did not know what to do and finally pulled off the aggressor by the tail.

Mrs. Crisler emphasized the lavish communication of wolves by gestures and sounds, their seeking to control by gestures and sounds first instead of by biting. In face and body, wolves can be among the most expressive of creatures—a fact abundantly documented by the studies of Rudolf Schenkel on captive European wolves. Their ceremonies have a great deal of meaning.

Much of a wolf's personality develops from individual experiences. The Crislers noted a change—a new confidence—after young wolves had killed their first caribou. In courting the friendship of another wolf (or of a sledge dog, in one outstanding instance), a wolf may have been repeatedly and painfully rebuffed, then the courted animal may have been converted, and a new permanent friendship established. Or a conversion may establish an enmity. Or a change might come that seemed to have no relation to anything or perhaps be only an outgrowth of maturity. As the wolf matures, it normally shows much more authority in its behavior, in indicating what it does not like.

It can still be ceremonious, even courteous, as well as authoritative, using a paw or taking hold with jaws in warning. A person who insists on being a wolf's master, without being polite to the wolf or permitting it to be a little authoritative, could conclude that a wolf gets mean with age. To the contrary, Mrs. Crisler did not find that wolves became fierce or treacherous or unpredictable as they grew older. She found that friendship with mature wolves became deeper, stronger, and more satisfying than ever, that the mature wolves are "completely trustworthy, after they get you trained!"

The Crisler accounts are full of wolf frolics, with their own kind or with human beings or—I think most revealingly—with ravens that enthusiastically entered into the games. Frolicking might celebrate making a kill and having a good meal. It might be in response to finding the first thawed clay bank of the year, with scampering and somersaulting. It might be responsiveness to fall snowdrifts or new ice. Meeting a friend or a return to camp might touch off a frolic. Pimlott's tame wolves could be notably frolicsome when meeting their favorite human friends, the Pimlott children, after substantial intervals.

The games of both the Crisler and Pimlott wolves might consist of simple pursuit. A leader carrying a trophy might be chased. There might be mischief games, seizing and running with caps or mittens. Mrs. Crisler described nabbing at bootlaces and braided hair, untying earflaps of a cap, and other manifestations of inventiveness. All together, as she indicated, wolves have potentialities for a tremendous gaiety and social zest.

Wolf games may be rough, though the tame wolves of which I know were always careful about using teeth. This I particularly noticed, first hand, during a brief acquaintanceship with the Pimlott wolves. Of course, it does not always have to be that all playful wolves must be careful with their dangerous teeth. The sportive bob-tailing of calves that wolves once did on western cattle ranges was rough, but the bob-tailing was not within the normal social relations between the wolves and their friends. The roughness of the Crisler and Pimlott wolves consisted more of violence in body-to-body contacts, as in running into a person.

A wolf's nature allows for gloominess too—recognizable in part by the position of the tail. The Crislers could talk a gloomy wolf into a happy mood.

*

Hunting methods of *Canis* may vary considerably with species and individuals. The smaller members tend to be more fox-like; the larger, to depend more upon strength or stamina.

Coyotes seek prey by ears, eyes, and nose, and their own ingenuity. They may stalk, they may pounce or dash, they may follow in direct pursuit or await an opportunity to seize prey running past them. Their hunting may reveal much originality. The reputed foxiness of coyotes is not without factual basis.

Coyotes may behave in ways suggesting that highly individualistic animals may go to a great deal of trouble to catch some one or a few kinds of prey that they particularly want. Such prey may be commonplace, as the voles and rabbits that are relished by many flesh-eaters. Less frequently, the specializing may be directed toward grouse, domestic fowl, or some other gallinaceous birds; and some of these birds may be abundantly available to certain coyotes at times or extremely difficult for them to get, depending upon circumstances. Specialists may search after bird nests, become sheep killers, or take advantage of drought-exposed muskrats. Specializing may be directed toward something that the coyotes do not relish as food—such as weasels—or toward non-animal foods, such as melons and juniper berries.

Some coyotes may not seem to be at all imaginative or particular as to what they eat. They may prey upon medium-small mammals and birds, plus the more palatable and easily caught of cold-blooded vertebrates, large insects, and crustaceans. They may eat coarse livestock carrion of fields, often living upon this type of food almost entirely where it may be safely obtained in quantity.

Their hunting behavior can overlap with the hunting behavior of other dogs. In the farming communities of central and north-central United States, food habits of coyotes actually may not differ much from those of foxes. Moreover, coyote food habits may resemble those of feral house cats living in the same localities. Coyotes may be so wary of man that they seldom go near farmsteads or have opportunities to kill livestock of manageable sizes—the sheep, calves, and pigs.

Coyotes are famous for their teamwork in hunting as pairs. They may use relay techniques used against swift prey, distraction techniques against wary prey (with one animal drawing attention while its mate stalks). Both animals may work together to find something or to dig out something or to scare out something. Sometimes, coyotes may associate in a so-called pack, but this is not the usual coyote behavior while hunting.

Wolves hunt small game (also some large game) in a coyote-like fashion, as individuals or as pairs or small groups keeping together for company. In the absence of really clear data, the celebrated wolf pack is believed to consist principally of a family group—sometimes a family group and old friends. Young animals may be expected to go their own ways as they mature or as the numbers in the pack grow unwieldy, but a nucleus of socially adjusted animals seems to remain. Larger packs, formed as a unit of convenience, could be effective in hunting large game during hunger-winters, but their biological disadvantages would offset their advantages when they become too big to allow the socially less dominant animals opportunities to feed at a kill. It certainly is probable that members of a large pack split off to form whatever associations may be more advantageous to them. The largest authentic pack of which I ever heard was one of thirty-five, observed from the air in Alaska in the spring of 1957.

Whether led up to by a reconnaissance, a stalk, an ambush, a pounce, a short rush, or an endurance contest, the act of killing prey represents a recurrent climax in the life of a normal, free-living wolf. As an act, it is a result of innate psychology and individual experience, of anatomy and all that contributes to the totality of an animal.

Before I knew anything about wolves, I had supposed that the behavior of a hunting wolf pack reflected a mass single-mindedness, with more or less equal participation in killing large, tough, dangerous game. This was a wrong supposition; the degree of participation in the killing varies greatly; even in a large pack, the actual killing may be done almost exclusively by one or a few capable individuals. In watching wolves hunting moose on Isle Royale, David Mech noted that the predatory activities of one wolf appeared outstanding, but he did not know if it were the same wolf in all instances. The aggressive wolf not only led the attacks on the moose but broke trail during overland journeys, running twenty-five to fifty yards in the lead of the large pack of fifteen.

Although possessed of good equipment for killing big game, the Crisler wolves at four months of age were timid in the presence of caribou, that staple prey species for Arctic wolves. Emboldened by a sledge dog, the young wolves helped to kill ailing caribou in a hesitant manner at first, closing in on victims already lying helpless on the ground. A young wolf learns much from parents.

Large prey may be hamstrung (though hamstringing does not represent standard behavior among wolves), seized by the nose, knocked down or pulled down, have its vitals ripped open, chunks of flesh torn away. The wolves often bite at the juncture between leg and abdomen, thus severing large blood vessels and letting out the viscera. To do all of this, wolves need the suppleness of body, the powerful neck and jaws, and the sharp teeth that make them the formidable predators that they are.

The biting equipment of a wolf is also a precision instrument. Mrs. Crisler described a surprise she once had when lying with eyes closed. She felt fine pricks on an eyelid, as from a row of needles. One of the wolves was picking up the skin of her eyelid with its teeth, giving her grooming nibbles.

✳

Versatility in their feeding, advantageous social customs, and ability to use teeth do not represent all that wolves have to adapt them to a predatory life. They have long legs, with long spreading paws. Mrs. Crisler referred to their fineness and delicacy of articulation, to the rippling and flowing of their bodies in motion. She was particularly impressed by the ability of the wolves to leap. She described a wolf leaping six feet sidewise, a wolf whirling in midair as if its forefeet were pivoting on an invisible turntable, and a wolf making a perpendicular leaping—called the observation leap.

I am not sure that the wolves of the central North American forests, with which I happen to be the most familiar, are quite as graceful as the Alaskan wolves studied by the Crislers and the Murie brothers. Whether or not the northern Minnesota wolves that I examined really had less agile and more powerful bodies, my observations left me feeling that power and endurance might rather characterize the North Woods timber wolves. In the North Woods, the deep, fluffy snow might be the more selective for power and endurance, and I recall how the wolves could almost endlessly plow through it.

Wolves have still other adaptations for living their lives. Even for mature wolves, much hunting effort is unsuccessful. A species having so many uncertainties in its day-by-day feeding must be able to maintain its strength during long fasts—and to make up for its fasting when it does have access to a bountiful food supply. That is what the wolves can do, as predators adapted to prey upon or eat on the carcasses of large animals not always available to them.

Their capacity for gorging also has an important biological function in carrying meat for their young. The Crislers noted the excellent condition of the meat when disgorged for the pups. In the case of the stomach contents of a wolf that must have carried his load eighteen miles, only the last portion disgorged was tinged with brown; the rest was still fresh and red in appearance. Maximum stomach capacities have been recorded as up to twenty percent of the weight of individual wolves.

Caching or hiding or defending stores of food for possible future use may vary from elaborate burials to spirited attempts to guard kills from aggressive competitors. Small quantities may be disgorged at scattered places, or large pieces may be dragged or carried long distances. One of the Crisler wolves cached meat wherever meat was available for caching, whereas a litter mate was satisfied to eat of the same kill but would not cache unless fearful that strange wolves might get the meat. Even though a kill of a large animal may attract wolves other than those doing the killing (as well as attracting many other opportunistic flesh-eaters), a large carcass left where killed may serve as a wolf cache.

The equivalent of-storage killing is so well known among predatory mammals that its occurrence among wolves should not be surprising when prey of favorite types may be abundantly available. It seems especially likely to be done near prospective den sites for young wolves. Sigurd Olson, an outdoorsman and field ecologist of long and intimate experience in the Quetico–Superior wilderness, appraised the killing of large numbers of deer in areas having many deer as storage acts, though the wolves often did not feed upon the killed deer at any time. On the other hand, the Alaskan wolves studied by the Muries and the Crislers did not do a great deal of killing at any one time. But this may have reflected either a psychological disinclination to kill or few opportunities.

Distinctions between storage-killing and sport-killing may not be very finely drawn in cases of conspicuous killing of big game or livestock by wolves living in regions where they have reason to fear traps or poison. Wolves that follow their ancient behavior patterns in storage-killing yet dare not later utilize their kills may easily be charged with what man would call wantonness. Yet sport-killing, as such, should not be an unexpected outgrowth of playfulness in a playful species. This is the sort of thing that could either arise spontaneously in response to moods and opportunities or be picked up or passed on by example as a form of rough play.

(Possibly sheep-killing domestic dogs might better illustrate the wholly playful basis of sport-killing. The sheep may not be bitten at all but merely be chased until dying from exhaustion. Or they may be killed or crippled by the biting, a few individuals to an entire flock. The chasing or killing of sheep tends to be contagious among a community's dogs when some dogs learn how much fun it can be. Basically, it does not differ much from the milder forms of sport, such as chasing rabbits without the urge of hunger—or from the chasing or killing of game done under the control of human hunters.)

The influence of curiosity on the behavior of wolves should not be overlooked. Wolves have a curiosity that may go beyond food and fear. Add curiosity to the motivations that govern what a wolf does, and we get a partial answer to what may be preliminaries of attacks that are not carried through and to oddities in behavior that might not otherwise fit into anything comprehensible.

For myself, I learned something about dog-wolf nature from a hound that we had at our family's farm in South Dakota. He played our game of fur hunting if he understood it and if it suited him. He did not chase rabbits or anything other than carnivores, probably having had the rabbit-chasing beaten out of him long before I knew him. If the carnivore that he treed turned out to be a neighbor's cat instead of an animal with a salable pelt, we could take it or leave it. He was capable of controlled ferocity when ferocity was in order. I saw him shake loose a mink that was clamped to his nose and seize the mink again and kill it without a growl, without an unnecessary bite, an unnecessary motion, or anything unnecessary at all. A minding-its-own-business dog, he had in him, so far as I could see, neither unfriendliness nor servility toward anyone.

I liked to think of him as an old pro. If he got lost to us for hours, as when getting on a coyote trail and running far beyond our ability to keep up with him or to hear his baying, he would reappear at the farm the next day, his own unabashed, unreproachful, independent self. As a trapper, I was impressed by the knowledge he displayed concerning the traps I had out on or near the farm. The traps could be set for mink or fox or badger, they could be beneath a snowdrift, they could be as odorless as I knew how to make them, but that hound always knew where they were. He avoided them with his invariable lack of extravagant demonstration. He made just a little jog in the trail at the right place.

He did the thing to do, and I could see in him some of the wolf of the past that had inclinations to hang around human camps together with some of the wary wolf of the present.

*

In considering the nature of wolves and the differences in behavior that one might expect for different animals and circumstances, one may not be quite entitled to say that anything can happen. The full range of differences, however, is wide, and the extremes embrace opposites.

As concerns at least North American wolves, the extremes include the very exceptional individuals that would, as healthy animals, try to take human beings as prey. The usual wolves are those respecting man's living body or having no interest in him as huntable game. In their social relations with their own kind, the wolves may show both extremes of animosity or friendliness, with all individualistic variations in between. And the same species that frequented the camps of Indians and white bison hunters of the past century, and can be so gentle and tame, can furiously assault dangerous bears in defending property rights.

Members of *Canis lupus* may show both restraint in killing and the capacity for mass slaughter of livestock, as on the western plains. We should not have to go far to comprehend how it could be that wolves, partly stereotyped and partly individualistic in behavior, may kill relatively little or relatively much prey. Their reactions may be conditioned by inclinations for peaceable and easy living, by the allure of excitement, or by awareness of dangers either in hunting dangerous game or in feeding upon non-fresh meat. Behavior patterns must be compromises between what wolves have done in the past and what they must do now—and with the little whims and idiosyncracies and behavioristic luxuries that the rigors of selection still permit an intelligent and resilient species to have.

While their hunting and killing may be characterized by either restraint or rapacity as extremes, a statement may be justifiable that wolves commonly respond to ready availability of acceptable prey by killing freely though not senselessly. Similar statements may apply to their utilization of the prey that they kill: They may eat all of it that is edible or they may not eat any of it, but, in between, their degree of utilization may be termed moderate, consistent with their convenience and tastes, their needs, their safety, and their overall behavior as wild dogs.

As wild dogs, the wolves live their own lives, and only as wild dogs— with their racial and individual differences—may they be realistically thought of. They do not try to emulate human virtues in what man might call their exemplary family lives—nor in any other way. The expression wolfish nature may properly describe a wolf's friendliness and fidelity as well as its predatory behavior. The Crisler wolves exhibited capabilities for great sympathy: toward a dog with his nose full of porcupine quills, toward a sledge dog that had lost face, toward a new sledge dog chained and crying, toward a sick wolf, toward a human friend who had hurt himself falling on the ice.

Wolfish nature should not connote anything fiendish. Wolves are predators adapted to prey upon large animals, and predation upon large animals can be messy. But to regard wolves as creatures of evil, per se, is not defensible.

They are just wild dogs.

CHAPTER 3

Of Wolves and Wolf Prey

Since the last Ice Age, man has, most unwillingly, contributed domestic animals to wolf diets over the world.

Considered apart from emotional extremes, a simple generalization as to wolf predation upon domestic animals should not be far wrong; the greater the degree of domestication, the less chance a prospective victim usually has against wolves that are disposed to attack and have an opportunity to do so without human interference.

Feral pigs and horses and the longhorns of the old American West could do well in taking care of themselves against wolves. The weak or clumsy or stupid livestock could not. Under human protection, the livestock breeds were developed for qualities other than defensive prowess, and they had to remain under human protection as long as they had such an effective screening agency as wolves to work on them.

But, by now, few North American large wolves have opportunity to prey upon domestic animals. Call them buffalo wolves, timber wolves, or lobos, these large wolves have been practically extirpated from most parts of the United States and Canada where their depredations could concern anything man has any more claim to than wild game.

The remaining large wolves of North America now feed chiefly upon the types of prey that they have lived with for many thousands of years. While the continental glaciers advanced and receded, modern wolves and their wild prey adjusted to each other and underwent their own respective evolutions. Since long before the writing of human history, native predators have been testing, attacking, killing, and exploiting native prey; and prey species have been appraising, trying to escape, escaping, and defending themselves against their natural adversaries.

What North American large wolves eat reflects their habits and preferences and responsiveness to availability. The food has to be acceptable to them, and they must be able to get enough of it to supply their needs.

It does not have to be big game, though big game tends to be more of a dietary staple—perhaps an almost exclusive staple—wherever most large wolves still live. Sigurd Olson wrote of predation by northeastern Minnesota wolves upon rodents, grouse, and cold-blooded vertebrates during the warm-weather months and upon snowshoe hares as well as upon deer during the winter months. The wolves (like coyotes) may prey upon waterfowl and fish when they have opportunities, or they may dig into muskrat lodges to reach muskrat victims of epidemic disease.

Many of the species of small prey upon which wolves feed vary tremendously in numbers from year to year. The grouse, the mice and voles, the rabbits and hares may reach astounding abundance-peaks or become astoundingly scarce at times. In some instances, mouse-like rodents or hares may be hundreds of times more abundant during one year than during another. Over a whole block of Wisconsin counties, I have seen vole populations that were literally swarming everywhere during a summer, fall, and winter; then, with relative suddenness, the voles were all but gone.

Or the population trends of some of these prey species may be decidedly up or down over a long period of years. Changes in human land use, climatic cycles, and dominance of plant successions may push one species up and another down. The heath hen became extinct, and other prairie grouse may fade until not so far from extinction themselves, but their brushwoods relative, the ruffed grouse, may expand its range until the ecological balance goes against it, in turn. Human patterns of exploiting game or fur species may change; a species may greatly modify its living habits or it may at a given time find things much more to its advantage than before, whatever the cause.

The raccoon furnishes an example of what can happen. After supplying the collegians of the 1920s with their coonskin coats, it lost its popularity in the fur trade to the extent that few trappers bothered about taking it. Once considered dependent for den sites upon the hollow trees of deciduous woodlands, it responded to deforestation by taking refuge in holes in the ground, in tile openings, in junk piles, and by accustoming itself to ranging farther and farther into open fields. Whatever it ate before the white man came, it is now a grain-eater, a fruit-eater, a scavenger, an eater of mice and fish and frogs, an eater of crayfishes and large insects. While more doubtless remains in the raccoon equation than can be explained from present knowledge, the species has dramatically increased and spread in Minnesota and South Dakota. It has spread, for one thing, far up northward from the timber wolf country of northern Minnesota into places where local people would not have known what a raccoon was during the years of my youth.

But abundance of animal life suitable for predator food may not be all that determines what will be most available to the predators of an area, to wolves or to lesser predators. Abundance itself need not be synonymous with availability—either strictly or approximately.

Helplessness or inexperience of young or weakness or disability from any cause may predispose certain members of a population to exploitation by predatory enemies. Biological surpluses—meaning more animals than should be trying to live in their habitats—are special targets for predation. Victims may be taken while moving restlessly about or while preoccupied with fighting or with the tensions of overcrowding. They may be strangers in strange places, not knowing what they need to know, which may mean the difference between escaping a predatory attack and not escaping. They may lack confidence, which is something that predators may recognize when deciding whether to refrain from attacking, to feint, or to follow through with a serious effort. More and more, evidence from a vast amount of field research points up the role of psychology in governing predator-prey relationships in at least a considerable variety of vertebrate animals.

Predation victims may not necessarily nor even usually be physically unfit. As individuals, they may be full-fleshed and healthy, but they may have lacked the good fortune to have been living in a suitable place in numbers that could have been comfortably accommodated. They may have lacked the good fortune to have been hatched or born in numbers that their parents could have taken care of or to have been hatched or born at a favorable time of year.

My most detailed knowledge of predator-prey relationships has grown out of investigations of two prolific wild species native to the north-central United States. One is a member of the partridge family, the bobwhite quail. The other is a wetland relative of the voles, the muskrat.

Neither species is classifiable as main staple wolf prey, but the studies of both have been sufficiently informative to illustrate the things that should be kept in mind in appraising wolf predation upon small game— that is, when it occurs.

Both the bobwhite and the muskrat have many predatory enemies or potential enemies. The list of species known to have preyed upon them could be made most imposing. Bobwhites and muskrats are also considered by many people to be limited in numbers and distribution by the losses that they suffer from predation; yet, in analysis, the population status of neither proves to be governed fundamentally in our north-central region by differences in the kinds and numbers of their predatory enemies.

The population status of the bobwhite and the muskrat may depend more upon food and other environmental features, upon luck with respect to the weather, and upon their own social tolerances. Predation may usually be regarded as operating more incidentally.

The incidental nature of the predation may be revealed by the tendencies of bobwhite and muskrat populations to conform to mathematical patterns. Except when scarcity itself may impose a biological handicap, the *lower* the breeding populations with respect to the supporting capacity of an area, the *higher* the rates of population increase may be. Many of such rates of increase, in their mathematical conformities, seem to be remarkably little affected not only by wide differences in kinds and numbers of predators but also by wide differences in the actual losses suffered through one kind or another of predatory enemies.

Within the mathematical patterns, much natural substitution of one type of loss for another occurs. Counterbalancing and adjustment offset many of the differences in what we call limiting factors, including predation. When more than enough bobwhites are hatched or muskrats born to fill an area's mathematical quota, the overproduced ones tend to be eliminated somehow. Since much if not most of this elimination of the overproduced occurs at immature stages, it is somewhat comparable to what happens when a plum tree loses its excess flowers or fruits. Whether elimination of the overproduced occurs through predation or not, a natural shaking-down to fit wild populations into their habitats must have the sanction of much evolution.

No one, to my knowledge, has intensively studied wolf predation upon small game. Assuming that the wolves are not on a straight diet of big game, I should not expect wolf predation upon small game to differ significantly from other predation suffered by small game. Accordingly, even when heavy, it might have little or no influence on the population levels reached or maintained by mice and voles, rabbits and hares, grouse and waterfowl. The years of maximum numbers of wolves on the North American prairies coincided in part with what may be regarded as the wonder years of the prairie grouse and waterfowl.

The mere fact of a predator being formidable or killing large numbers of prey should not be overrated in appraising population effects. If the bobwhite and muskrat findings be considered in detail, it may be seen that the very formidable great horned owl may have killed more bobwhites and the very formidable mink may have killed more muskrats on some of the study areas than any other non-human predators. The exploits of foxes with respect to both bobwhites and muskrats may have been decidedly lethal at times. Even so, there are plenty of case histories of bobwhites and muskrats thriving in the midst of the horned owls, minks, and foxes—and case histories of population surpluses of bobwhites and muskrats having been eliminated in the total absence of the horned owls, minks, and foxes.

*

Wolf predation upon large animals is what arouses the most interest and emotion. This is quite to be expected. Wolves are adapted to kill and are usually dependent upon large prey, and that prey may be man's favorite game species as well as his domestic animals.

The categories of wolf predation upon really wild and adaptable big game are not too clearly distinguishable. So much in the way of relationships between wolves and big game may seem to be a matter of gradations. At one extreme, big game populations can live with evident security from wolves. At another extreme, wolf predation can look severe, almost annihilative. And, in so many of our efforts to appraise the population effects of wolf predation upon big game, we may be confronted by questions as to human influence either affecting the game outright or the place in which the game lives or tries to live.

At first, when we think of how pitiably helpless domestic sheep can be against wolves, it may be difficult to visualize the conditions under which their progenitors managed to exist before they came under the protection of human shepherds. Surely, the frequent biblical references to wolf depredations on sheep suggest no special ability of sheep to cope with wolves then. The early history of domestication of sheep leads into the obscurities and unknowns of prehistory sufficiently soon to discourage efforts to get much farther than the idea that sheep have been on earth for a long time.

Wild species of sheep—somewhere around a dozen species—do live as natives in different parts of the world. Those living in North America are mountain dwellers. Their adaptations to a peculiar environmental niche, their fantastic agility, and the formidability of the rams as fighters explain a good deal of how they can live with wolves. It may be not only futile but dangerous for wolves to attack mountain sheep in the type of terrain in which the sheep can find secure refuge. If sheep such as these were the progenitors of our domestic sheep before the time of human shepherds, we need not postulate any long period of evolution in wolf-less places.

Adolph Murie's study of wolf predation upon the Dall mountain sheep of Mount McKinley indicated that the sheep were reasonably safe from the wolves as long as they stayed in their proper habitat and did not overpopulate it. He thought that the mountain sheep and the wolves may have been in equilibrium, with wolf predation probably being important in holding sheep numbers in check within the ordinary limits of the food supply. When the sheep left the more suitable parts of their range, they were much more severely preyed upon. It could be that the wolf predation might restrict the sheep to the superior places in which they may be said to belong.

Murie's data show impressive evidence of wolf predation upon diseased or weakened mountain sheep. This may or may not have selective value for the Dall sheep as a species. The sheep may have been vulnerable because of old age, and thus may have lived out their lives to the point where, biologically, it made little difference what happened to them. Or the vulnerable lambs may have been those simply not having enough to eat. As Murie wrote, it is hard to say just what effect on the species the wolf predation may have; it may be important along with other natural forces. Perhaps the wolf is important in maintaining the type of sheep that can live in equilibrium with good range.

The North American bison and musk ox are believed to have evolved group tactics for defense against wolves. Douglas Clarke wrote about how admirably the circle formation of the musk ox—adults outside, calves inside—affords protection against predators other than man, and how the musk ox did not seem to regard the wolf as much of an enemy. In one cited case, a pack of seven wolves circled a herd of four musk ox cows and their calves, and the cows did not even bother to rise to their feet. Instances are known of wolves isolating and killing musk oxen, but Clarke considered that such occasions must be rare.

For a species that is so very nearly wolf-proof as the musk ox, what does operate as the limiting factor in the absence of anything to be called effective predation? That takes us back to the differences between good and poor ranges. There are the commonplace—though undoubtedly valid—considerations such as of food resources. I am not sure that anyone knows what else. Clarke noted that the places where the now much reduced musk ox still survives on the Canadian mainland are those where the species was most numerous a century ago.

Wood Buffalo National Park in northwestern Canada may be about the only place where present-day North American wolves have any chance to prey upon bison in native bison range. There, the wolves also have an abundance of other game—game easier to get than bison—to prey upon. From Dewey Soper's study of the park bison, one may conclude that obviously well-situated animals suffered wolf predation only occasionally. It was mainly the senile or the handicapped young that fell victim. Mature bison in vigorous health were unlikely to be successfully attacked, and Soper felt that such animals may also be capable of protecting their calves. Bison were often observed to be indifferent to the presence of wolves.

Soper referred to wolf predation upon the bison of Wood Buffalo National Park as having been not nearly as destructive as it apparently had been upon the bison herds of the Great Plains. Undoubtedly, wolf predation upon the plains bison was sufficiently conspicuous for many people to witness, but, here too the descriptions of the plainsmen and early writers suggest that such predation was mainly centered upon stragglers, overaged animals, and undefended or poorly defended calves. The plains bison—indifferent to the wolves under normal conditions—could be dangerous to the wolves themselves in the event that the wolves did attempt an attack. The idea of the bison having been trained on wolves is not misleading.

George Catlin's description of hungry wolves working on an old, outcast bison bull illustrates bitter fundamentals. The desperately resisting bull had its eyes, nose, and tongue mostly torn away and the skin and flesh of its legs raggedly torn. But on the ground lay the crushed bodies of some of the desperately attacking wolves. Apart from the sympathies that human observers practically always feel for prey that suffers so much in the process of being killed, one should find it quite understandable how the wolves, if their hunger gave them any choice, might prefer to eat something that came more easily.

Clarke once pointed out to me that the bison, unlike the musk ox, lived on rich forage and had a high calf production along with extraordinary longevity. By 1939, there were still considerable numbers of earmarked cows over twenty years old in the Wainwright herd, still in good health and producing calves despite deliberate human culling; and a vigorous herd bull at Banff reached the age of fifty years before it was beaten in battle. This longevity combined with a high rate of calf production must have added up to a heavy loss of calves in any system of natural balancing. As long as a preponderance of cows each had a calf a year for up to twenty years, the bison herds must have contained immense numbers of potential wolf prey, even though the individual availability of calves to the wolves may have varied greatly with the circumstances.

Northern forest regions comprise the world range of the moose (genus *Alces*, including the Old World elk). As large animals, moose require much food of certain types, especially the shrubbery and small conifers that follow fires or cut-everything lumbering. Balsam fir, young pines, willow, birch, and aspen are among the staple moose foods listed in the literature. Aside from overexploitation by man, moose populations seem to be determined primarily by a subclimax or intermediate stage of the forest.

Randolph Peterson wrote in his book on the North American moose that the maturing plant succession tended to outgrow low moose populations. The range would thus be made still less favorable for the moose unless something happened to set back the succession again. Moderately heavy browsing, on the other hand, may stimulate some of the choicer food-plants to increased proliferation and so maintain or improve carrying capacity for a time. Willow, birch, and mountain maple are among the food-plants that best withstand browsing. In areas overpopulated by moose, the browsing can be so severe as to suppress the regeneration of important food-plants.

A notable example of overbrowsing was studied by Adolph Murie on Isle Royale, Michigan. The moose exerted such pressure on the vegetation that the population collapsed, and the island's carrying capacity for the species was drastically reduced for many years. At its peak, the Isle Royale population may have averaged as high as fourteen per square mile on a total area of about two hundred and twelve square miles. Following relief from browsing pressure, and after fires had renewed the browse, the moose population and the carrying capacity of Isle Royale for moose seemed rather stabilized at about three moose per square mile, as of the late 1950s. By the latter time, a wolf population had become established on the formerly wolf-less island, and the wolves had been forced by lack of alternative foods to subsist for the most part on the moose.

Peterson considered that a moose per square mile would be a relatively high density and that two or more per square mile would approach maximum carrying capacity for most large regions occupied by moose in eastern North America. In western North America, carrying capacities may run higher, many figures indicating between two and six per square mile. Some Rocky Mountain valleys may have temporary winter concentrations up to or exceeding thirty per square mile, but such figures must be far in excess of any normal carrying capacity of moose range. In Alaska, the range of the moose apparently has greatly expanded in recent decades. This in part may be a result of a gradual warming of the Arctic climate. Mostly, according to Starker Leopold and Fraser Darling, it resulted from extensive fires in southern and central Alaska.

Even spectacularly top-heavy populations of moose do not inevitably lead to spectacular die-offs or ruination of range. The moose may be sufficiently hardy to get through a normal winter on the poorer foods, after the better foods have been eaten. Although the moose can starve during periods of deep or badly crusted snow, overcrowded moose are ordinarily less likely to die off than to decrease their production of calves.

Except when wolves have nothing else to prey upon, they are especially apt to prey upon moose that are handicapped by ice-glazed snow. Starving moose may have the hide worn off their legs in trying to get around through the crust. Animals may be weak from massive infestations of parasites, they may be diseased, or they may lie dead or helpless from miscellaneous causes.

When in good condition, adult moose have great strength and endurance. If they cannot escape wolves by keeping away from them (as in deep, soft snow or in heavy cover or by taking refuge in water), they can still be difficult and dangerous prey as long as they do not just panic and run. A single wolf can kill a moose that continues running when overtaken.

Published accounts relate to a lone bull moose beating off an attack by five wolves, to dead and crippled wolves lying about sites of attacks upon moose, and to evidence that wolves avoided attacking in places where the moose had firm footing. Of course, moose may suffer injuries, even in victorious battles with wolves. Adolph Murie thought that wolves might worry many moose, possibly even in sport, yet be unwilling really to take chances from the deadly hoofs. Much seems to depend upon the psychological responses of the wolves when the moose have advantages in the lay of the land and refuge cover, together with evident stamina and a will to fight.

Despite an impression observers may get that the larger wolf packs should be able to handle about anything that they tackle, questions persist as to how much unnecessary risk they may care to take. This is a consideration that always should be kept in mind as applying to any difficult, dangerous game. The wolves may often find it easier, simpler, safer, and more satisfactory to subsist upon something else, upon something like deer or caribou, their more usual staple foods, wherever large wolves still live in North America. Wolves may in fact ignore moose if they do not have to feed upon them through necessity.

The formidable defensive prowess of adult moose naturally confers some degree of protection upon the calves. There is a widely stated view in Scandinavia that the custom of the bull moose staying behind weaker members of family groups represents an adaptation for intercepting wolves coming up along the trails from the rear. Undefended moose calves discovered by hunting wolves or those that the wolves succeed in keeping separate from defending adults have little life expectancy. But David Mech found in his Isle Royale studies that if the cow and calf can keep close together they seem to be invulnerable; the cow kicks at the wolves behind her, and the calf charges the wolves in front of it. When running, the cow stays close behind the calf and threatens any wolf that comes close.

Moose as well as other kinds of big game have often shown steady increases in areas having abundant wolves and have maintained their high numbers along with the wolves. The Alaskan situation illustrates this clearly. It also seems clear that, once the moose population of a large area gets out of bounds biologically, more than wolf predation will be required to control it.

At the opposite extreme, low moose populations have no assurance of becoming thriving populations merely through human elimination of the predatory enemies that might prey upon them. It might as well be recognized that, whatever the reasons, many places in the geographic range of moose are not suited to moose. Biologically, the moose do not belong there.

At their more moderate levels, moose populations living in places favorable to them show the adjustments that one may expect of species that have long lived successfully in boreal regions. So far as we know, wolves have been with the moose throughout the adjustments that they both made before the coming of the white man. It is possible that the presence of a normal wolf population may select for a healthy balance between moose and moose habitat in those places that genuinely are suited to moose.

Overpopulations of American elk or, better named, wapiti have their almost-standard troubles. They may suffer from malnutrition and disease. Reproductive rates may be depressed, calves lost through many agencies, including not particularly formidable predators such as coyotes and black bears.

In the Jasper and Banff national parks of Canada—very nearly the only North American region where wolves still have a chance to prey upon wapiti—Cowan reported a marked favoritism of the wolves toward this species as food. A large proportion of the wolf victims were taken in their prime years of life rather than predominantly as diseased, senile, or young animals. As of 1947, as much as fifty percent of the wapiti population might be classifiable as a vulnerable surplus. Despite the fact that remains of calves and adults were equally represented in the summer wolf droppings, no significant differences were found in survival of young wapiti in park ranges that were hunted over by wolves and in those that were wolf-free.

The overcapacity game herds of these Canadian national parks had developed largely since 1930 at a time when human interference with predators had been light or lacking. The predator populations of all kinds—of coyotes, cougars, and wolverines, in addition to the wolves—had not succeeded in taking the annual increment of the game herds, not even removing the cull group, a large part of which ultimately became carrion.

Although the subjects of wolf-caribou and wolf-deer relationships will both be reserved for fuller treatment in the following chapters, a few generalizations as to what wolf predation upon these staple prey species may signify should help in rounding out this preliminary sketch.

Clarke observed that the caribou-eating wolves of the Canadian tundra had to work hard for a living and tended to be somewhat underfed. While Adolph Murie found that caribou were the main food of wolves in Mount McKinley National Park, he not only regarded the caribou as adapted to withstand the losses but also not tending to worry about the presence of wolves unless chased. This apparent unconcern of caribou in the presence of wolves has been repeatedly noted. However, references may be seen to caribou being apprehensive and not lingering in the vicinity of special places where wolves might hide. The caribou prefer to keep their racial enemies in sight.

Whether wolves of caribou country feed upon caribou as staples because of genuine preference, because of habit, or because these are easiest or safest to get, wolf predation upon caribou can vary according to time and place. Murie's detailed observations showed that most wolf predation was borne by stragglers and calves. The Crislers did not consider calves as necessarily vulnerable to wolf predation unless they did the wrong thing. Some of the most careful observers have concluded that a chief source of wolf food consisted of diseased or injured individual caribou. At least sound adult caribou might be more sure-footed than wolves. Murie described caribou quickly leaving a wolf behind when they reached rough ground. Francis Harper thought that a pursued caribou may choose to try to escape by running on ice, as if aware of its relatively greater sure-footedness there. During seasons of open water, caribou may escape by swimming rivers and lakes or by taking refuge on islands.

Starker Leopold concluded, on the basis of years of research in the North American southwest, that deer populations were determined by the quality of their range, and that predation was unlikely to do more than to remove the surplus. His studies were carried out under a great diversity of conditions, from wolf-less California to the Gavilan wilderness of northern Mexico, having a near-primitive population of large predators, including wolves.

Irrespective of all that remains unknown or little known about wolf-deer relationships, it seems clear that wolves, if present where deer live, may be expected to prey upon top-heavy deer populations on a conspicuous scale and to take advantage of starving or otherwise handicapped individuals.

There are many instances of North American deer increasing up to the point that they starved after human extirpation of wolves (or other formidable predators); and these might make a cause-and-effect relationship between the fortunes of deer and their predatory enemies seem self-evident. Still, great changes also occurred in North American deer ranges during this period. Also, there is much evidence of the deer changing their living habits to adjust to human land use. There are also differences due to human hunting practices.

*

In certain ways, the beaver, though on the whole not a very important food of wolves over North America, provides some of the best evidence of fundamentals in predator-prey relationships. Cowan's observations in the Rocky Mountain national parks of Canada illustrate distinctions that can be made out if one looks beyond the mere fact that predation can occur.

There, very heavy beaver populations could live in superlative beaver range despite an abundance of predatory enemies. But, in one place, nearly half of the droppings from young wolves consisted entirely of beaver remains. After their range had deteriorated because of overuse, the local beavers were more important as wolf prey than the deer and wapiti combined.

I do not need to visit such an area to visualize how the wolves would respond. In beaver country, from Montana and Wyoming eastward through the Lake States and northward, local beavers work progressively farther up the smaller streams. They cut and they dam, and the aspen and willow and other of the choicer foods may virtually disappear for years, until the beavers themselves disappear and give their food-plants a chance to come back. The beavers have no safe passage to a large river or a lake, and distant places may be no better for them than the ones they have left. As the food goes, the beavers become increasingly active over the land, and Nature's answer is starkly simple—fewer beavers.

There could be many wolf droppings made up of beaver fur along trails and loafing sites if the wolves were hungry enough to clean up a beaver kill. A beaver has much fur on thick skin tightly grown to the body, and the pelt does not peel away from the meat so easily as to encourage the kind of cutting and tugging that lays back big clean patches of skin to be left gathering frost on the snow. If a wolf is hungry enough, it eats large quantities of fur along with what else of a beaver's body it can reduce to swallowability.

Wolf predation is just part of the exploitation of the exploitable that occurs wherever living creatures live. Details of exploitation of prey by predators may differ according to species and circumstances, but, as an overall phenomenon, what counts most of all in determining the predation that a prey species may draw is the availability of that species as prey.

Wolves are no more able than other predators to prey upon what is not available to them; and, to the extent that a predator does not prey upon what it can neither catch nor handle, this is all most simple. It is when we go deeper into questions of availability of prey and population effects of predation that the simplicity becomes illusive.

At North American research centers there are records of thousands upon thousands of meals of predatory mammals and birds that lived on the same areas where populations of prey animals were investigated on a year-after-year basis. From these records, it may be seen that rabbits and mice, for example, may come close to being year-round prey for many predators. Yet, the local food habits of typical rabbit-eaters or mouse-eaters may switch to some other prey—and many of these switches are not really forced by what might be considered necessity. The populations of regular prey may be just as abundant, just as exploitable as before, but other sources of food may be still more exploitable, if only very temporarily.

During a couple of weeks in spring, the chief predators of an area may be living on large beetles in combination with something like young flickers and barn rats. Some predators may suddenly be getting young screech owls, or there may be waves of blackbirds, pocket gophers, garter snakes, young pheasants, blue jays, or meadowlarks showing up in the feeding debris of wild hunters. When summer comes, the flesh-eating and insectivorous animal life that is able and disposed to do so may gorge upon grasshoppers and crickets.

Much general predation is centered upon biological windfalls. The windfalls may be literally that, as when storms increase the vulnerability of many species to predation. Not only does this occur through the physical beating of individuals and the places in which they live but also through evictions by floods or fires, forced wandering in strange and inhospitable

Wolf with Rabbit, by Charles W. Schwartz. Charles W. Schwartz Collection, the State Historical Society of Missouri.

places, and an endless variety of aftermaths. Other crises include those brought on by droughts, deep snows, thick glazes of ice, thaws exposing snowdrift tunnels, trampling or heavy grazing by livestock, farmers hauling in corn shocks or cutting brush along roadsides or removing woodpiles or plowing fields or draining ponds.

Opportunistic predation was shown by a mink killing and dragging to its den sixteen young muskrats that had been sitting, storm-evicted, along a lakeshore—by a mink that evidently had not succeeded in preying upon muskrats at any other time for weeks preceding and following the storm. Opportunism may be manifested over a longer period, as by predation upon bobwhite coveys trying to winter where environmental deficiencies made their situation hopeless. One such vulnerable covey lost twenty-one out of its twenty-three members almost exclusively to a pair of great horned owls, whereas a neighboring but well-situated covey totaling thirty-two birds wintered without loss, though living much more within the regular home range of the owls.

Any kind of emergency that leaves prey animals exposed or trying to live at a disadvantage means windfalls for predators. Gulls picking up earthworms behind a plow, a raccoon searching puddles in a drying stream for minnows and crayfishes, a red-tailed hawk taking a flood-marooned cottontail from a hummock, human hunters shooting mallards attempting to alight in a waterhole during a snowstorm, all exemplify opportunistic predation.

Man repeatedly charges natural enemies of his favorite game species with obeying no game laws and mercilessly hunting the year around. This can be true in words, but, in many ways, predation by wild enemies upon well-adjusted prey species living in good range conforms to natural rules that tend to give increased protection to the prey when protection is most needed and decreased protection when protection is needed less. Furthermore, a large proportion of the non-human predation suffered even by the favorite game species is not actually in competition with human hunting. There are distinctions here that the public is unlikely to perceive without help.

Calculations as to population effects of this predator or that predator, or of more or fewer predators, or of increased or decreased predation, may become nothing more than nonsensical when assumptions are made that do not come anywhere near the truth. Some natural factors—notably those linked with weather and environment—may so completely dominate some populations that all else becomes of secondary or of no real importance, with predation then becoming a mere symptom of unbalance. Natural safeguards protecting common animals from excessive predation may be more than fecundity to outbreed the toll taken by predators. They may be more than the obvious means of concealment, escape, or defense. A great amount of automatic taking up or letting out of slack characterizes certain ancient predator-prey relationships. Population effects of increased losses from one agency may be nullified by decreased losses from other agencies, or through increased production of young in compensation. The chances of survival of young may depend upon how many of the same species the older animals may tolerate. Death of one individual may, in short, make possible the survival of another of its kind.

Complexities in natural relationships have surely been a part of Life as long as Life has been on our planet, and surely Life has been acquiring complexity in relationships as it has been acquiring complexity in its forms. Life has had a long time in which to make adjustments—animals to animals and to plants, plants to plants and to animals, animals and plants to their physical environments and to the stresses of emergencies. Thriving forms of Life have demonstrated their successes in making adjustments by the fact of their thriving. Their long experience with their racial enemies is itself proof of successful adjustments. Bobwhites lived with horned owls, muskrats with minks, caribou and deer with wolves, long before any modern biologist tried to analyze population mechanisms.

The public generally overrates the population effects of predation upon wild animals, at the same time generally underrating the effects of the less spectacular factors that may operate more fundamentally. The effects of intolerance within a species and of changes in environment are particularly easy to underrate when enough bloody predator kills may be strewn about. I do not imply that predation cannot be important as the dramas of living things mesh and intermesh. Man, himself, has demonstrated by his own hunting of certain species to extinction how predation can be more than a species can endure, but man is not a typical predator, and such cases are not typical. Predation upon at least the commoner mammals and birds is more likely to center upon the annual overflow and wastage from Life's fruitfulness.

From this broader perspective, it may be possible to get closer to the truth in appraisals of some of the relationships existing between wolves and wolf prey. Wolves may show specializing and selectivity in their hunting, killing, and feeding, and their hunting in packs introduces its own special cases, but there are still biological limits to what wolves can or will do and to what racially adjusted prey species have to withstand from wolf predation.

CHAPTER 4

Of Wolves, Reindeer, Caribou, and Human Mistakes

The genus *Rangifer*—comprising the reindeer and caribou—has several important species (or subspecies) native to the bogs and tundras and Far North forests of the northern hemisphere. The reindeer of Lapland and the caribou of the American Arctic and Subarctic are known for their large herds and for the conspicuous predation they may draw from wolves.

Wolves rank very high indeed in public estimation of factors limiting reindeer and caribou populations. One can get the impression from much of the older, practical literature that nothing really counts like wolf predation. So we may still be told or still read in today's literature. Moreover, the wolf predation, we may be reminded, is something that we can keep down.

Wolves can and do prey heavily upon reindeer and caribou whenever they have good chances.

✻

Of course, as relates to wolf predation upon Lapland reindeer, the disadvantageous effects of domestication must be considered. The Norwegian biologists Yngvar Hagen and Aage Wildhagen told me that the genuinely wild reindeer stock of Norway's Dovrefjell region was incomparably better adapted to live with wolves. The ancestors of the wild stock had lived with wolves for many, many millennia before there were Lapps or any herdsmen to soften life for them.

Semidomesticated reindeer were imported from the Old World to Alaska late in the nineteenth century, and Lapp herders were brought over to take care of them. Close herding kept predation losses negligible. In some places, rates of increase were almost as high as the reproductive potential. When the reindeer herds later collapsed, wolves were blamed not only for outright killings but also for scattering herds. There is no doubt that the poorly herded or neglected reindeer could draw wolf predation and that the listing of wolves by Eskimos and whites as the most serious cause of loss could seem convincingly logical. There is no doubt also that too many people concerned with the introduced reindeer in North America have a deficient knowledge of the reindeer's ecology.

Any decline of reindeer as precipitous as from the peak numbers of over a half million in the 1930s to an estimated twenty-five thousand by 1950 would have to be explained. Much was said and written about what happened.

In reviewing the testimony as to careless herding, wolf predation, and excessive human slaughtering, Starker Leopold and Frank Fraser Darling remarked how little attention had been paid to the deterioration of the range brought on by the reindeer themselves. They considered that the reindeer in Alaska furnished a grand-scale, well-documented example of the rise and fall of an animal population subject to few checks. The reindeer could graze or browse more than the annual increment of food on their range and still go on increasing and apparently thriving; and the people interested in the reindeer tended to look at the animals only and be content as long as they were increasing and thriving. Yet, the condition of the range—particularly the winter range—was the crucial factor.

Although studies of Alaskan reindeer range had been in progress since 1920, early estimates of carrying capacities had been optimistic. As evidence that the rise and fall of the reindeer was in fact a range phenomenon, Leopold and Darling cited situations on various islands where the customary reasoning simply could not have applied. On Nunivak, St. Lawrence, and St. Paul Islands, the reindeer had had no chance to stray or to run away with wild caribou, wolves had been absent, and killing by native people had been very limited—and the reindeer herds had built up and collapsed in the same way as on the mainland.

The collapse on Nunivak Island occurred between 1946 and 1948, after the reindeer had reached a peak of about twenty-two thousand in the mid-1940s. Inspection of the range in the early 1950s showed that the nutritious and palatable lichens had been largely eaten away. The surviving reindeer had gone over to a diet predominantly of willow, a food of uncertain value for them in the event of a severe winter.

In Scandinavia, the Lapps recognize the necessity for rotating reindeer grazing on lichen ranges. There, herds must be moved far and often to avoid passing a given locality more than once in ten years. In North America, Leopold and Darling wrote that neither Eskimo herders nor most of the whites (except the transported Lapps) seemed mobile enough to follow any such grazing schedule. Overgrazing and ultimate exhaustion of the coastal ranges may be regarded as a natural consequence of poor husbandry.

It should not be forgotten that the Alaskan reindeer situation remains essentially a domestic animal situation. Unless constantly tended, the reindeer herds often scatter, and, in wolf country, the strays are easily run down by wolves. Wolf-reindeer relationships in Alaska differ significantly from those between wolves and the racially tested wild reindeer in Norway's Dovrefjell.

✿

Alaska is also the site of some of the most penetrating studies of ecology and population dynamics of native caribou.

Leopold and Darling discussed the nature of the winter range required by caribou and what disturbances in that range mean in the ecology of the caribou. During the times of year when herbaceous foliage is frozen or unavailable under snow, caribou subsist principally on branching lichens (called reindeer lichens or reindeer moss) and willow browse. The lichens of the genera *Cladonia* and *Cetraria*, which seem to be the basic elements in the winter diets of the caribou, are members of various climax plant associations of boreal regions. They tend to reach maximum abundance as an understory to the sparse forests of white spruce that occur in the drier places, on ridges, benches, knolls, and well-drained uplands; they are lacking in muskegs and wet tundras. Because of their very slow rate of growth, they withstand only light grazing. Fire eliminates them entirely. After burning, these lichens may require up to fifty or a hundred years to regenerate; and, when fires have burned down to mineral soil, recovery may take much longer.

Although caribou wander over and eat a great variety of vegetational types in spring, summer, and fall, and do not then require lichens, these seasons are not critical in the lives of the animals. It is in winter that the caribou's usual dependence upon the lichens makes it a member of a climax biota and a member that must have what it needs.

Leopold and Darling wrote that even the most casual inspection of caribou ranges in Alaska would reveal relatively little climax lichen growth remaining south of the Arctic Circle. In the coastal range of western Alaska that had been occupied by the great reindeer herds, the lichens have been grazed out to the point of ruining the range for caribou. In central Alaska the destruction of wintering range for caribou seemed to be due principally to burning.

There were lightning and Indian fires before the coming of the white man, but the evidence suggests that fires increased greatly in both size and frequency after settlement. During the gold rushes, the miners burned the timber on an enormous scale; afterward, a large population of trappers and prospectors stayed on in Alaska, and, as a group, they were no more careful with fire than the original miners. Leopold and Darling did not inspect any large part of the original wintering range of caribou of the Alaskan interior, but, on the samples that they did inspect, fire had played such a dominant part in destroying the lichens that they felt safe in attributing to that one factor the major blame for the decrease of caribou.

They also wrote that, contrary to the situation in central and southern Alaska, caribou in the north were at least as numerous as fifty years before and perhaps even more numerous. Since the truly Arctic tundra does not burn and has only been grazed locally by reindeer, the caribou range there may be as good as it ever was. But, in their view, it appears relatively poor winter range, lichens being sparse at best. Large herds visit the Arctic slope in spring, summer, and fall, but they usually spend midwinter on better ranges lying to the south.

Where does the wolf fit into any modern reconsideration of the interactions of a native predator and a native prey in a changed and changing scene?

Human campaigning against wolves has been, expectedly, a prominent part of what has gone on under the name of big game management in

Alaska. Much of this campaigning has been for the protection of caribou, that hereditary wolf prey.

In view of the limitations and vulnerability to overuse of caribou range in Alaska, Leopold and Darling felt obliged to point out the dangers in campaigning against the wolves as a catchall management measure; and, in this connection, they used the Nelchina herd as an example. This herd near Anchorage was built up from four thousand in 1948 to seven thousand in 1951 through intensive campaigning against the wolves. With a hunting take of only seven to eight percent per year and a high survival rate of the calves, the prospects are for continued increase. The winter range of the herd was an unburned block surrounded by many burns of varying sizes and ages. Any further increase of the caribou would have to be accommodated on this one block, which was already fairly heavily browsed. There was nowhere else for the animals to go. (Adolph Murie wrote me in 1960 that, because of the beneficial aspects of the wolf predation on the Nelchina area, the wolves are no longer campaigned against there.)

After looking at the Alaskan caribou ranges south of the Arctic Circle, Leopold and Darling generalized that the western portions have been all but destroyed by reindeer and the central four-fifths by fire. The capacity of the region to support caribou is therefore more circumscribed than it was in the past. It would take a great deal more than regulating human hunting and keeping down losses from wolf predation to restore the herds to anything like the original level. Decisions as to where, if anywhere, exploitation by either man or wolves may need more stringent control should be based upon examination of local winter ranges in relation to current numbers of caribou. If the role of wolves in depressing caribou populations is being considered from the standpoint of caribou management, it would be appropriate to consider whether an increase of caribou would be desirable.

Throughout Alaska, the protection of caribou from both hunting and wolves almost always has been on the apparent assumption that the range would carry the increased caribou herds. If the northern caribou ranges are in fact inferior in carrying capacity, with caribou numbers being quite high and hunting pressure low, there could be an incipient danger of overpopulation and damage to the caribou range. A recent drive against wolves in the Umiat region eliminated over two hundred and fifty wolves through shooting and poisoning in an area where the natives usually killed about a hundred additional wolves per year for bounty. All of this was for the stated purpose of giving caribou protection that they very likely did not need and should not have received.

While the inherent nomadic wandering of the caribou herds would tend to distribute their grazing over wide expanses and thus work to prevent destruction of the lichen complex from overgrazing, the caribou do not seem to have a fully automatic, built-in safety factor that protects their range from overuse. The possibility still exists that an age-tested relationship between caribou, caribou range, and wolves may still need all of its major components. And, it may be not only a matter of wolf predation being of direct benefit to the caribou in preventing overpopulation and damage to the caribou range.

The role of wolves as culling agents for the caribou herds has been discussed by a number of close observers. Francis Harper considered it significant that the two regions of the world where caribou or reindeer have not long lived with wolves are those having the runts of the whole caribou-reindeer tribe. The Crislers felt they could recognize, within the first few seconds of wolves chasing caribou, if an unfit—lame, diseased, or parasitized—animal were in the band pursued. Some authors have made at least reasonably good cases for the sanitation value of wolves in their elimination of caribou afflicted with serious diseases or parasites; and, in a review of Lois Crisler's book, *Arctic Wild*, William O. Pruitt, Jr., wrote that the wolf, "instead of being doomed with a price on his head and agonizing poisons served to him should be, in a land governed by civilized and rational humans, recognized as the master herder and rigidly protected."

＊

The barren-ground caribou of northwestern Canada has declined most alarmingly during the present century. According to calculations made for the Canadian government by Frank Banfield and John Kelsall, the reduction has been from about one million seven hundred and fifty thousand to about six hundred and seventy thousand in the first half of the century, then to about two hundred and seventy-seven thousand in the next six years. The numbers in some herds have dropped to a quarter or less in the 1950–1955 period alone: one from two hundred and twenty thousand to fifty-nine thousand and another from thirty-five thousand to five thousand.

The quality of much of the barren-ground range has been adversely affected by fire, but evidently not quite to the destructive extent as in Alaska. However, Kelsall wrote that the winter range of the Yellowknife area had been almost completely burned during the past sixty years and that large areas around Great Slave Lake had been purposefully burned by prospectors to expose the rock. He attributed much burning to carelessness on the part of both natives and whites, whose mobility has been so greatly increased by motor transportation. The burning during the last three-quarters of a century seemed greatly to have exceeded any normal burning that preceded it.

Despite man's often serious and sometimes ruinous impacts on the barren-ground caribou's range, the prevailing view seems to be that man exerted his heaviest influence on the species through direct killing—and also that wolf predation exerted a significant influence in accelerating the caribou decline. Yet, Douglas Clarke considered that very low calf crops noted during the years of sharpest decline did not represent a likely biological response to either human or wolf predation on the part of a herd living on good range; and, while he did not try to explain the entire decline in terms of damage to the range through burning, he rated the burning as of outstanding importance.

Wolves and barren-ground caribou are always intimately associated except for two months in the summer when the migrating caribou have moved and the wolves still must not get out of reach of their young in the dens. For most of the year, caribou-hunting wolves are as nomadic as the caribou are; they stay with the herds, preying chiefly upon calves or upon isolated, sleeping, sick, or crippled adults. Banfield remarked that, in large herds, the caribou would sometimes remain bedded down within fifty yards of passing wolves, becoming accustomed to the presence of the wolves associated with the herd. He estimated that the annual wolf predation probably did not exceed five percent of the total caribou population of the barren grounds even during wolf abundances.

When the caribou are abundant, wolves may kill in excess of immediate needs, to cache pieces of meat deliberately or merely to leave the killed prey, possibly to revisit it in the future. Much of this heavy killing is in the vicinity of dens at which pups will be born and cared for. The wolves may do much scavenging on both the older wolf-kills and upon carcasses of animals dead from other causes. Of slightly under seven hundred caribou carcasses discovered, Banfield ascribed the deaths of one hundred and seventy-four to wolf predation, in contrast with four hundred and eighty-three killed by man. Continued, large-scale feeding by the wolves on caribou carrion has been recorded for two months after all of the living caribou had departed from the hunting area of the wolves.

If it be conceded that human and wolf predation in combination may impose more of a toll than the barren-ground caribou can withstand, it might also be conceded that campaigning against the wolves could be good management. The caribou is to the natives dependent upon it about what the bison was to the Plains Indians. On the face of it, this looks like an example of wolves competing with man for a resource that man wants and needs.

Nevertheless, as concerns this persecution of wolves on behalf of the human hunters who want and undoubtedly do need the caribou, I find it impossible to avoid consciousness of a big question, a great big "Why?"

The caribou hunting practices of the Indians, Eskimos, and some European trappers are scandalously wasteful—to me, incredible according to modern standards of ethics and good sense. For firsthand information, I admittedly have nothing: I have never been on the Canadian Barren Grounds, I have never seen a caribou speared or shot, I know nothing about it except from what I have read or have been told. But the reputable literature on caribou hunting so describes conscienceless waste that there cannot be any doubt about it. I have witnessed the despairing anger of one of the top game administrators in Canada upon hearing more examples of fantastic irresponsibility with firearms among dwindling caribou herds, the same herds that are assiduously protected from wolves and non-resident hunters for the benefit of residents and especially natives.

Caribou may be singularly vulnerable to shooting with firearms. Hunters in a good position to shoot caribou may stop for no reason other than running out of ammunition. Banfield, in a recent summary of the plight of the barren-ground caribou, wrote that Indian and Eskimo hunters generally make no effort to conserve caribou while hunting. Nor, except rarely, do they attempt to kill escaping wounded animals, nor to find wounded animals that have died at a distance, as long as other animals remain available for more killing. Killing may go on in excess of anything even remotely approaching needs, according to ancient custom. Or killing may be for sport. In sport, there can be shooting with small-caliber rifles (which are still capable of serious wounding or killing) into passing herds, with no intent to utilize the victims.

Even when primitive methods are used, such as the spearing of swimming caribou from canoes or kayaks, reports may tell of at least as many escaping wounded as were killed. Banfield wrote of killings at crossing points that resulted, each year, in the abandonment of thousands of caribou carcasses. Some photographs show windrows of rotting bodies along the water's edge.

Aircraft passengers misinterpreted the visible evidence of a slaughter of up to five thousand caribou by local hunters in one area, reporting great numbers of wolf-kills on the lakes. Surely, the wolves could be expected to feed upon such a concentration of available food, upon caribou killed and left by hunters making no real efforts at caching. Often, these kills are never revisited by the hunters, or the hunters allow the meat and hide to spoil, anyway, or utilize it wastefully.

Banfield further noted that bullet-crippled caribou commonly trailed the migrating herds, yet the wolf predation was insufficiently severe to eliminate them. Wolf packs could probably winter in southern Keewatin District without killing any caribou, just by eating the carcasses that human hunters left on the tundra.

As long as they are attending the caribou herds, wolves can be vulnerable to what is euphemistically called wolf control. Whether through the use of aircraft, poisons, or skilled hunters, or all modern methods in combination, methods of wolf control—let us call it plain killing—exist that are sufficiently effective to reduce wolf populations to remnants over vast portions of the regions occupied by barren-ground caribou.

When the wolves are reduced to remnants over the Canadian (and Alaskan) North, where shall we go from there?

We return to the certainty that man, caribou (or reindeer), and wolves have existed together for thousands of years in suitable parts of the northern hemisphere. Wolves have been part of a biotic community, and the functioning thereof was good enough to endure. Now that the human member of that community has acquired modern weapons and transportation to implement a Stone Age psychology, I do not think that the resulting combination of power and irresponsibility has survival value. Man can continue to burn what is burnable of the caribou range and slaughter the caribou while they last; and, while he does it, he can surely, if he tries hard with poison and light plane and buckshot, wipe out his rival, the wolf of the tundra. Maybe, in need and recklessness, man can otherwise make his existence felt by the biotic communities that evolved with him since the coming and going of the ice sheets.

I have my sympathies for northern natives, whose lives can be hard and whose personal generosities great. I have known Indians whom I admired, and some of them were intelligent and civilized according to any meaningful criteria. That Indians are capable of restraint in the harvesting of wildlife has been demonstrated by Canadian experience with registered traplines. That some Indians can be sensitive to the subtler natural values is something of which I have been sure for a long time. Even so, Indians and Eskimos can be wretched conservationists on their caribou ranges.

If we destroy one member of the ancient man-wolf-caribou association merely to give squandering man a little more time to destroy the third member, is that really intelligent?

The changes over the caribou range are not of the kinds made inevitable by human occupation of the world in any ordinary sense. The tundras are not being taken over by agriculture nor by urban expansion nor by anything else that so thoroughly upsets what we might loosely call any primitive Balance of Nature. The tundras are still wilderness, still peopled by hunters, and there can be little doubt that immense tracts will remain that way for a long time to come. As yet, upsetting the whole tundra relationship between animals, plants, soils, and climate cannot be defended in terms of progress or advance of civilization. It is a man-made bungle of disheartening magnitude.

CHAPTER 5

Of Wolves and Deer and Deer Range and Man

One of the recent newspaper photographs that the American reading public may have glanced at before discarding was of three big timber wolves from the Ontario–Minnesota border, stretched out dead and frozen in a winter scene. The wolves had been killed in part of a wilderness and backwoods region now having nearly all of the last free-living timber wolves of the United States—north-central Minnesota eastward across part of northern Wisconsin to the Upper Peninsula of Michigan.

✻

On the whole, timber wolves are now killed in the northern Lake States for the expressed reason that they kill white-tailed deer. They do kill deer. When able to, wolves may subsist principally on this item of food during the winter months or over the whole year. Furthermore, when the deer overpopulate their range or are available to wolves in great numbers as victims of emergencies, the wolves may kill them on a conspicuous scale. Milton Stenlund cited as an extreme the case of nine wolves in a pack killing seventy-two deer in four days at a time when northeastern Minnesota's deer had reached a population peak. Adolph Stebler wrote of storage-killing in Michigan: A pack of six wolves killed a dozen deer in early April within a three-mile radius of the den that a wolf mother-to-be had chosen for whelping.

The irony in man's reaction to the timber wolf as a deer killer lies in the fact that the most critical problems in deer management in the United States are due to overabundance of deer—that is, overabundance in relation to the supporting capacity of their winter range. Deer problems have their local variations but are likely to have the common denominator of more deer than the occupied areas can accommodate on a year-round basis.

Behind the attitudes of the public toward wolves killing deer is the failure of sportsmen, tourists, and other laymen to understand what the actual situations may be with respect to deer and deer range. These situations differ greatly with the area and with the season of the year.

Appraisal by the public may be especially faulty in places where plenty of deer food is available except in winter. Even greatly overbrowsed deer ranges in the northern states may be lush with leafy vegetation in summer, at which season the deer may feed on many kinds of plant life. An observer must know what to look for to see the old sign of winter overbrowsing after it is masked by new growth. One must think, not of summer greenery, but of dead, chewed-off stubs of twigs, of differences in palatability and nutritive quality of shrubs, saplings, and lower branches of trees, and of how much the ground cover will be withered and dry or under snow by midwinter.

Few laymen ever get out in the northern deer range in winter or visualize the intensive utilization of browse that can take place in a deeryard. Yarding behavior is itself quite the opposite of the freer movements of the snowless months, the bounding over hills and across valleys that the hunter, fisherman, or motorist sees. Snow, accumulating to a depth of three or four feet by late winter in the northern Lake States, may shrink a deer herd's immediate world to restricted areas in which excessive browsing may leave little that is edible between the surface of the snow and the heights to which deer can reach. When one considers that the height of the deer line in an overbrowsed yard is determined by the feeding of the deer that can reach the highest, it is easy to guess how badly the deer of smaller sizes get along in this sort of competition. White-tailed deer of the Lake States seldom learn to utilize food under the snow—other than, for example, to scrape away a thin covering to eat acorns on the ground— hence a deceiving feature of some overbrowsed yards in summer may be conspicuous low growths of unutilized winter browse.

A population crisis among the deer may not be manifested by denudation of the land of all vegetative cover, nor always by such things as damage to agricultural crops or mass starvation. Both fat and starving deer may be found in the same area at the same time. Deer may starve in one place while good food remains not far away. No one should impute to the deer more adaptability than they have, for their behavior is not always advantageous to them. The same individuals that rapidly become wary when hunted may not respond at all intelligently to the gradual onset of the greater perils resulting from their tendencies to gang up and overbrowse their favorite winter retreats.

The ecology and behavior of deer is a special field of study in which competence is not easily gained, either by formal training or by exposure to outdoor air during the hunting season. Complex, imperfectly understood situations exist in every region occupied by any species of deer, and there is much that no one knows and probably much more that no one ever will know.

It may not be easy to say what really constitutes deer range. I can recall when deer were absent or at least very localized in the farming country of the Dakotas, Nebraska, Iowa, Minnesota, and Wisconsin. Now, they occur over the prairies, in the wood lots and along the streams of those same states in sufficient numbers that one may now and then see deer or deer sign almost anywhere. They can now be highway hazards or farm nuisances in places where the sight of a deer would have been most unlikely thirty years ago. The deer have gained some range by adjusting to modern agriculture. That, in itself, may be nothing that many other wild species may not have done, also—Iowa's beavers no longer need the streamside timber and brush that they once did, now that they have learned to feed in cornfields—but it points up the difficulties of trying to define things exactly.

Even so, certain elementals may be demonstrated over and over again. Among the plant components of grazing or browsing lands are what are called indicator species. Varying degrees of utilization of these reveal the condition of a deer range in essentially the same way that they do the condition of a livestock pasture. Like the trained and experienced husbandryman inspecting a pasture, a man trained and experienced in deer management should better be able to judge what is happening on a deer range than should lay observers. Yet, it is strange how readily laymen who pride themselves on common-sense practicality may ignore or challenge biological findings on overbrowsed deer ranges, though they may not have been near a crisis area at the right time nor competent to interpret correctly what evidence may have been before them. This is in somewhat the category of insisting that a dairy farmer has an abundance of food for his herd on the basis of the uneaten bull thistles in his pasture or a moldy straw stack outside of the barn.

Milton Stenlund has described the rise and decline of deer in the Superior National Forest of northeastern Minnesota, on which he carried on a careful study of wolf-deer relationships. Although the hardwood forests and the edges of prairies in central and southern Minnesota are said to have had large deer populations in the 1980s, deer were then scarce in the part of the state that was to become the Superior National Forest. Moose and woodland caribou were the important big game species of northeastern Minnesota. Later, as logging and fires transformed an almost deer-less mixed evergreen forest into a second-growth hardwood forest, the deer found living conditions favorable, and the moose and caribou did not. The ascending deer population had access to ideal wintering areas in the thousands of white cedar swamps that had not been previously used by large numbers of deer. The deer had the temporary advantage of unduly protective hunting restrictions, which probably served in the long run to accelerate the deterioration of the range and the decline of the deer.

Stenlund considered that 1946 represented the last of the golden years of the deer in the Superior National Forest. Most hunters attributed the subsequent decline of the deer to wolves and overhunting. However, the deer declined in areas having neither wolves nor human hunters. The most influential single factor in reducing the deer from a peak population in the 1930s was range deterioration, accompanied by starvation and lowered productivity of the deer.

The general range deterioration had four causes. First, the slow-growing white cedar became almost eliminated as deer food—cedar swamps that had hundreds of deer in the 1930s were almost abandoned by the mid-1940s. Second, the heavy deer population overbrowsed the preferred brushy foods. Surveys of five wintering yards showed a fifty percent decrease in the amount of available deer food from the beginning to the end of the 1940s. Third, the second-growth woods of the cutover areas matured, and their full canopies of crown leaves shaded out the food-producing shrubs beneath. Fourth, the change or succession in the dominant types of trees was from deciduous to evergreen forest, with balsam fir and spruce forest occupying sites formerly covered by second-growth hardwoods.

It may be emphasized that, for a first-class winter diet, northern deer need much more than just forests or brush. The expanses of hardwoods and conifers to be seen from roadsides do not necessarily have much good deer food. Modern forestry and conservation practices often tend to bring about changes unfavorable to deer. The resulting plant successions or natural changes are in the direction of the deep-woods type of forest cover. Fire protection combined with little cutting of forest growth can work inexorably against an animal that is primarily a native of the mixed hardwood forest or more open places.

(I do not here imply that forestry and conservation practices should be otherwise, except when special objectives are sought. Personally, I would rather see a beautiful pine forest, with relatively few deer living around the edges and along the streams and swamps, than mile after mile of brush-grown, cutover, and burned-over land full of deer.)

For a first-class winter diet, the deer of the northern Lake States need the foliage of white cedar and the maples, buds and twigs of dogwoods, viburnums, elderberry, and a limited number of other trees and shrubs that grow when and where conditions are right for them. These are the ones that, overbrowsed by too-abundant deer, fade out over the years as overbrowsing continues. The real supporting capacity of the deer range can go down and down, despite the profusion of green plants to be seen in the summer. As winter emergencies become pronounced, and the choicer foods are gone or become unavailable, the deer may begin stuffing themselves on balsam fir, jack pine, or black spruce. Heavy browsing on the balsam means that the deer are in trouble. The animals may die with stomachs full.

Not only may continued overbrowsing of the key parts of a deer range cut down its supporting capacity for the deer, but recovery from advanced deterioration, if it comes at all, may require many years. This is something that should be thought of not in terms of a growing season or two but in terms of decades. In problem areas of northern Minnesota, I have seen tracts of land where virtually the only mountain maples to bear fruit were those having tops out of reach of the deer. These were the plants that had grown up before browsing pressure became so intense. Only the ability of the lower stands to sprout profusely following each winter of browsing back saved them from being killed. The mountain maple is an outstanding deer food in this region because of its recuperative powers as well as its palatability and nutritive qualities, but there are limits to what it can withstand. Stenlund observed that a third of the stems of mountain maple clumps on one of his areas died from overbrowsing. Other choice winter foods cannot tolerate such severe treatment either. The ground hemlock is one, and it has been largely killed in overpopulated deer range. Formerly, this hemlock was rated as the most desirable winter deer food occurring in abundance in the Upper Peninsula of Michigan.

Unpleasant though it may be to read of the starvation of deer—of fifty thousand starving to death in Michigan in one winter—the longterm damage inflicted by those deer upon their environment while they hungered is really the more ominous. There are published descriptions of stunting and death of deer on overbrowsed deer ranges and of great damage to the range, itself, from the Pacific coast and the Rocky Mountain States across the country to Pennsylvania, New York, and New England.

One should not always visualize an overpopulation of deer as a starving horde. An overpopulation may not involve immense numbers at all. An overpopulation may be present when an area does not have a numerically impressive population of deer. There may not be as many deer as the hunters wish to have, nor enough to justify an open season. Overpopulation is relative, and some deer ranges in their existing condition simply cannot accommodate many deer. Wild places may be found in the Lake States and adjacent Canada where any deer would constitute an overpopulation.

Mass tragedies on dozens of areas show the absurdities of our collective attitude toward the biggest problem of all in deer management—especially the disbelief with which many influential people maintain that the problem does not exist. Demands by an uninformed or a misled public must be considered as a political force—perhaps a dominant part of the whole equation—but population crises among the deer may not remain shouted down indefinitely. That complex mechanism we think of as Nature operates with a most impersonal disregard of human glibness, vehemence, accusations, alibis, and misstatements.

*

A recent inventory by the U.S. Fish and Wildlife Service gave a total population of nearly two and a half million white-tailed deer in Minnesota, Wisconsin, and Michigan. The legal hunting take was slightly over two hundred thousand for the same year. This harvest rate, averaging about eight percent annually, is dangerously low compared with the rate of increase of deer even if we make allowance for the unreported, illegal kills and the unsalvaged victims of bullet wounds.

Populations of white-tailed deer are partly self-limited; that is, their breeding slackens somewhat as environmental conditions become unfavorable. The well-studied, controlled herd on the George Reserve in southern Michigan showed a tendency for reproductive rates to fall off as the herd increased. It has been rather generally observed that larger numbers of does failed to breed or conceived single fawns, in deer-crowded areas, than in areas having healthier deer range. But annual increases of thirty to fifty percent recorded for poorly situated deer herds should be warning enough that neither man's hunting (as hunting is usually practiced in the problem areas of the Lake States) nor the self-limiting tendencies of the deer are effective in coping with the white-tail's fecundity.

Without here attempting to resolve differences in regional deer problems, we may say that population control through the agency of malnutrition, if not outright starvation, affords about the least desirable of solutions, particularly from a long-term standpoint. This, nevertheless, is the agency we may confidently expect to operate when conditions become extreme for the surplus deer in the problem areas of the United States.

*

Histories of areas having deer problems do sometimes show destructive ascendancies of deer following extirpation or near-elimination of deer-killing predators. Recorded instances of overabundances of deer in the years prior to intensive campaigning against predators are rare. Deer apparently did reach destructive abundance-peaks at times then, but not, so far as we can judge, nearly to the same extent as in recent decades. Some of the most favorable balances between deer and deer range now to be observed are in parts of Mexico and Canada that retain more or less natural populations of large native predators.

These parallels do not conclusively show that deer populations increased wholly or mainly because their predatory enemies declined. Effects of changes in human land use on deer ranges must also be appraised, and such appraisals may be very difficult and should not be undertaken without minimal knowledge of the relationships involved. Genuine effects of predation by wolves, cougars, man, or lesser predators are hard to dissociate from effects of other factors in the more complex of situations.

We may, however, remember Starker Leopold's view that the size of deer herds that he studied still seemed to be a function of their food supply. He has known parts of Mexico having numerous cougars and wolves where poor ranges supported few deer and good ranges supported many deer.

*

The apparent ease with which a single wolf has killed a deer has been noted by many people. Stenlund commented that wolves generally have little trouble bagging their game once they have set after it—yet also that they may give up chasing certain deer, though continuing with their hunting. Hunting as packs, they may drive much as human hunters drive and thus gain an effectiveness in tactics that the less imaginative predators do not have. Pack members separate to outflank driven prey, especially when approaching on the ice an island on which they might find a deer. As some wolves drive through the island, the others go around to await any deer coming out. Another variant of driving techniques is for the wolves to line up abreast while hunting in brush or timber in which visibility is limited.

In reading the descriptions of others and remembering what I have personally seen, I keep thinking of the possible differences in security of the deer populations. Patently, there can be differences between the places where wolves catch few or many deer, where wolves stand the best chance of successful attack or the deer stand the best chance of escaping. I wonder how much the islands in lake country, as in the Quetico–Superior region, may, at least in winter, be marginal environment for the deer, how much of the killing of deer out on lake ice may represent elimination of genuine biological surpluses. I wonder if the strongest deer range may not occur as larger blocks, as on the mainland, in which the deer can be more elusive or have a wider variety of alternatives or run better than the wolves can run. When it comes to detailed analyses, I do not have much to offer, but my impression is that strong deer in a deeryard may neither be easy for the wolves to approach nor to kill. Soft snow may favor the deer over the wolves in direct overland pursuit.

I wonder how much protection the right psychological attitude may itself confer upon a healthy deer, how much panic may contribute to the chance of a deer being overtaken and killed by wolves. This illustrates the sort of thing I believe we need to know more about if we are to come closer to the truth in appraising wolf-deer relationships.

Likewise awaiting analyses are the subtleties in the behavior of deer in relation to environmental niches, which determine an animal's sense of belonging or not belonging in a place, its feeling of well-being or otherwise. One need not go to extremes philosophically to recognize that an intelligent animal knows something about peace or lack of peace and the gradations between these two contrasting psychological states, and to recognize that its behavior with respect to the resources it has or does not have may condition its reactions at times of danger.

I do not know how to appraise wolf predation upon fawns. It can be heavy (representing about half of the summer wolf droppings) in places having carrying-capacity populations of deer as well as those having chronic overpopulations. Douglas Pimlott believes that the killing of deer by wolves in Algonquin Provincial Park, Ontario, actually increases in summer because of the many fawns killed. Still, the deer population thrives.

*

I should question that any intensity of wolf predation that is likely to occur would, of itself, effectively reduce any general overabundance of deer in the Lake States problem areas. The severest wolf pressure that I have seen described in the literature should eliminate only hundreds of deer from sizeable problem areas, compared with the thousands of deer that starve there.

Stenlund considered that a pack of three wolves would, on the average, kill a deer every four days from November through March on the Superior National Forest under conditions prevailing during the early 1950s; and at about two-thirds that rate from spring to fall. He estimated that two hundred and forty wolves on about four thousand square miles should thus kill about six thousand deer annually, which would represent about sixteen percent of the area's deer. Wolf predation and human hunting together removed about twenty-four percent, or approximately the annual crop, of the deer; but Stenlund did not conclude that, in the absence of the wolves, the hunters could have consistently harvested more deer. He felt that intensive campaigning against the wolves would produce more deer for a time in the areas accessible to hunting, yet it would also hasten the deterioration of the deer range and lead to greater starvation losses during severe winters.

Deer outnumbered wolves in the ratio of eight thousand to one in the Upper Peninsula of Michigan, where Adolph Stebler carried on his wolf study. During the twenty weeks of the yarding season for the deer, at the rate of a wolf killing a deer per week, a population of twenty wolves would kill four hundred deer, as against a starvation mortality estimated at ten thousand deer. The wolf-kill would thus have to be increased twenty-five times to bring the peninsula's herd within its winter food supply.

It has been indicated in an earlier chapter that timber wolves are not the creatures to tolerate large numbers of their fellows as close neighbors. The social order of a wolf pack calls for generous *Lebensraum*. A single wolf pack, with hunting grounds extending over several townships of land, typically consists of about a half-dozen individuals, though larger temporary gatherings occasionally may be formed.

To be realistic, one should think of winter numbers of timber wolves in present-day wolf country wildernesses of North America as perhaps a wolf per ten to one hundred square miles. Wolves at these densities may give the impression of being more numerous than they are, for groups may either follow hunting routes more than fifty miles across or hunt intensively about game congregations. Reports of an area overrun by wolves or implying the presence of hundreds in a locality may signify that someone saw evidence or heard howling of wolves in different places. Exaggerations easily grow from an area being frequented by any wolves.

The possibility should be recognized that, while the more notable overpopulations of deer in the northern Lake States would appear impossible for existing or prospective wolf populations to control, wolf predation might exert some controlling influence on more moderate deer populations or, in particular, on low deer populations trying to live in unsuitable range. Wolf predation might result in sufficient reduction of deer to relieve population stresses locally. Wolf predation might operate to prevent some overpopulation crises in the deer from becoming quite so destructive to deer range as otherwise might be the case.

There may not be any wholly satisfactory management measures to apply to the problem areas. Palliatives such as artificial feeding may have popular appeal, and, in places and at times, the food supply may be improved by management. Nevertheless, when overabundance of deer for the supporting capacity of the range not only results in their starving but also in extremely serious damage to that range, the supreme need in the management of the herds is that plenty of deer be killed, and that the reduction take place before the deer do further damage and so indirectly—and too late—reduce themselves. Whatever may be the uncertainties in wolf-deer relationships and the doubtful effectiveness of wolf predation in regulating high deer populations, reasonable sportsmen might well be glad to have wolves killing deer that are present in excessive numbers—as they are over immense tracts of land from northern Minnesota to northern Michigan.

Under such conditions, the deer do not need greater protection either from human or from non-human hunters.

CHAPTER 6

Of Man and Wolves and Labels and Morals

Man's motivations for killing remnants of wolves in wilderness regions are more special, more personal than the protection of the game or livestock that those remaining wolves might prey upon. Man is motivated by more than apprehension that those wilderness wolves might increase, spread into settled areas, and again become more troublesome to him. He lives in a society in which it is not customary to like wolves.

Wolves have not always been hated by all peoples. The popularity of personal wolf-names—Adolph, Rudolph, and the whole list of Scandinavian variants incorporating Ulv or Ulf—goes back a long time, and it is not like man to name himself or his beloved after anything he really despises. Today, we can still see respect for the sagacity, teamwork, courage, and formidability of wolves in some of our words and symbols. We have advertisements and trademarks featuring wolves. We have cub scouts and pack meetings and wolf insignia with complimentary meanings.

Yet, the attitude of modern man toward wolves as he conceives wolves to be remains one of animosity. With some people, it can be a great animosity.

Part of this animosity must surely be due to fear of wolves, to human ways of reasoning or distortions of reasoning, to the labels man puts upon acts and characteristics of non-human creatures.

＊

Long after the passing of my childhood fears of wolves, I had recurrent wolf nightmares. Occasionally, I still have one. I remember a dream that I had about the time I began writing this book: I was out in the darkness calling for my own lost child while wolves howled all around. The vividness of that dream reminded me, if I needed reminding, that people can be afraid of wolves, not that the wolves themselves should be so fearsome to modern man.

In North America, there have been few authentic records of wolves preying upon man since the days of the earlier white settlements. Killings could well have taken place that were difficult or impossible to verify, but the rarity of records is an indication of the rarity of such events under North American conditions. Stanley Young, in *The Wolves of North America*, quoted fewer than a half dozen specific instances of wolf predation upon man and about a dozen instances of apparently intended human victims escaping or defending themselves or being rescued. In other instances, it was difficult to judge the behavior of the wolves, and the degree of provocation to attack. Sometimes it was difficult to judge whether a person was a victim of wolves or had died from other causes. Young also commented that, in the twenty-five years (as of 1944) that the federal government had aided in cooperative wolf control, no unprovoked attacks of wolves upon man had come to the notice of the service personnel.

A similar picture can be traced for the Scandinavian Peninsula, which truly has a history as wolf country. Except for the distressing predation upon local children by a single wolf (sometimes accompanied by a second wolf) in central Sweden during the last century, I have found practically no definite records in the literature. In the Turku area of neighboring Finland, I did visit a tract that had been the site of a single wolf (possibly a pair) killing and partly eating twenty-two children during the early 1980s. Talking with the ornithologist Lars von Haartman, whose father had told him of the dangers of walking alone in the country at that time, I could appreciate the grimness of fear that the presence of man-eating wolves could instill in people who had reason to be afraid. Of course, a realistic picture requires consideration of the instances, however rare, in which wolves may prey or attempt to prey upon man.

(Fair appraisal of wolves as a source of danger to human life also requires consideration of that deadly madness, rabies. Rabid wolves, as well as other rabid animals, may act tame in man's presence; and, if the apparent tameness of a species that normally avoids man be due to rabies, the problem calls for intelligent action wherever it arises. Despite medical advances in protection against rabies, a rabies outbreak can be a terrible thing. My files contain a clipped news article that describes the visit of a rabid wolf to a sleeping Iranian village. It bit twenty-nine people, mostly about the head. Certain parts of Eurasia have been especially known for their rabid wolves. Bohemia, I believe, once had such a reputation, and I understand, moreover, that it also had been a center for werewolf tales. The thesis has been proposed that rabid wolves and the people contracting rabies from wolf bites comprise the factual basis for werewolves—with the superstructure of fantasy built on it. In North America, the western and northern parts have their own histories of rabies epidemics among wolves and coyotes; and, in Ontario, eight recent [1954–1959] cases of rabid wolves—including coyotes—have been reported by the Diagnostic Laboratory of the Canadian Department of Agriculture, according to records sent me by David Fowle of the Ontario Department of Lands and Waters. Also, in recent years, the reputable *Journal of Mammalogy* published an article describing an attack by an Ontario wolf upon a man who was not having an easy time defending himself with an ax when relieved by other people, and discussion continues among the mammalogists of that region as to the probability that this wolf was rabid. Nevertheless, at least the Lake States' timber wolves have never been, to my knowledge, anything of a rabies hazard. Richard Parker, Chief of the Midwest Rabies Investigation of the U.S. Public Health Service, wrote me that he was unaware of any rabies reported in wolves in Minnesota, Wisconsin, and Michigan in recent times.)

It still remains true that, in the wolf country of my familiarity, the northern Lake States and Manitoba and Ontario, man may in effect consider his person exempt from wolf predation. A tourist hearing a wolf howl in northern Minnesota, Wisconsin, or Michigan might appropriately worry much more about getting home alive through the highway traffic. A city deer hunter walking back to camp after dark in an area having wolves might meditate upon his real chances of dying from a heart attack or a bullet of a fellow hunter. In that whole region, a person would be in less danger of being attacked by a wolf than by someone's grown-up pet deer that had turned vicious after having been bottle-raised.

Apart from the wolf stories that are represented as truth, we have the great amount of printed space and movie footage made up of fiction, all perpetuating the old popular concepts of wolves and wolfish nature. The fictions of people being pursued, attacked, besieged, or devoured by wolves, or rescued from them, make for thrills and suspense—and reinforce further the public's unrealistic attitude toward wolves.

I was particularly conscious of the advertising that man-eating wolves continue to get as I watched a movie filmed in a Lapland setting. As a wolf pack came up from behind to grab a young lady from a sled, I doubt if many of the Oslo audience sitting around me questioned whether that was the sort of thing that wild wolves did in Lapland or anywhere else. Thrilling, yes, but what bad press added to what has so long gone before. And the shabby old tales about the Russian travelers seem to hold on with much of the public, generation to generation, even in their details of human sacrifices to the wolves pursuing the sled.

I have a boyhood memory of a melodrama shown at the old hometown opera house, and while many details are far beyond recalling, its overall effect on my susceptible psychology stays with me. The title may have been something like *Wolf Moon*, and the advertising had such a fascination that I very literally could not have stayed away for any reason short of inability to have gotten into the theater. The play was honestly consistent with the advertising, and I sat on the edge of my seat until finally hero, heroine, and their families, friends, and lovers were happily reunited. The tension build-up was based upon the dangers of a countryside that might have been called wolf-infested, upon overdue travelers and off-stage howling.

One story that I remember had for its hero a man whose efforts to rid a "wolf-infested" area of its wolves had been so mighty that the ghosts of the dead wolves returned to howl their hatred of him at a time when he found himself inconveniently occupied with their still-living brethren. The tense action, the spectral howling, the triumphant human virtue, and more dead wolves strewn about the winter landscape doubtless contributed the reader-satisfaction that the story was intended to give.

By adding to the publicity brew from the myth wolves the undoubt-edly genuine reactions of human beings who do not like wolves, we get a concoction that could not help having an influence on public opinion. We may read at random of the wolf howl being the most dismal sound ever heard by human ears, of howls so frightfully piercing as to go through a listener's heart and soul, of howling as an infernal chorus, of mournful cadences, down to the just routine horrid, hideous, and bloodcurdling howls. (Not many people who write about wolf howls seem to have had the experience of participating in social howls with wolves.)

We may read about there being nothing so vicious in its cruelty as the wolf's method of taking prey, about a wolf destroying and mangling ten times as much prey as it devours, delighting in slaughter, tearing flesh and sucking blood, about a wolf being a cruel and cowardly animal of a disposition to kill and kill merely to gratify its thirst for blood. It is called raging, greedy, voracious, rapacious, wily and fierce in its looks, a gray monster, and, doubtless to aid the reader in forming an opinion of loathsomeness, its color also may be described as a dirty gray. There is the superstition that a luminous appearance of wolf eyes at night is due to feeding upon human cadavers. When once having fed upon human flesh, the wolves are said to become more fierce and daring, inflamed with greater fury. "Incarnation of destruction," so we may read; not only that, but we may also read of their powerful jaws equipped with shark teeth.

The Crisler wolves seem to shrink to such weak and un-wolfish crea-tures under the weight of man's epithets. What kind of wolves could these be? Wolves that liked to be fondled by people when they came home after hunting and killing their own game, coming home with blood still on their faces? The biggest wolf that liked to be picked up and carried, legs dangling? The hunting pack of wild ones that came up to the Crislers and showed neither threat nor fear?

*

Undoubtedly, much of man's dislike of wolves may be traced to the old custom of judging wild creatures as good or bad. Without belittling in any way the fact that wolves have afflicted mankind, no justification remains for continuing to impute to wolves malignancies that never were more

Gray Wolf, by Charles W. Schwartz. Charles W. Schwartz Collection, the State Historical Society of Missouri.

than inventions. We may learn about human psychology from a movie that has scientists injecting wolf serum into a man to transform him into a werewolf—with shaggy head and gleaming teeth and horrendous savagery—without learning much that is true about wolves.

Of course, the gruesomeness of wolves feeding on human corpses may arouse fear in an observer or thoughts as to just what might happen if a defenseless person met up with wolves that ate human flesh. After reading an account of wolves terrifying a Swedish village by trying to bite and dig their way into a mortuary, I could understand the reluctance of the villagers to leave whatever safety they had in their own dwellings as long as the wolves were behaving in an unrestrained manner outside in the darkness. I can frankly say that, under those conditions, I should not want to go outside, either, despite the usual lack of personal fear in my mature attitude toward free-living wild wolves.

I do not share the emotions that some people show with regard to the immediate fate of corpses. To me, the words about ashes to ashes and dust to dust and the corruptibility of flesh have literal significance; and, once a human body is dead, I cannot see that it makes a great deal of difference what happens to it through utilization by other forms of Life. My years of early manhood were spent in such a way that I then considered it very possible that my own body would ultimately (but in the comfortably distant future) be eaten upon by wolves, and the thought caused me no horror, nor does it now.

Man's revulsion toward violation of human flesh by beasts must nevertheless be considered in our analysis. Since at least early written history, the feeding on corpses by anything larger than maggots has aroused feelings of outrage; and the wolves surely have not endeared themselves to man by feeding upon his dead as they had opportunities over the long centuries leading back into prehistory. A considerable variety of modern farm animals would do much the same thing if given the opportunities, yet man is more apt to excuse them as being only irresponsible animals rather than ghouls indulging evil appetites.

It is perfectly natural for non-human creatures to eat food as they know it and wherever found. There is no issue of moral delinquency on the part of scavenging poultry, livestock, dogs, or wolves, whether the objects scavenged upon be human remains or not. The morals of a chicken or pig that never got a chance at the forbidden flesh, or of the sheep or cow that did not eat flesh of any sort, are neither better nor worse than those of the dogs or wolves that dug out a pioneer's grave or fed on the body of a starved coolie. To almost any flesh-eater, meat is meat, eaten according to its own properties and the needs and tastes of the eaters.

Let us regard the wolves as but the species of wild dogs that they are, no more the vehicles of perversions than any other wild animals that live, where, how, and because they can. It should be possible to regard wolves for what they are, without mythology and sensationalism.

As concern labels and morals and one-sided justifications, man can indulge in some peculiar reasoning when he becomes sentimental about the deer that our remaining North American wolves may hunt or kill. The deer are big-eyed and innocent-looking, and the fact or prospect of their being dragged down by wolves is revolting to persons who consider themselves right-minded or true sportsmen. Deer are possessed of so many idealized human qualities, so knightly, stately, sensitive, and brave that when they die they deserve peaceful deaths, or at least merciful deaths, as from hunters' bullets.

The statement that hunters' bullets bring the most merciful of deaths to wild creatures is, with reservations, true. When a high-powered bullet, without previous warning of danger, hits the base of the brain of a deer, that deer may be said to have been mercifully killed. Those breaking the neck, smashing through the heart, or cutting vital blood vessels are also merciful by reasonable standards, but not all bullets strike these places or any other places where they bring even prompt death.

From years of hunting and some professional study of the subject, I know that crippling losses incidental to a game harvest can be, at their worst, wasteful and sickening. The more that the unskilled public participates in a game harvest and shoots erratically and at long range, the more wasteful and sickening the crippling losses may be. For those who doubt this, I might prescribe a visit to almost any area where wildlife is subject to mass hunting. There, one who looks may find some of the victims, the dead and those still able to care for themselves, the strong animals and the weak, those with puffed out, greenish, stinking bellies, with legs or wings or jaws or tail bones broken and every other kind of wound from random projectiles.

I want to make it clear that I am not opposed to hunting that is conducted with care and good ethics, even if some crippling is inevitable. To the extent that the escape of game with gunshot wounds cannot be helped, I can accept it without great emotion. I think, however, that it is inappropriate to extol the mercy of hunters' bullets compared with talons or teeth of wild predators as long as public hunting performances have so many regrettable aspects.

The fact that wolves may terrify deer on occasion does not mean that a deer population lives in constant terror of wolves. The deer that tamely frequented roadsides of a Canadian provincial park were not disturbed by the playing of tape-recorded wolf howls, though the wolves were the main check on the local population of deer. As has been brought out earlier, the testimony of observant outdoorsmen since the days of the early fur traders indicates that North American deer (as well as other native hoofed animals) are wary in the presence of their racial enemies but show no particular fear except when under attack. Even under attack by wolves, the deer have long-tested answers to many problems if they are physically strong, psychologically steady, and if environmental and weather conditions are in their favor. Even an attack seems to be a matter of acute interest only to the animals most concerned as individuals.

It may be said that deer do not like wolves. Neither do they like human hunters. I have seen deer running out of an area a mile or more ahead of a hunting party. It would be surprising if wolves under any conditions ever made a deer population more jittery than those subject to ordinary hunting season gunfire in the northern Lake States.

People who disapprove of deer dying from bullets as well as through the agency of wolves should consider that neither is starvation a nice way to die, nor are some of the other ways that deer die. For wild deer that do not want to die in any way whatever and are not lucky enough to intercept the more merciful of the not-invariably-merciful hunters' bullets, I cannot see that death from wolf predation is any worse than most other deaths likely to befall them.

But here we may get into another round of human sentimentality—which is exactly where our social influences from childhood may be expected to lead us. Love of animal life is itself a worthy feeling to be instilled in the minds of youngsters. That is, it could be a worthy feeling, were it not so restricted to what people fancy as attractive kinds.

I recall an animated cartoon, a movie that left the audience, myself along with the others, with strong sympathies for the deer that lived idyllic lives except when beset by hunger and cold, forest fire, hunters, and hunters' dogs. My sensitivities are not so finely drawn that I cannot enjoy a well-done fantasy of humanized wildlife or of elfin personalities out of a fairy story; but the movie also illustrated how a sentimental lack of balance and faulty ecological concepts relating to deer and to deer enemies could be perpetuated in a susceptible public. The scenes of winter starvation left an impression that Life could be hard during the crueler moods of Nature—not that overabundant deer could ruin their habitat. In contrast with the lovable deer, the hunters were uncouth and brutal madmen. The dogs pursuing the deer were portrayed as having a ferocity not calculated to arouse sympathetic feelings toward them, for all of their faithful performance of the duties their masters assigned to them. The dogs were, in short, caricatures of wolves, as the public conceives wolves to be.

*

Wolves, being wild dogs and natural predators, surely can enjoy hunting and the excitement of a kill—so can tame dogs and so as everyone knows can human beings. The howling of wolves is no more infernal than the baying of hunting hounds, but one may carry menace and the other pleasure for human ears. What happens to a deer hunted by wolves or to a fox hunted by hounds may be within the choice of neither deer nor fox, but man's ordering one and not the other event has a bearing upon his responses.

Hunting spirit is on one hand a prized quality to be bred into tame dogs and a manifestation of bloodthirstiness when possessed naturally by wild dogs. One is called good and the other bad, but the criteria for labeling in anything such as this are as variable as human whims and backgrounds.

If the wolf became thoroughly domesticated, if it became a mild and obedient house dog, man's creature but wolf-like in form, if it even remained a wolf in every way except that it would be subservient to man, I have no doubt that it would be considered among the prize breeds of dogs. As a man's dog or as a family dog, it would be loved and taught to show its submission in numerous ways, to accompany its human masters on walks, to protect children, or to entertain guests.

In individual cases, man has more or less successfully domesticated wolves—up to a point. As I write this, I have before me an illustrated article in a national magazine about a wolf trained as a hunter's game-bird retriever. But, apart from a few exceptions, wolves have remained very definitely their own dogs despite human efforts to domesticate them. They can be friendly with man when having reason to trust him, but the friendships have to be more between equals than man is usually satisfied with.

*

When it comes to judging the nature and morals of wild animals, one should consider both the wolves and the deer that they prey upon as only living their natural lives. From the standpoint of a natural animal's morals, I should say that it makes no difference that the wolves are adapted to flesh-eating and the deer to plant-eating. The wolves are not morally bad because of killing deer that hunters want to shoot nor morally good because of killing deer that threaten to ruin a forest. Neither are the deer morally bad because of their damage to forests nor morally good because they are vegetarians, graceful, and fit for trophies, targets, and human consumption. Similar statements could be applied to non-human animal life all the way through, to weasels, rabbits, mice, songbirds, house cats, vultures, snapping turtles, ducks, pheasants, tapeworms, whatever they do or look like, be it to man's liking or not.

Although deer should not be judged according to human moral standards any more than should wolves, people who justify careless labeling with reference to wolves might consider how such reasoning would backfire if applied to the deer that the public more customarily admires and defends. They might remember the fight-ridden promiscuity of the mating season of the deer and the strictly me-first behavior of the deer at all times of the year except when helpless young are under care of their mothers. They might remember that there is hardly a more treacherous pet than a white-tailed deer that has grown up to lose its fear of man. This is nothing that needs to be developed much further, only to illustrate where we would logically arrive as long as we persist in the fundamental illogic of holding wild animals morally accountable to man for their natural behavior.

Certainly, one should not allow an overly strict preoccupation with facts to spoil one's enjoyment of an artistic creation as delightful in its way as Prokofiev's *Peter and the Wolf*; but, at the same time, we should not allow the fanciful to color our reasoning in matters of serious appraisal and action.

*

Man, who has amply demonstrated his own capabilities for cruelty or callousness (whether for reasons of vengeance, sport, or convenience) can become furiously aroused at the thought of wolves eating on a deer before the victim is quite dead—or of a snake swallowing something alive, along with other manifestations of messy predation. As a student of predation, I have seen many things that meant suffering to the victims, but one impression growing over the years is that, except for human contributions and the debatable exceptions of predatory play, very little deliberate cruelty occurs through predation in the Animal Kingdom. Predation tends on the whole to look as matter-of-fact as any kind of natural exploitation.

There may be defensible reasons for encouraging one form of Life and repressing another. That in no way changes the fact that man should be outgrowing his barbarous habit of passing life-and-death judgment on amoral creatures on the basis of whether he considers them moral or immoral, innocent or guilty. When he kills, let him do so forthrightly, for his own advantage, but let not the killing be punishment for a wild creature merely being what it is.

PART III

Toward Appreciation
of Wolves as Part of What
Is Wild and Free

CHAPTER 7

Of Wolves and the Big Bog

At eighteen, I had finished high school and was paddling a canoe up Thief River from Thief River Falls, in northwestern Minnesota. I had never been there before, but somewhere, in some suitable place, I planned to spend a winter fur trapping. A winter in the North Country—I had been planning for it since my early teens.

I did not immediately see much that conformed to my idea of a northern wilderness.

The day after leaving Thief River Falls, I had come to the desecrating channel and lower spoil banks of a ditch draining those formerly splendid game and fur marshes, Mud and Thief lakes. I did not then recognize the magnitude of the Mud and Thief lakes' drainage program in terms either of the ruination of outdoor values or the economic fiasco that it brought about; nor could I foresee that it ultimately would serve as one of the most publicized examples in arguments against unwise drainage. To me, this simply was nothing that I wanted further to see. The exposed rocks and puddles in the original streambed reminded me of the stripped skeleton of something that once had been beautiful. I was glad to get out of there and try again to find some place offering more promise for a trapping expedition.

Red Lake River was the route that I had considered the best bet, anyway. It was part of the drainage of the Big Bog country, which I had heard referred to as a vast swampy area. There on Minnesota road maps, occupying most of the north-central part of the state and extending up to the Canadian border, lay one of the biggest blank spaces in the United States. Somewhere, in the millions of acres of lands and waters represented by that blank space, I felt that I should find wilderness, a place to establish hunting and trapping headquarters, and sufficient game and fur to make a winter in the woods pay out.

It was the mellowest of Indian summer weather in late September, as I headed upstream through the Red Lake Indian Reservation, en route to whatever places were as far into the Big Bog as a canoe could take me. The leaves were turning color, and the air was delicately fragrant with wood smoke. As the last of the white settlers' buildings disappeared from sight, few signs of man were to be seen from the river, for mile after mile. Tops of dark conifers protruded more and more like great pinfeathers from the hardwood forest. Slowly, the panorama changed. The stream borders became marshy. There were growths of wild rice; there were muskrats and ducks, muddy game trails between water and woods. The game trails showed small footprints and large ones, of rabbit and mink and skunk, of deer and dog-like animals.

The dog-like tracks among the hoof marks seemed narrower and less fleshy of foot than ordinary dog tracks. These were the track characters I had learned to look for. I could not always be sure of them when I saw them.

✲

I particularly remember Red Lake River and Lower Red Lake for their campsites during that Indian summer, so benign and comfortable after the passing of the mosquitoes.

I remember at one place a peculiar tinkle, which came from a pool so full of minnows that they looked almost solid in the rays of a flashlight. When pike drove through the massed minnows, the minnows popped into the air to fall back into the water with the tinkling sound. I remember awakening one morning with a ruffed grouse looking in at me through the opening of my little cruiser tent, about a yard from my face.

One night, I could not find any dry campsite and had to wedge the canoe into a reed clump and sleep in the bottom. The cruiser tent, lying loose between the litter-stuffed bows, made a passable sleeping bag to keep the dew or light frost off bedding and clothes.

Another night, I pulled up to a sand ridge at the marshy outlet of Lower Red Lake. I was tired and did not bother about the cruiser tent but just wrapped up in blankets under the canoe. A storm whipped sand into blankets, clothes, and hair, and into a kettle of boiled ducks. In the morning, I rinsed out what sand I could from the ducks, but the duck grease still held enough so that my teeth gritted with every bite.

In opposite directions along the sand ridge, the wooded lakeshores stretched away and disappeared into only water and sky. As I cleaned up and shook out and repacked, the sun hazed over, and sky and quieting water became suffused with yellowish light. I had thoughts of being alone on a beach between a marsh and a sea in an otherwise man-less world. Except for my outfit and me, the scene could have gone back a million years.

That part of the world did have something of the real wilderness then, in 1920, before the building of a bridge and road across the outlet.

My next camp was on a hilltop, on which tame ruffed grouse strutted or budded in the aspens. The wild creatures—even a lynx that looked me over in the dusk—had the tameness of those that never had reason to fear man.

Between my hilltop camp and the lake beach lay a narrow strip of white cedar swamp. The outermost cedars extended out on the sand ridge of the beach to within ten to fifteen feet of the water's edge; and there were no cut stumps, no ax or saw marks, no cans, bottles, cigarette packages, no junk either along shore or in the strip of cedar swamp. Neither were there deer lines, where deer had overbrowsed the lower cedar growths, though a lakeside trail had tracks of deer as well as of wolves. (There may have been tracks of Indian dogs as well as wolf tracks in the trail—again, I could not always be sure.)

The lakeside fringe of cedars was so solid that one had to push through it to enter. Inside, the sights and smells gave the impression of unlimited age, of primeval Life and a clean and wholesome and beautiful decay as a part of Life. Trunks of the living cedars were two feet or more in thickness, and seedlings and saplings grew where they could. Dead and living cedars and balsam fir stood or leaned partly uprooted or laid their weight on each other. There were open spaces through which one could walk and tangles of trunks and boughs and roots that one walked around or climbed through or over. Mosses and lichens covered everything, hanging, clustered, growing in mats. On the ground, punky down-logs lay partly sunken into the swamp floor, partly settled into themselves, and partly overgrown with peat moss. Still-older down-logs were only peaty ridges, going back into what they had come from centuries before.

The chipmunks were what gave this place active life during the daytime hours. They sat, they fed, they streaked over the down-logs and over the sand ridge. But, in my memory of the cedar swamp, nothing can compete with the lynx. As the local deity of an ageless sanctuary, the lynx did not seem quite to lose its unreality by any full materialization.

I was scouring the supper grease from the frying pan with lakeside sand when I first heard the lynx squalling, perhaps a hundred yards away. More and more squalls, closer and closer, until they came from directly in front of me, about ten feet away, as I stood at the edge of the lake. The lynx was inside the wall of cedars, and it squalled and squalled so that I knew exactly where it was. I knew that it was standing with its forefeet on the sand ridge, watching me through the hanging cedar boughs.

The dusk became dark as I waited, not knowing what I should do, feeling more than a little spooked yet intensely wanting to make the most out of the experience.

The lynx was still not quite distinguishable in the flashlight rays, though the squalls were coming almost from within reach. After some ten minutes or so of this, I began to worry about whether the batteries might burn out. Earlier, in the shaded daylight of late afternoon, I had slipped off a log, gone up to my hips in soft peat—in fact, had grabbed a limb to keep from going deeper. That swamp was no place in which to be groping around without a light, lynx or no lynx, though it would not be so dark on the other side, on the hill where the cruiser tent was pitched.

I walked straight for the wall of cedar with lighted flashlight. My approach made the lynx lose some of its brashness. It became silent, but I am sure that it stayed close for a time, that it kept me company part of the way across the swamp. There were shiftings of shadows that could have been due to no movements of mine. Twice, I glimpsed what I thought was a square face with tufted ears among the lit-up and shadowy tree trunks and the drapery of moss and hanging boughs.

Halfway across, I was sure that the lynx had left me. I worked carefully the rest of the way on fallen logs to the base of the hill, climbed the hill to the tent, spread out my bedding, appraised the extent to which my wet socks, pants, and underwear had dried on me since the afternoon's slight mishap in the swamp.

One last squall, quite faint, from down along the lakeshore.

During the night, something carried off a new slab of bacon left, forgotten, near my wet-down supper fire on the beach. The bacon was no sad loss, having been a poor buy, too wormy to be appetizing and too expensive to throw away outright. Its disappearance settled the question of what should be done with it.

It could, of course, have been taken by an Indian dog—or by a wolf or whatever had been leaving the dog-like tracks in the game trail. In retrospect, I like to think that it may have been taken by my lynx.

Whatever may have happened to the bacon, I like to think of that experience with a very special wilderness creature living where it belonged, in its own proper wilderness, along with other wilderness creatures that also lived and belonged there. That big, curious, squalling cat and its preoccupation with a stranger and a flashlight.

*

A friend who was interested in homesteading or buying a backwoods farm joined me for a time in northern Minnesota. Together, we were to spend about a month looking over the Big Bog country, he as a prospective settler, I as a trapper. He had brought with him most of my trapping outfit, but we decided to store at the freight depot everything not needed for our preliminary trip. We took with us in the canoe a bedroll and the cruiser tent, a pack sack full of spare clothes and cooking equipment, and guns and ammunition for living on game as we traveled. For meat, we depended upon mallard ducks as long as we could travel by canoe and upon ruffed grouse when we traveled overland.

The Tamarack River was the only stream on the map that showed any promise of taking us by canoe into the Big Bog country from the Red lakes. At its mouth, the principal building at Waskish was the Chippewa Trading Post, a long two-story wooden building heated by a five-foot box stove. A smaller two-story building was a hotel. A third building was a combined residence and post office. Those were all of the Waskish buildings that I remember, as of the beginning of the 1920s. Upstream were a few log cabins, some occupied but most not. One of these unoccupied cabins seemed fairly inviting as wintering quarters.

There were some settlers in and about the Big Bog, including a married man who had attended an agricultural college. He expressed disappointment that people came but did not stay, or proved up on homesteads and left afterward. His faith that "this was the coming country" did appear to be borne out by his neat log buildings, the haystacks in his meadow, and the vegetables in his cellar. The vegetables were impressive, especially root crops—they were as big and firm and perfect as the winning exhibits at the Brookings County Fair back home.

This settler and my companion talked about taxes and prices, about winter employment at lumber camps or cutting cedar posts or spruce pulpwood to sell on one's own, about clearing land, about what crops would grow and what would not, about distances from markets, and about what could be done to open up the country and make it attractive to the right class of people. My attitude, as I listened, was one of agreeable teenage naiveté. I hoped that they got what they wanted and, to that extent, went along as a very temporary disciple of progress. I trusted that somehow we would all be happy, though, for myself, I was seeking only land that remained wilderness.

There was wilderness left, some of it remote from both land-clearing settlers and lumbering operations. The Big Bog was timber wolf country and had the last herd of woodland caribou in the United States. It had some fishers and lynxes, prize furbearers of remote wildernesses. Moose, deer, and coyotes (called brush wolves) lived in environmental types suited to them. Natural streams and drainage ditches alike had beavers. Muskrats, minks, weasels, striped skunks, red squirrels, horned and gray and Richardson's owls, sharp-tailed and ruffed grouse all lived where they belonged.

Among my special memories are those of a white cedar swamp. Brooklets trickled through miles of the swamp, often hidden under a deep mat of sphagnum moss, to draw together and become part of the upper Tamarack River. Beyond the white cedars lay a small isolated creek, banks overhung with hardwoods, and here lived beavers, minks, and otters.

Sandy hills were grown to park-like stands of white and Norway pines and protruded island-like from the panoramas of bog and swamp. The low ground itself was varied in appearance, with great blocks of cedar and spruce amid the tamaracks and the open bogs.

The banks of the Tamarack River had a thick fringe of ash and elm along with the commoner birches and aspens, practically as far upstream as banks remained above water. In its mid-stretches, a savannah of sedge, redtop, and reed separated flowing water from the bogs and swamps. Upstream, perhaps fifteen miles from the mouth, the river narrowed down to a rocky channel.

✻

I moved into the unoccupied cabin on the Tamarack and started winterizing it. It required a lot of chinking and repairs but did not really have to be rebuilt.

Soon the freeze-up came, after preliminary freezes and thaws. When I got on heavy woolen underwear, the early cold lost its pervasiveness. It seemed almost surprising that I could be comfortable, as if I had not quite been expecting to be comfortable, just because of being in northern Minnesota.

I was still a little lonely, a little scared.

✻

The transition from fall to winter was very pleasant, very peaceful.

Snow fell steadily, settling down through windless air. Ruffed grouse almost as tame as the chickadees and Canada jays, walked into the cabin clearing. If alarmed, they flew off, dodging among the tree trunks. They sat in the aspens, eating buds, in plain sight of the cabin.

Beavers and muskrats came out on the ice and tracked up the first snow. The trails of minks ran along the stream edge from one open patch of water to another. Bounding weasels marked up the snow almost everywhere. There were tracks of snowshoe hares and red squirrels and deer. There might be something else: a porcupine trail, the signs left by a horned owl killing a snowshoe hare, the tracery of mice and shrews and small birds. There were fox tracks, in straight strings, in crooked trails, going through or laid down as the foxes had hunted or investigated wherever they had wanted to.

One morning, I saw, not fifty yards from the cabin door, the trails of three timber wolves on the river ice, each track the size of my closed hand imprinted in the few inches of snow.

✷

The snow often fell heavily and continuously for hours at a time. In places out of the wind, it remained undrafted and fluffy from about the middle of November to early spring. It piled up in perpendicular walls on fallen tree trunks. It loaded the tops of spruce and cedar. By late winter, the fluffy snow reached a depth of about five feet on the level and lay even deeper where gentle wind eddies piled it without packing.

Immense drifts combined with ice ridges lined the shore of Upper Red Lake, and the more or less bare lake ice reached a thickness of between four and five feet. At the river near the cabin, under four feet of snow, I had to cut through as much as three feet of ice to reach a new source of camp water whenever an old water hole became unusable. It took 20 to 40 degrees below zero Fahrenheit to freeze all that ice.

The cold had a bite to it that sought out the thin spots in four pairs of heavy wool socks. It tightened skin of face and shot little pains—like slight electric shocks—through the sides of nostrils as they hardened; and then I had to put up mittens to keep the freezing from going deeper. I did nothing with exposed hands for very long out in that cold—a trigger had to be squeezed very quickly, a match had to be lit very quickly, lacings had to be tied very quickly, slipknots and loops in snare wire had to be made very quickly. In cleaning game or in skinning anything in that cold, I held the knife in a mittened hand, after opening the blade very quickly with bare fingers. I did not clean or skin much of anything, anyway, in that cold—mostly an occasional porcupine for food—and steaming, warm tissue hardened as I looked at it, and bloody surfaces grew pale.

✷

At night, the ice might boom and the tree trunks pop; a wolf howl carried well in the brittle air.

Out on the ice fields of Upper Red Lake, wolf packs might run. They cut across the lake between the chief deeryards south of the Tamarack River and the woodland caribou range far off to the west and northwest. Distances meant little enough to the wolves when they wanted to travel. Maybe they liked to cut across other parts too, but I cannot be sure. I do know that their inclination to run on Red Lake ice got them into trouble years later, after hunters started shooting them with buckshot from light aircraft.

When the wind blew, the lake might smoke and the drifts gather beyond ice-heaves and buckled beaches and in the fringing tree growths that caught blowing snow. Little signs of the running of wolves might show, only the pressed-down prints and the claw marks. Up on dunes of hard snow there might be dog-like claw marks.

When the wind blew and the lake smoked and the temperature dropped down and down, maybe down to 40 or to 50 below zero, or conceivably lower, it is just possible that the wolves did not care to be out there.

On one such day, with a strong wind coming off the lake, I could not face it at all and had to take off my snowshoes and walk backward across the mouth of the Tamarack River from the shelter of the woods to the Chippewa Trading Post at Waskish. On another such day, sixteen years later, some scientific colleagues of mine were traveling by dog team in the Big Bog at a temperature of 52 below zero; they barely made it to a patrol cabin and finished up by carrying the dogs.

✳

The Tamarack River cabin, itself, was nothing to promote sentimental memories, for it was only a place to stay, with comforts that were at times scarcely minimal for a trapper's needs. It is the general setting of the cabin and the wildlife of the setting that I remember with sentiment.

A creature of the wilderness lived inside of the cabin with me—a white-footed mouse that I enticed with prune pits to come within the circle of light from the lantern. Outside, the Canada jays and chickadees stayed all winter, and at least some must have been the same birds from the beginning. Sometimes in the night I heard the hooting of horned owls. Upstream, where the river's edge became marshy and marsh and bog and meadow spread out toward the woods, there were early winter trails of minks and foxes among the muskrat lodges of grass and sedge. One wide beaver trail led through the snow from a hole beside the beaver lodge to an aspen thicket until the cold sealed the water hole permanently.

With the intensification of the cold, a weather-conscious mink might stick its head out of a hole in a beaver lodge or a stream-edge snowdrift. As the snow deepened, the minks did not come out at all. When I shoveled away snow with a snowshoe and chopped down through the ice in the right places, I saw that they were living down below where the muskrats were. On splashed icy shelves there were fish heads and scales, frog eggs, clam shells, blood, bits of vegetation, and sometimes remains of thin bodies of muskrats. Beneath the shelves, dark passages would lead still farther out of sight.

Except for the snowshoe hares, the extremely abundant weasels were the principal animals to leave tracks over extensive surfaces of the snow from midwinter to the first of the spring thaws; and it was apparent that the weasels were getting most of their living beneath. Their trails would quarter back and forth, and then there would be a hole in the snow at the end of a trail and another hole at the beginning of another trail. Sometimes, there would be a hole with several weasel trails leading in and out. The snow-buried marshes and bogs and meadows always looked as if they particularly belonged to the weasels. Often, the bounding trails would go on across the snow as if the makers were only using up energy, in little jumps and big jumps, in soft snow and over the wind-packed. Short-tailed shrews frequented the weasel holes too, and one of them hollowed out a trapped weasel for me.

The pine-covered sand ridges protruding here and there from the surrounding bog lands were delightful places, with their bright colors, their majesty of tall, virgin timber, and their red squirrels. The squirrels dominated the pine ridges, though the weasels tracked up the snow there too, and so did the foxes. The squirrels worked over the snow and dug for buried things; they ran through the pines; they fed on cones and sat and barked.

My trapline was strung out along one of several distinct game trails on the sand ridges, but, after the deepening of the snow, only the foxes and I followed the game trails. Wolves had been around earlier, and I was convinced that those ridges had meant something special to them during the warmer seasons, as offering some of the driest and most secluded den sites in the Big Bog.

✳

From the cabin, I usually maintained from two to four partially over-lapping traplines, all in the form of loops that were up to ten miles in circumference. Each trapline was covered by walking about once a week. I had no fear of trap victims escaping or being left alive to suffer need-lessly in the great cold, so did not have to adhere to a regular schedule of trapline runs. Sometimes, I covered one trapline in a morning and another in an afternoon. Sometimes, I did not cover any trapline for a day or two. The most pressing day-by-day job was keeping enough firewood cut and ready for stuffing into an oil-barrel stove at night.

Then, if I did want to do something different, other than cover another trapline, I could usually do so, particularly if the spare woodpile along one wall inside of the cabin was reassuringly heaped up nearly to the roof. I would head off with gun and snowshoes and some fried venison in a pocket to see what I could find.

In these explorations within a walking radius of the Tamarack River cabin, I did find places where nobody lived. Some were places where I sus-pected no other white man had ever been. Others were places where white men had been and gone. Away from a few maintained roads on ditch banks, the Big Bog stretched away for miles and miles. I liked to prowl these man-less places in the hope of shooting wolves, foxes, or other prof-itable prey—with the two-fifty if prowling during daylight hours, with a double hammer gun loaded with buckshot if prowling at night.

White cedar swamps were the winter retreats of the deer, and an exten-sive deeryard lay not many miles from the cabin. On bright nights, I could sometimes hear the howling of wolves as it came faintly from what I thought was this yard. Sometimes, just now and then, the howling might be quite plain, but I doubt that I ever got very near to the wolves by trying to work up to them with the shotgun.

Nevertheless, I was not always sure where those wolves might be. I would go crouching through thick clumps of spruce or cedar, breaking trail with snowshoes, trying to keep dislodged snow from falling in the collar of my mackinaw, and looking backward to see if some of the heavier shadows had moved. Or, I might go to Waskish in an evening for mail and listen for wolf howls. I hoped that a wolf pack might follow me out of curiosity, with a nighttime tameness, and obligingly circle within range of those buckshot loads. The idea of getting a hundred dollars in pelts and bounties with a few shots in an adventurous way appealed to me very much.

By midwinter, I still had shot no wolves. I had not yet learned about snaring large animals. Nor could I afford any outlay of cash for wolf traps—and I was not confident I could catch wolves if I had the traps. Therefore, I intensified my efforts to hunt them, and, whatever may be said of my methods, I tried. With the flat-trajectory two-fifty rifle, I stationed myself at a number of strategic lookouts to wait for daybreak. After a series of terrifically cold mornings, I finally gave up. Economically, I did better trapping weasels at forty cents apiece and cutting cordwood at fifteen cents an hour for the five-foot box stove in the Chippewa Trading Post at Waskish.

I never did get any real timber wolves, that winter or any other. I did not see any of the particular northern Minnesota wolves that I had been trying to hunt. They were most circumspect in their behavior toward man. The nearest that they ever came to me was that one night when the three of them had loped past the cabin on their way upriver.

And their mobility was so much greater than mine. They could, on occasion, bound through deep snow with a power and stamina that made my trail-breaking on snowshoes look slow and feeble.

I appreciated still more the adaptations of the wolves for getting through the snow one night when, returning to the cabin over a trail-less route, I broke a thong on a snowshoe binding. I could not see to retie the broken thong, and my hands stiffened so badly in the cold that I could not do anything by feeling. The only alternative to building a bothersome fire for warmth and light was to take off the other snowshoe and wade perhaps two miles in snow that was nearly up to my armpits. I waded but had to do a lot of resting before getting in.

A little lake lay off by itself in some of the most beautiful surroundings in all of the Big Bog country. Beside the lake stood an old cabin. In the cabin clearing, the top of an ornately carved wooden cross stuck out of the snow. I never learned who lived and died there, but often thought that it must have been some Finn or Swede who chose to do so because it reminded him of some lonely setting of woods and waters in which he had lived before.

The little lake was one place where I might find wolf tracks. The wolf tracks might be along the shore, heavy trails partly filled in with drifted snow, the tracks evenly spaced or in bounds. A mind-picture that I have is of wolf trails going past a partly fallen-down log barn and of walking tracks around one corner of the barn. I am not sure, at this distance, that the wolves used the corner of the barn as a scent station, but I think that they did.

✳

Slush and mud and remnants of the five feet of snow—and I was riding in a bobsled toward the railroad town of Kelliher. On the sled were canoe, camping equipment, traps, guns, and everything I wanted to take out with me. I had already disposed of my fur and sent home to my mother in South Dakota a fine deer head for mounting. At the end of seven months in the Big Bog country, I was leaving without waiting for the spring breakup and the opening of the ice on the lakes. It took four to five feet of ice longer to melt than five feet of snow covering.

I suppose that poetic fitness should have called for a last memorable experience or adventure concerning the Big Bog wolves as an ending for this chapter. I did not have any, but that is all right. It is all right that I never had as much to do with those wolves as I wanted. I am glad to settle for what I have of Big Bog memories, whether in matters of wolves or a squalling lynx or a white-footed mouse that cached prune pits in my footwear.

CHAPTER 8

Mostly about Coyotes and the West River Country

The sparse human population living in western South Dakota in the early 1920s referred to that area as the West River country. In this region there were sand hills and badlands and expanses of erosion-cut river breaks and flatlands having towns fifty miles apart. The main highways were not even graveled except in or close to a few of the towns. There were not even many graded roads away from U.S. 12, 14, 16, and 18. In dry weather, a Model T Ford could be driven to most places where people lived. In wet weather, the sticky gumbo was unnavigable by any motor vehicle having wheels to bind under fenders. (I remember getting stuck in the rutted wet gumbo that was the middle of U.S. 16 west of Kadoka and camping there for three days while the road dried out.)

When West River people wanted to go anywhere and be sure that they got there, they usually rode horseback. They might ride over to a neighbor's and back or they might ride a hundred and fifty miles toward Rapid City. It was customary for agreeable strangers to stop at almost any occupied dwelling for a meal or a bed. I shall not label this hospitality of the Old West—for the West River residents of that time would have laughed at being called Old West—and I shall not imply that such hospitality did not have counterparts elsewhere. It was a concomitant, perhaps, of a diffuse and rather non-competitive society in which people enjoyed the company of other people.

Nobody had much money. Some people who lived in log houses or tar-paper shacks must have handled less than a hundred dollars during an entire year. Sometimes, people experienced hardship: One family got through a winter mainly by eating hawks caught in a single trap. A half-dozen long-abandoned homes were in sight for every house still having human occupants. A drought about a decade before my time had impartially forced out those who could not withstand it.

Some of the larger ranches had extensive sets of buildings, either of logs or of mill-cut lumber. Some of the valleys had real farms, perhaps with irrigated croplands and flower gardens and no-trespassing signs and home-generated electricity. But these places were exceptional, and most land did not look like farmland.

The land had sagebrush, cactus, Spanish bayonet, juniper, wild plum, box elder, cottonwood, buffalo berry, poison ivy, the grasses and ground plants that could grow. It might be overgrazed by man's livestock, but there were large areas of grazing land where man himself was seldom on the scene and where his direct interference with native wildlife was negligible. Although lacking (except on reservations) its original free-living Indians and bison, the West River country had its un-despoiled high plains in the early 1920s. Wild land could predominate in the mile after mile of West River expanses.

North of the Black Hills, some of the West River country already had been tamed by irrigation; yet to the north of the irrigation district and making up the northwest corner of the state lay Harding County, a square of gumbo land fifty miles on the side. Here ranged a buffalo wolf called Three Toes. He had been known unfavorably to stockmen for many years. That wolf was said to have killed at least fifty thousand dollars worth of livestock, and I naturally did much thinking about him whenever in or near Harding County. He was not the only big wolf in western South Dakota, and some other wolves had reputations for expensive habits on about the same scale of annual upkeep; but, to me, Three Toes symbolized a number of things that I do not find easy to define.

Biologically, in terms of his own accomplishments in surviving, Three Toes certainly belonged in that great home range of his to which he contributed such a very special kind of wildness. There was no question about his dominance in his own way. He was a champion.

The story was that about all of the federal, state, and private trappers west of the Missouri River had made a try for him at some time or other after he had become famous. He had been in traps twice—that was what had happened to his toes. He was an educated wolf still in possession of what he could claim as his.

I admired Three Toes and not with any grudging admiration. The epithet "renegade," so liberally applied to Three Toes, was farcical. Destructive of human property, yes, but unfaithful or traitorous to whom?

Nevertheless, under the circumstances, I could have no feeling that Three Toes belonged where he was. He was too expensive, in an area where ranching comprised the most generally desirable and defensible type of human land use. My sympathies had to be with the ranchers. Three Toes imposed upon the local people an economic burden sufficiently intolerable to allow only one major conclusion.

He was just too downright expensive.

✳

I knew the South Dakota Badlands fairly well. Sometimes in summer I went deep into the jagged parts to walk along gullies or climb among the spires.

By then, I had read enough geology to understand something of what I was seeing and I remember finding, halfway up a steep surface, a stratum of pig-like fossils. These animals had originated in the Eocene Epoch, apparently to range in great herds during much of the Oligocene and Miocene. The pronounced canine teeth gave their jaws a rather wolfish appearance, but this was only a superficial resemblance not indicating any close affinity with wolves.

The Eocene–Oligocene–Miocene times did have their flesh-eaters, of which one, known by the suggestive name of *Hyaenodon horridus*, was nearly as large as our modern black bear. Although the cats and weasels had their early representatives (including saber-tooth and an animal something like a giant wolverine) to take advantage of that early meat supply, the dogs or dog-like forms were right in there too. A very abundant fox-like form was thought to have hunted over the country in packs; another had been about the size of a coyote; and a third had been as large as a full-grown buffalo wolf. Add to these, another dog-like animal about the size of a grizzly bear, and we can imagine quite a predatory complement and one anticipating the genus *Canis* before the appearance of any true *Canis*.

The fact that these precursors of modern wild dogs had small brains did not alter the fundamentals of the predator-prey equations. Their competitors and their prey had not been especially gifted with large brains in those long-ago times either. So far as I was concerned, that ancient mammalian fauna did not have to show modernity in any way. As exemplifying the eating and being eaten of natural relationships, it was acceptable to me as it stood.

In that wilderness of subdued, contrasting colors, I always felt a reverence for the antiquity and integrity of Life. I could feel it even while being bitten by mosquitoes as I clung with both hands to the side of a slope. It was still a place for eating and being eaten.

Some of the little juniper-grown canyons had horned owls and bobcats. Overhead there might be a golden eagle or a turkey vulture or a buzzard hawk—occasionally one almost as large as an eagle. Stream waters ran chalky with silt. Their margins had tracks of raccoons, jackrabbits, and coyotes, of the smaller sizes of rodents and land birds, of some insect life. A few Indian horses wandered around, and, from their condition, I could see that they might feed the coyotes from time to time.

✳

The northern edge of the Badlands straggled off into the gumbo. Pronghorn antelope lived on some of the vast flatlands, usually well away from what roads there were—the pronghorns did not lack space. Hardpan flats had prairie-dog towns, and a prairie-dog town might have a black-footed ferret (though the only black-footed ferret that I ever saw in South Dakota was a bloated one lying beside U.S. 16). Flat-topped buttes with near-perpendicular sides might have a pair of golden eagles or prairie falcons. The singing of coyotes that carried to my night camps often seemed to come from such high places.

The common West River wildlife congregated in brushy and woody creek valleys: the magpies, meadowlarks, sharp-tailed grouse, striped skunks, bull snakes, garter snakes, cottontails, screech owls, flickers. Horned owls nested on the ground in the buckbrush when they had no better nesting sites—no tree cavities nor hawk nests large enough for them to take over. The animals of dry places and the animals of wet places came close together at the creeks—the salamanders of the pools, the pocket mice and ground squirrels, sometimes porcupines or sage grouse.

The young horned owls, at last learning to be self-hunting by late summer, fed upon grasshoppers, snakes, young rabbits, and other catchable prey of bottoms and hills. So did the buzzard hawks. So did the coyotes. Yet the coyotes also came to the streams for the good living to be found there. The coyotes always took advantage of what was favorable, living and hunting and adjusting.

The larger streams—the White, the Cheyenne, the Moreau, and the Grand rivers, all running eastward across the western half of South Dakota—were western-type in appearance. They had their erosion-cut breaks. Their flows could thin to crooked trickles over the silty and pebbly bottoms, or dry up entirely. Or new water could rush down the channels, scouring, undercutting the cottonwoods of the banks, lodging drift ten feet or more above the streambed, washing away bars in one place and building them up in another. The old oxbows to the side of the main channel might have wetland wildlife, from fishes and frogs to beavers and ducks, and the deeper eddies in the channel might have catfishes. Higher up in the breaks would be the gullies, partly grown to brush and trees in moister parts, sometimes as far as a person could see.

*

The winter of 1924–1925 was for me one of hunting, trapping, and very economical living. Except for a twenty-dollar bill reserved in a metal match case for emergencies and a little pocket change, I was broke; and I was hoping to raise enough money from fur to put me through the coming spring term at South Dakota State College.

The Fairchild ranch, which I was to make one of my trapping headquarters, lay twenty miles or so northwest of Philip, the biggest town between Pierre and Rapid City on U.S. 14.

My first sight of this ranch came in late summer at the end of an all-night drive in a Model T. The place seemed so delightfully far from a main highway, so delightfully deep in the miles and miles of hills and hardpan, so peaceful and cool and beautiful in the dawn. The impression of peace and coolness passed with the awakening of the younger Fairchilds and the rising of the sun; but the ranch was genuine, and Haakon County stretched off toward horizons. To the north, it might almost be said that there were not any towns for as far as the North Dakota line other than Faith and Dupree up in the sheep country. There were the Cheyenne River breaks, and, north across the Cheyenne River itself, the Cheyenne River Indian Reservation, with its agency at Cherry Creek.

The Fairchild ranch lay near the edge of an area having considerable land under cultivation or planted to alfalfa. Its salient natural feature was Plum Creek, an intermittent stream usually having water in isolated pools. The climate had been on the wet side for the preceding few years, and this had resulted in an increase of such wetland wildlife as waterfowl and muskrats.

The deeper pools of Plum Creek had muskrats—more muskrats than the local people had ever observed before. All up and down the creek, the muskrats tracked the mud margins, wore trails from pool to pool, foraged on the greener of the streamside growths, dug and plastered with mud. They raided an alfalfa field and bounded back along their trails toward the water, with alfalfa sticking out of their mouths like mustaches. They still were not well situated in anything resembling good muskrat habitat, and some died as they fought among themselves, or as horned owls and coyotes hunted the places where muskrats lived most insecurely.

✱

Some miles to the north of Fairchild's the Cheyenne breaks began. The first time I went into them, I was one of three people on a horse and buggy trip. The old-timer among us drove his buggy with our simple camping equipment into backcountry that no then-existing motorcar could have traveled in any weather. The days were sunny and cool, the nights were chilly, there were no other people for miles and miles. We fed well and were in no hurry.

We camped beside a marshy oxbow of the Cheyenne River and ate fried catfish for supper. The coyote chorus came as the afterglow faded, and it sounded right.

We talked about coyotes and we talked about wolves, about buffalo wolves—the lobos—that sometimes came over from the west. The old-timer thought that Three Toes of Harding County must still be alive if he had not died of old age.

We did a lot of talking about this and that. Of the few prairie chickens that occurred now and then among all of the sharptails in the West River country, of the black-footed ferrets living in a prairie-dog town on the tableland above. Of how high the water had to be in the channel of the Cheyenne to flood the oxbows and how fast it came up at such times when it left drift marks on tree trunks beyond the reach of a man standing on the top of the bank. Of whether any minks appeared as the muskrats increased in the creek potholes. Of ducks and muskrats being only pioneers and how they would shrink away during the next series of dry years. Of how the land would again belong to what could eat cactus, sagebrush, and willow, and to what could eat the flesh of feeders upon cactus, sagebrush, and willow.

We talked of game and fur and predators and prey, of wild things in wild places and, finally, of nothing more for the night.

After the talking ceased and I lay in blankets under the open sky, I heard wings and saw blobs that were blue-winged teal flying over and alighting upon the water of the oxbow . . . sounds of munching from the horses. . . .

Dew on the blankets and on my face, and I was crawling through the morning wetness with a borrowed ten-gauge to get fresh meat for breakfast.

As we drove down into the Cheyenne River bottomland, we found the cottontail rabbits living in the willow growths in such numbers that dozens were in sight at once. They were not only in the willows but well up among the prickly pears and sagebrush of the hills. They were spreading their range into everything that they could occupy and hold.

The coyotes, bobcats, and everything else predatory that could eat cottontails had plenty of good feeding. Maybe something bigger than coyotes and bobcats might be attracted by those rabbits. Harding County was not an impossible distance away for a wolf to travel and, then again, there might still be buffalo wolves other than Three Toes living in the West River country.

I was not ready to move into the Cheyenne River breaks and bottoms to stay, but this was a good time to make arrangements for trapping territory and headquarters.

The ranchers assured me that I could have that part of Haakon County practically all to myself for my hunting and trapping. Moreover, my welcome from the ranchers included offers of places to stay overnight and horses to ride whenever I might need them. Any time I happened to be coming by, I should be sure to drop in for a meal. For my main headquarters, I could share a cabin with a congenial bachelor living next to a stream called Straighthead Creek a couple of miles from the Cheyenne River.

*

From late fall to the first of December (when the trapping season opened on muskrats and skunks), I shot wild meat for the Fairchild ranch, then stayed on at the ranch while trapping during the month of December.

I was too busy with some quite profitable skunk and muskrat trapping along Plum Creek to bother about trying to catch coyotes during my December stay at Fairchild's. Besides, most of the coyotes seemed to have left Plum Creek by the first snowfall, presumably to retire to the rabbit-teeming Cheyenne breaks and bottomlands. Plum Creek looked just a little too civilized, with too many people around and not enough privacy during the snow months when a coyote would be conspicuous out in the open.

By the time I left for my trapping headquarters in the Cheyenne breaks soon after New Year's, I had made enough money from the muskrats and skunks to go back to school, so I no longer had to worry about the trapping expedition paying out. The rest of the winter—that part reserved for the breaks—could be more of a leisurely outing if I wanted to make it one.

I would return to Fairchild's for a short stay in the spring, before going on to Brookings.

*

In my Cheyenne River trapping territory, occupied sets of buildings perhaps averaged five miles apart. They usually were either down at the base of the breaks slightly above the river flood plain, or at the edge of the high tablelands slightly below the upper edge of the breaks. Between flood plain and tableland lay a belt of rough land of varying width and steepness of slope.

I saw a ranch at the edge of the breaks where I felt I might be happy living out my life. I knew a bit of temptation not to go back to school, just to settle among quiet, friendly people, in surroundings of beauty and peace.

The ranch buildings lay in the upper part of a juniper-grown gully, protected from the wind and out of sight from any road on the tableland. Behind the buildings, I walked among junipers and followed a spring-fed brook down and down, while thinking of bobcats and the shy life of evergreen coverts. It was the sort of place in which one might expect to find a saw-whet owl sitting. It was the sort of place where chipmunks might be sleeping.

Straighthead Creek was only as long as the breaks were wide. Its headwaters thinned out and disappeared among the junipers below the tableland.

At the edge of the tableland, blowing snow often looked like a smoke cloud, below which snowdrift anvils grew deep and overhanging and collapsed in short-run avalanches. I did not climb up to the tableland just anywhere along the rim, and neither did the coyotes and jackrabbits. I went up one day to look at the prairie-dog town where black-footed ferrets had been seen; but I could make out no signs of anything special on the blown surface—only the raised islands of packed snow representing coyote and jackrabbit tracks.

There really was so much more of interest down below that I seldom left the breaks and the bottomlands. Mostly, I could get all I wanted of the tableland by looking up at the snow-clouded rim and the white anvils poised above the valleys.

Above one spring pool, an area of about a square yard remained wet and exposed, except for partial frosting-over, throughout the winter. A muskrat came out in midwinter to feed on algae and mosses and other green growths not covered by deep snow. After a time, I saw no more of its tracks. It did not belong there but it was doing what it could with itself as long as it could.

The main stretch of Straighthead Creek was fringed with hardwood trees. Yellowish-colored porcupines hung in the elms, and heavy, dragging porcupine trails led to holes in the creek banks. Magpies flew across valleys, searched and sat among the trees, pecked on whatever dead flesh they could find, and called and called. Horned owls hooted during the cold moonlit nights. Sometimes the hooting sounded soft, sometimes brassy, always wild.

The coyotes had a broad crossing zone some hundreds of yards upstream from the cabin on Straighthead Creek. On clear and quiet nights, their singing might carry down to me in bed. It was almost a personal challenge, especially in the early part of my stay. I had no success in catching coyotes at first and sometimes wondered if I would catch any at all. I had to get some coyotes. I had moved into the breaks for the stated purpose of doing so and felt that I would lose face if I failed completely. I had to get some.

I did like to hear the coyotes sounding so happy and independent, whether they were challenging me or not. If only I could get a few, enough for a halfway respectable showing. . . .

I had not expected that they would be easy to catch. In fact, I had had a disquieting hunch that I was up against something while out in a snowstorm on my first day of exploration of Straighthead Creek. The snow had the fresh trail of a big coyote that I suspected already knew of my presence, though I had not been away from the cabin for fifteen minutes. The trail went in bounds across the creek valley and up over the nearest hill.

As I followed for a short distance, I noticed that the trail was somewhat odd, that it did not seem wholly complete. It was not complete. It was the trail of a peg-leg, a coyote that had lost a hind foot in a steel trap. I did not need more insight into the nature of coyotes to recognize that Peg Leg would probably be one of the most trap-wise coyote in the Cheyenne breaks. There he was, right in my backyard, no doubt to confound me for the rest of the winter.

The Cheyenne River flood plains still had cottontails massed by the thousands in the willow thickets. They were in all of the choicer bottomland places for cottontails as well as upon the surrounding hillsides. Up on the hillsides and along the brinks of steep gullies, the cottontails slept

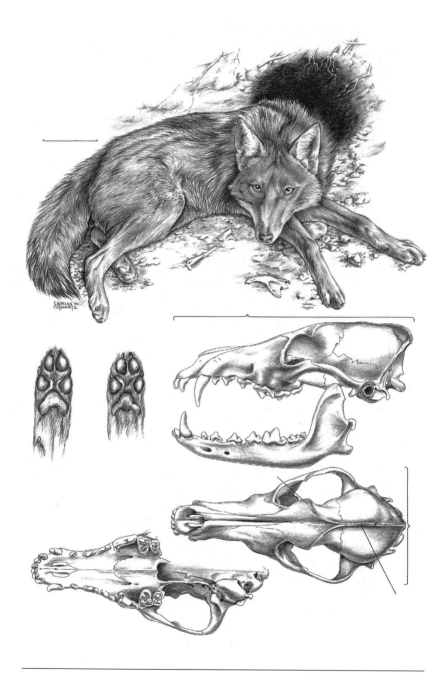

Coyote, by Charles W. Schwartz. Charles W. Schwartz Collection,
the State Historical Society of Missouri.

or sat. They ate cactus and were all ready to dive into holes if alarmed. Sometimes, four or five cottontails would run, single file, into a hole at my close approach.

Actually, the rabbit abundance was restricted to neither the breaks nor to the cottontails. Out on the plains, the jackrabbits sometimes massed as thickly as did the cottontails of the bottomlands—or more so. Once, I saw jackrabbits streaming from a three-acre cottonwood grove like a flock of hundreds of sheep. From a distance, I first mistook them for sheep. They ran strung out in bunches of twenty-five to fifty or as a long line following a fence. But no rabbit populations that I ever saw, then or any other time, ever compared with those of the Cheyenne bottomlands during my coyote-trapping winter. A picture that I took with a vest-pocket camera shows fifteen cottontails sitting in an area of about a sixth of an acre.

I knew, even then, that such abundances of cottontails and jackrabbits could not last, that they really were biological excesses that must come to a natural termination somehow. Meanwhile, they made the winter lush for predatory creatures.

In addition to the coyotes, I tried to catch bobcats, but the bloody bait-rabbits left in the likeliest places never drew a bobcat near them. Nothing but magpies and the occasional winter-active skunk seemed interested in dead rabbits. The golden eagles, rough-legged and red-tailed hawks, prairie falcons, horned owls, coyotes, and everything else that could prey upon cottontails acted sated. Goshawks were there too, surely drifters from either the mountains to the west or from the northern wilderness.

Very nearly the whole wildlife economy was dependent upon or adjusted to or to some degree influenced by the rabbits.

*

My old-timer friend of the horse and buggy trip had told the ranchers how I inoculated coyotes with my two-fifty rifle, but I still had some inoculating to do to live up to the advance advertising. I was sure that I could hit a coyote with that rifle if I had a good chance within three hundred yards.

One afternoon, I had two chances.

The first came when I was walking between the Cheyenne River flood plain and an adjacent hill. Outlined against the sky on top of the hill and at a distance of about a hundred and fifty yards, a coyote sat looking at me. At my shot, the coyote disappeared. I reached the top of the hill in time to see what must have been the same coyote running down the side of another hill about a half mile away. The bounds of the coyote down the steep hillside became so great that I wondered how it could keep its feet—then, it lost its footing and went into a sprawling roll. It got up again and continued bounding out of sight into the breaks. At the moment, I could see humor in the coyote's spill, if nothing else.

While I was up on the hilltop, I took three shots at a part of a bleached cottonwood log that lay near the place from which I had shot at the coyote. The bullets all struck at about the same place, though a foot to the side of my point of aim. I still was not convinced that the sights could be so much out of line, but planned to try more sighting shots the next day when the light was better.

On the way to the cabin, late in the afternoon, I was walking through the breaks, and, behold, there was a coyote sitting up watching me, this one on a level with me and at a distance of less than a hundred yards. It watched me sit down and wrap my arms around my knees in a steady firing position. I could not bring myself to aim to the side to allow for any misalignment of the sights, so I aimed dead center on that coyote's chest and squeezed the trigger. This coyote too bounded out of sight into the breaks.

I had no further adventures with curious coyotes as I plodded on toward the cabin, in the shadows and changing colors of sunset, in the dusk and the darkness.

(On one other occasion toward spring, I thought that I might be able to shoot some coyotes. I was on the rim of the tableland when I heard a daylight coyote chorus, so loud that it seemed to come from directly below the rim. The clamor was so great, and so many voices were sounding in unison, that I thought there must be several animals in the group. When I peeked over the rim, I had a splendid view of a valley and long, sloping hills, but nothing at all of coyotes.)

During my coyote-less first two weeks in the breaks, I had been carrying on a baiting campaign in an effort to get coyotes accustomed to visiting strategic places. Rabbit baits for the coyotes turned out to be futile under the circumstances, but I did establish one genuinely attractive bait station: an old horse that a rancher gave me for that purpose. I shot the horse and left it in the crossing zone of the coyotes upstream from the cabin.

I did not go near the horse carcass until the coyotes were visiting it with patent confidence and approaching by definite trails. Then, I hollowed out a space under the floor of the main beaten trail, at a point about fifty yards from the horse. A wolf trap fitted neatly in the hollowed space, in such a way that it had a crust of snow suitable for a covering yet a crust weak enough to break through under a coyote's weight. Only this one trap—nothing next to the horse, where the coyotes would be most likely to suspect traps and to smell around with special care. The trail set seemed perfect.

By morning, the coyotes had pawed away the snow to uncover one of the trap springs, urinated upon it, and thoroughly trampled the vicinity of the trap.

I left the evidence of the insult to my trapping skill exactly as the coyotes had left it, the trap spring exposed for all interested coyotes to see or smell. That night at the cabin, I dipped traps in fresh, hot paraffin to seal in the odor of the steel. Then, early the next morning, I set two or three of these paraffined traps about the unparaffined, coyote-anointed trap of the original set.

Two days later, after living in the Cheyenne breaks for almost three weeks, I had my first coyote, a young one. It was worth four dollars for bounty and ten dollars for pelt.

The misfortune of one of their number terminated all coyote activity at the bait horse for the rest of the winter. The coyotes even quit using the crossing. Peg Leg would no longer go within a quarter of a mile of it.

With the contents of the urinary bladder of my coyote, I made scent stations and set traps to take advantage of coyote doggishness until I had out nearly all of my traps that were at all suitable for coyotes. These were fifteen wolf traps and fewer than a dozen fox traps that I thought might hold a coyote if set double.

I chose my trap sites so that I could visit all of them at least every two days. This meant two separate traplines of about ten miles each, but, insofar as the most promising sets were within a few miles of the cabin, the close-by parts of both traplines were covered daily. At times, when feeling especially hopeful, I would cover both full traplines in a day, but that was too much for any bearable daily routine, with all of the uphill and downhill walking. (Horseback riding was impractical for my hunting and trapping because borrowed horses responded unpredictably when shooting had to be done and I had trouble keeping warm while riding in cold weather.)

No coyotes were caught at the scent stations made with the urine from the young animal caught in the trail leading to the bait horse. The coyotes seemed able to make all of the distinctions that they needed to make.

I finally caught Peg Leg, about six weeks after our initial discovery of each other in the snowstorm. The other coyotes responded to scent stations made with his urine as if they had confidence that the stations were his and that any place he inspected and passed would be all right for them to examine. Three coyotes got in the traps in as many days, but two of them were caught in the fox traps, and they pulled loose after presumably acquiring information useful to them in later life.

*

In some ways, I was sorry that I caught Peg Leg. Had I been more mature, I think I would willingly have let him go with my good wishes for his peaceful future, after about the first month that he so consistently outsmarted me. Still, I must admit that I do not, even now, feel sorry about succeeding in a feat that I long thought would be beyond me.

Peg Leg did nothing as extreme as abandoning his established home range because of my presence. He seemed unafraid of my trails in the snow but made detours of fifteen to twenty feet around each trap site that he passed. When I made new sets, he detoured around them also, if he went that way.

I schemed and schemed as I studied where he tugged at some stock carcass in the hills. Whether I set a trap either in a trail leading to the carcass or in the beaten space around the carcass, he always knew about it. Whether I walked with gumbo balling up on my feet during thaws or with a mitten held up to freezing face and the wind cutting through wristlets, I seemed not to have what it took to put Peg Leg's tracks very near a trap pan.

On a clear day, I might stand on a high point and look off to the west, where I could see badlands and buttes in the far distance, and think of that real wolf, Three Toes, over there somewhere. Thinking again of Peg Leg and how well he was living with what natural endowments he had, I could understand how Three Toes grew to be an old wolf, despite the best trappers in the country. Surely Peg Leg had no economic notoriety to compare with that of Three Toes, and no one other than myself was trying hard to get him. Besides, compared with that of Three Toes, Peg Leg's home range was small. I always knew within a few miles where he was and that sooner or later he would be back at approximately the same places. Therein, I felt, lay my only chance of catching Peg Leg, to take advantage somehow of the fact that he did come back to the same places.

I kept watching to see if Peg Leg had a special habit that might be exploitable and ultimately saw that he did have.

A cavity about twenty feet wide and half as deep had eroded away between creek bank and a hill slope to one side. This left a little natural bridge over which Peg Leg crossed when he ran along the creek bank. The natural bridge was in a position so that the prevailing northwest winds blew across it from the creek-bank side and out over the twenty feet of space over the erosion cavity. It seemed to me, if a trap were set on the bridge, that the odor would be blown directly away from the trap and dissipated over the top of the cavity. When Peg Leg crossed the bridge, he would not be moving into wind-borne scent, whichever way he walked.

About a week earlier, a state predatory-animal hunter had looked me up and spent an afternoon with me. In the course of our conversation, he told me about a trick he used to catch coyotes in their first passage over a trap set in a trail. He said that, when a coyote stepped over a stick or stone, it centered the object in its normal stride, and that, by proper placing of such an object, the coyote's foot could be guided right to the two-and-three-quarters-inch trap pan.

Accordingly, I measured Peg Leg's stride and took half of the length as the distance at which to place stride breakers on opposite sides of the trap pan. When studying the nearly bare ground where the trap was set, I was afraid to introduce any wholly strange objects, so I bent over some rose canes that were growing on the natural bridge at the right distances from the trap pan. I did my picking up and brushing and got out of there.

The next day, a jackrabbit awaited in my perfectly made, last-bet set for Peg Leg. I reset the trap and tidied up as well as I could. The scent of the unlucky jackrabbit as well as the trap scent still seemed to be blowing across the top of the erosion cavity.

Peg Leg did not come around for two or three days, and then a warm day took the snow off the hills fast. Sheets of water converged and poured through the erosion cut and under the natural bridge. Early in the morning of that day, I took a look at the trap site and found it undisturbed. By late afternoon, Peg Leg hung over the edge, caught in the trap by a forefoot and drowned in the run-off stream.

✶

With what was marketable of Peg Leg on a stretching board, I could gaze off toward the northwest in the direction of Harding County and think of Three Toes. It was only daydreaming, however, for I knew that I stood no chance of getting him. I tried to think of what might be done against such an opponent. Watch for some idiosyncrasy, I supposed, such as Peg Leg's crossing the natural bridge—assuming that Three Toes showed favoritism for special parts of his vast home range. But I could think of no convincing answers and gave up Three Toes as being too much wolf for me to try for.

✶

I heard enough boom-talk to know that some of the local people of the West River country had ambitions. With irrigation water where it could be gotten and with scientific dry-farming elsewhere, the land could support a human population multiplied many times over—then, surfaced roads, thriving towns, community activities, and names instead of blank spaces on maps.

For myself, I could not see what necessarily had to be so desirable about more people living everywhere, though I do not recall that I ever expressed to the boosters any preferences for the so-called wastelands remaining as they were.

My feelings were due only in part to my love for the natural out-of-doors and for outdoor solitudes. I do not find it hard to admit that I felt that the coyotes and jackrabbits should be left to what was theirs. I also would think of the weathering ruins of buildings and farming machinery and windmills left by the too-many people who formerly had tried to live on land that should not have been treated as farmland. I was not forgetting that most of the earlier settlers had come in during a land boom when the talk had been that the West River country was undoubtedly THE COMING COUNTRY.

In the Cheyenne River valley, the abandoned houses and shacks were scattered both over the tablelands above and along the bottomlands below the breaks. I had looked through many of these while investigating their possibilities for trapping skunks.

The fact of those houses being there was of itself depressing. Sometimes, the evidence of the disappointment of people who had tried to make homes and a living could be pitiful. The broken-down stoves and beds, the old quilts and clothing, the ordinary worn-out left-behinds could be bad enough. What I seemed to notice more than anything else were the children's things, the pieces of trinket jewelry, the occasional pictures of weddings and family gatherings, the mementoes that once meant something to someone.

Most of the abandoned houses had packrats, and the packrats exemplified in my mind Life's opportunism. Whether man stayed or left, the packrats lived where they could. Now and then, one of them sat in plain sight and looked at me, so soft-furred and so tame and obviously in possession. Their tracks marked the dust on the floors, their nests might fill a cupboard or the corner of a room. Along with pieces of plaster and a scattering of small household items, their nests would usually be heaps of sticks, cactus joints, and dried horse and cattle dung. A nest might be a great mess of chewed-up paper mixed together with material carried from outside.

I caught two or three packrats accidentally in traps set for skunks. When I did, I felt sorry, for there never seemed to be more than one packrat to a house; and, with that one gone, an old house could seem lonely and empty indeed.

*

I did not work very hard toward the end of the winter. Mostly, I prowled the breaks and bottomlands with the two-fifty during those last days, more from wanting to see all that I could see than from any expectation of getting more shots at coyotes. Breakup came on the Cheyenne River, with grinding and crunching and tipping and piling of slabs of ice, building and breaking of ice jams, and rising and falling of water in the channel.

*

I did only a little trapping after I returned to Fairchild's. Some scent-station coyote sets made next to fence posts in the hills away from the ranch buildings caught only skunks that had come out of hibernation to paw about for insects at the bases of the posts. Thereupon, I took up the traps and kept myself usefully occupied until the spring term started at South Dakota State by picking what corn was left to pick in the Fairchild cornfield.

Mrs. Fairchild—I had come to know her as Ma Grace—told me that she was glad that I did not catch those coyotes near home. They were not numerous, and she did not want them cleaned out completely. She liked to hear them. She maintained that, if people kept a good dog and took care of their poultry and livestock, they would not have much coyote damage.

This was worth reflecting upon as I slogged through the spring gumbo, picking corn. Coming from a most practical and matter-of-fact ranch wife who felt that she could afford to hear coyotes howl, or to know that some were about, Ma Grace's viewpoint made sense to me.

*

I visited the Cheyenne River breaks and bottomlands during the summer and fall after I trapped there. The cottontail legions, though holding up until I left in the spring, were gone by summer. Neither did the jackrabbit abundance last long after it became top-heavy. Something had happened,

150 * Toward Appreciation of Wolves

the sort of thing that undoubtedly had happened again and again over the centuries. It looked like what the old-timers called the rabbit plague. I too thought that it must have been disease, but it was nothing that I could be the least sure about. The rabbits, to my eyes, merely were not there any more, neither there nor in any other places in the Cheyenne breaks and bottoms that I could easily reach by car or by walking.

In that same summer, a U.S. Biological Survey wolfer caught old Three Toes over in Harding County. The ranchers gave the trapper an engraved gold watch.

✻

A decade after my trapping in the Cheyenne breaks, I saw that the natural bridge where I had caught Peg Leg had washed out and that the erosion hole had lengthened into a deep gully extending fully fifty yards into the sheep-grazed pasture.

CHAPTER 9

Of Wilderness and Wolves

Aldo Leopold introduced one of his essays with advice never to revisit a wilderness. Returning to a place of favorite memories after long absence would not only be likely to disappoint but also to tarnish the memories.

I did not challenge the melancholy appropriateness of this advice in returning very purposely to northern Minnesota's Big Bog area where I had lived as a fur trapper twenty-eight years before. I knew that I would find changes that quite possibly might not please me.

Twenty-eight years after my winter in the Big Bog, Waskish was a small town with a U.S. highway passing through it. A highway bridge crossed the mouth of the Tamarack River. The downstream riverbanks were lined with summer cottages.

During the period between my wintering and return, all physical traces of my having lived there—that I could recognize—had disappeared. I could not find so much as one of my cut stumps at my former cabin site a few miles upstream from Waskish, and the cabin was gone. My old winter headquarters may now be said to exist only in memory, along with many other things antedating the summer cottages and the highway.

The Big Bog was no longer subject to the human exploitation and the promotional schemes of earlier in the century. In the mid-1930s, the federal government had resettled most of the remaining farmers in places where they would have a better chance to make a living. After its withdrawal from agricultural use, it had been managed by public agencies as wild land for game production, hunting, and related purposes for which it was adapted. As a wilderness, the Big Bog was not, in the late 1940s, anything much resembling the wilderness that the white man had found there; but it had regained some of the wilderness features lost during the boom period of human settlement. Perhaps it might be considered, battered as it was, a triumphant wilderness insofar as its human invaders had essentially withdrawn—that is, away from the highway, the summer cottages, and a few roads leading into one place or another.

*

An inland post office had become during the twenty-eight years a ghost of fallen, rotten logs. I did not find much left of the stands of pines, nor of the hardwood fringes along the Tamarack River, nor anything of the once-extensive white cedar swamps. The savannah was enlarged and the swamps and bogs less diversified and more open, similar in appearance to the vast Canadian wetlands hundreds of miles to the northwest. As before, the ditches had beavers, and probably more beavers than before. As before, a sand ridge along the north shore of Upper Red Lake was covered with a mixture of hardwood trees and berry bushes.

The last of the woodland caribou up there in the expanses of bog and swamp north of the lake had gone, though not before great effort had been made by conservation agencies to save them. Those caribou had been the last free-living remnant of the species south of the Canadian border. To the dwindling stock had been added animals live-trapped in Canada. They had gone too. The edge of a species' range had ceased to be range at all.

Some people blamed the wolves for the loss of the woodland caribou, and the wolves were known to have killed caribou, but the explanation is unlikely to be anything so simple and direct when a population disappears from an outskirt of its native range. Indian hunting could have been more than the fading species had been able to withstand, but that explanation does not take us far into fundamentals either. Neither wolves nor Indians explain the dwindling that had earlier gone on. Local extinction had been the culminating symptom of a biological impossibility. When I first knew that country, the caribou had probably been more abundant than the moose in the wildest parts of the Big Bog. As the caribou had faded, the moose had increased, and neither wolves nor Indians nor fires nor plant succession had prevented the increase of the moose. Moose country it had become, the moose belonged there, and the moose were there to prove it.

Other age-tested natives were there along with the moose and the wolves, wherever they belonged: the deer, the ruffed grouse and sharp-tailed grouse, the skunks and weasels and foxes, the snowshoe hares.

It was a quiet, sunny day of early fall when I walked along the north shore sand ridge of Upper Red Lake on the occasion of my return to the Big Bog country. The deciduous leaves were coloring, and the mosquitoes had given up. A bald eagle was flying overhead. I felt at the same time a great peace and a great longing.

I still wanted what my middle age had in family satisfactions; but I longed to be young, with youthful stamina and lack of big responsibil-ities, to be living in an interlude again, as a predator in wilderness soli-tudes, yet not so far into solitudes as to be out of reach of companionship when companionship was needed.

Walking along the lake beach, I pulled apart a wolf dropping contain-ing the remains of snowshoe hare. This wolf sign, more than anything else, aroused memories of a part of the world as it once had been com-pared with what it had become. This, more than anything else, was assur-ance that the Big Bog was still wilderness, despite the decades of human abuse and the new cottages along the Tamarack. Wolf country this had been since before the white man came, and wolf country it still was.

*

Farther north into Canada, the wildernesses that I know are wolf wilder-nesses. In these wildernesses, the wolves may not be the least obtrusive. One may, while traveling, think of wolves only now and then and not with any sense of their really dominating anything. To me, they fit into the northern wilderness scene, across the border north from Upper Red Lake and Lake of the Woods, as salt fits into a recipe, unobtrusively yet part of it.

When the wolves are there, one can see the signs. A portage trail that is not too exclusively packed with human tracks may show some wolf tracks. Game trails have wolf tracks among the moose tracks and rabbit tracks and the tracks of the other wild creatures that naturally use game trails. Wolf and moose or deer tracks show on riverbanks and mud bars and lake edges. Weathered wolf droppings may be found if one looks in the right places. Or, one may not actually look to find the droppings—they may just be there in plain sight, with the old deer hair or rabbit fur or feather butts sticking out of the clay-like body of a dropping. If a big carcass lies in some conspicuous place, maybe it will show tooth marks of wolves, but, except under certain circumstances, one is unlikely to find many carcasses, at any rate without looking for them and knowing where to look. The wolf sign is more unlikely to be tracks in places wolves frequent in their ordinary business of being wolves.

A hotel lobby may have walls decorated with wolf skins. A rustic bedroom may have wolf rugs on the floor. Among the old family hand-me-downs may be wolf coats or wolf rugs.

That wolf-country wilderness is vast, though I do not know exactly how vast from personal experience. I have seen it by air from commercial planes for hours at a time. Extending westward, northward, and eastward from The Pas, it looked all but endless—the lakes, marshes, swamps, bogs, the flat and the rough lands, the dense and the thin stands of trees and shrubs, the burned and the unburned, the panoramas of what the Canadians call "the bush."

At flying altitudes, the game trails were plainly visible wherever they were not overgrown by vegetation. The veteran northerner Tom Lamb flew me so low that I could look for muskrat cuttings and feeding platforms. In what was still woodland caribou range of central Saskatchewan, a lot of bog and open tamarack and spruce swamp and patches of higher ground looked to me very much as the woodland caribou range of northern Minnesota's Big Bog had looked when it had had caribou. Making allowances for the differences in details to be seen from skimming past in a light plane in summer and breaking trail with snowshoes, I could sense rather than explain why the Big Bog had the last of Minnesota's woodland caribou and why central Saskatchewan still has the species.

Neither place was beautiful according to the usual standards of scenic grandeur. They both had their solitudes. The Big Bog, itself, had its thousands and thousands of acres where people seldom if ever went. It had wilderness where people did not live, possibly never have been, maybe not even Indians.

*

My criteria of wilderness values are put forth only as my own, and I do not suppose that I can wholly define them. In part, wilderness values as I know them are those of naturalness, of cleanness and freedom. They afford a measure of peace to people whose tastes are like mine. They mean enough to cause some of us to fight for the preservation of wildernesses that we have neither seen nor expect to see. To those of us who see symptoms of biological and social unbalance in mankind exploiting and defiling almost every place within reach, the preservation of wildernesses anywhere is a source of comfort.

The quality of naturalness in a wilderness has its relative aspects and its anthropocentric definitions. We may quibble over what constitutes naturalness and, of course, maintain that anything is natural, including all of man's activities. For the sake of conveying a thought, let it be said that naturalness in the way that I mean reflects the working of what we call Nature in contradistinction to the workings of man.

In a North Woods wilderness there may be species that are beautiful according to nearly any human standards; others may be thought of as nothing special to look at, but still they belong. If the timber wolf were not beautiful, I would say that it still would have its place as a wilderness animal, but I think that it is very beautiful. I think that it is as beautiful as anything that it preys upon. Its beauty is that of power and ruggedness and movement, of the near-perfection of a natural type. It is adjusted to its way of life, a natural creature uncorrupted by human tampering. It is beautiful in the sense that a goshawk, gyrfalcon, muskellunge, canvasback duck, or an otter may be beautiful.

The sleekest, most superb, full-sized timber wolves that I ever saw were some snared in northern Minnesota. I cannot see any reasons other than fear, hate, jealousy, or misunderstanding why man should not appreciate the beauty of such as these. Theirs was the beauty of champions, if there ever were champions in anything, with heads that looked about a foot in width and powerful enough to bite a chunk out of any animal that they could take hold of, with necks, shoulders, and forelegs to match the heads. Surely, they were a tested product of much evolution, whether to be regarded as an enemy of man or not. Northern winters, with their periods of famine and great cold, have, moreover, molded in the timber wolf a species endowed with qualities other than crude strength and stamina.

While I learned long ago that there are people interested in northern wildernesses who do not agree with me as to how much wolves belong in a wilderness scene, I am certain that my views are shared by others. Such practical men as Ira N. Gabrielson and Stanley Young, with their great experience in predator control programs, cannot fairly be charged with being overly sentimental on behalf of wolves; yet they have expressed hope that the remnant populations of timber wolves found in the northern Lake States will not be exterminated. These men, among other naturalists, have suggested that, for biological and aesthetic reasons, preserves be dedicated to the wolves or that wolves be permitted to live unmolested in areas where their activities would not be in serious conflict with human interests.

*

The remaining wolves in the Upper Peninsula of Michigan and in northern Wisconsin are remnants, indeed. They are dangerously close to being lost as a species to those states. Perhaps they could not be saved on the Michigan and Wisconsin mainlands even if the public were to show far greater interest in saving them than it has shown to date. Northern Minnesota has its relatively strong stock of wolves to a large extent in spite of the public's animosity. The wolves are still killed by almost anyone having opportunities.

While I would not contend that there are any regions in the United States where free-living wolves should be given complete legal protection at all times, without any exceptions, it does not follow that wolves must be unremittingly campaigned against merely because it may be legal to do so. There remains the need for judgment, for rational policies and action.

The idea of a preserve for what Gabrielson referred to as "these magnificent predators" may be acceptable to many people in the abstract, but, when it comes to planning for a preserve of this type, all kinds of objections have ways of arising. Even though viewed without hatred, as wonderful animals and a priceless part of a wilderness heritage, even if

Gray Wolf, by Charles W. Schwartz. Charles W. Schwartz Collection,
the State Historical Society of Missouri.

one's sympathies are for the wolves, realities of damage resulting from
wolves must still be considered.

A fair and workable zoning policy or system of indemnity for *bona
fide* wolf damage might be prerequisite to the establishment of any real
wilderness-and-wolf preserve. Attempting to keep the wolves and other
wilderness predators killed off at public expense in order that someone
may try to raise a few sheep in out-of-the-way places in non-agricultural
country can be fully as absurd as would be the opposite extreme of toler-
ating the wolves where they would have real potentialities for damage to a
sound stock-raising industry.

I do not recall having heard of wolves destroying livestock about the
periphery of the Big Bog, though they surely must have done so. Even
in recent times, publicized wolf damage to livestock has occurred as far
south as central Minnesota, much outside of any consistently occupied
timber wolf range. The possibility of—especially—unsophisticated
young wolves straying into farming communities must be considered as

part of reality. However, I have been informed by predator-control people that such stray wolves are relatively easy to eliminate.

The Big Bog *might* be one of the areas in northern United States where free-living timber wolves might be left in comparative peace. Perhaps it is not; perhaps there are good reasons why not. If not, if this is just one more of the places where human interests and wolves are incompatible, if the wolves really must be kept down to the lowest possible level, I would not advocate anything to the contrary.

At the same time, if man—without really valid justification—succeeds in making and keeping the Big Bog wolf-less, by so much, in my opinion, shall he make this man-ravaged wilderness more nearly the worthless wasteland that some people call it.

*

My outdoor philosophies had not emerged in any clear, consistent, or final form after my earlier contacts with wildernesses. I probably recognized first the preciousness of solitude as an antidote to the overwhelming dominance of man. In addition, I should say that what has counted most to me in wilderness values has been the relative completeness of the living and non-living constituents of a given tract of wilderness. I do not want to see even my favorites among plant and animal life living just anywhere—only where they belong, marsh and bog life in marshes and bogs, plains life on the plains, desert life in deserts, and so on, according to what is appropriate in natural biological equations.

My views as to wildernesses and their essential constituents are not presented in this book as having originated solely with me. Other people certainly have arrived at the same or similar views. It is also true that no one really can trace how some concepts grow either in his own mind or in the minds of others. Before I ever met or corresponded with my Swedish friend, Kai Curry-Lindahl, I could see how parallel our thoughts were running on questions of Nature protection and preservation of unique and vanishing outdoor values. I could see that much of what he wrote about the importance of the natural out-of-doors and its creatures in a country's culture expressed not only my own sentiments but also those of Aldo Leopold, Frank Fraser Darling, and many other ecologists and conservationists, whether they wrote of the Americas, Africa, Europe, or Pacific Islands.

Curry-Lindahl's writings on exploitation of Scandinavian wilderness resemble those of Aldo Leopold regarding the American, as expressed, for example, in Leopold's celebrated essay, "Conservation Esthetic." Curry-Lindahl balanced the advantage of having as many Swedes as possible learn to know their mountains against the disadvantages of making the mountains tourist attractions. The enlistment of popular support in safeguarding the integrity of wilderness is one thing to be considered in the long view; so is the commercialization of wilderness, with its conse-quences in the form of roads, hotels, and towns. Gradually, one industry and community after another may then develop. And that kind of devel-opment, Curry-Lindahl pointed out, probably would mean the loss of the large wild predators of Sweden's mountainous region—the only region of the country where the greatly reduced stock of those animals stands much chance of persisting at all and the one region that still has the best claim to be called wilderness.

Aldo Leopold, in his article on conservation aesthetics, wrote of the proponents of wilderness having

achieved a compromise with the road-building bureaus which have the custody of our National Parks and Forests. They have agreed on the formal reservation of roadless areas. Out of every dozen wild areas opened up, one may be officially proclaimed "wilderness," and roads built only to its edge. It is then advertised as unique, as indeed it is. Before long its trails are congested, it is being dolled up . . . or an unexpected fire necessitates split-ting it in two with a road to haul fire-fighters. Or the congestion induced by advertising may whip up the price of guides and packers, whereupon somebody discovers that the wilderness policy is undemocratic. Or the local chamber of commerce, at first quiescent at the novelty of a hinterland officially labeled as "wild," tastes its first blood of tourist-money. It then wants more, wilderness or no wilderness.

In short, the very scarcity of wild places, reacting with the *mores* of advertising and promotion, tends to defeat any deliberate effort to prevent their growing still more scarce.

It is clear without further discussion that mass-use involves a direct dilution of the opportunity for solitude; that when we speak of roads, campgrounds, trails, and toilets as "development" of recreational resources, we speak falsely in respect of this component. Such accommodations for the crowd are not developing (in the sense of adding or creating) anything. On the contrary, they are merely water poured into the already-thin soup.

So it goes with very nearly every place that man can reach or exploit or tamper with in one way or another. If anything of wilderness or even of spontaneous wildness on a lesser scale is to be saved except by chance, it just about has to be through someone's initiative and sustained and well-directed effort. The public can, it is true, respond magnificently when something it wants to keep is threatened—which has been demonstrated by its most heartening support of campaigns to safeguard national parks and national monuments in the United States. But I am afraid that the public influence is likely to be more bad than otherwise as concerns the preservation of natural values over the country as a whole.

The push is on via the bulldozers, draglines, trucks, the new factories and apartment houses, the spreading suburbs, the roads everywhere. Into the north, what is tillable is tilled, the military agencies take over tremendous areas, and the processes of change shrink the wilderness almost irrespective of where it is.

In my emphasizing wilderness, I am not underemphasizing man and the needs of man—just the opposite. I am convinced that modern man, in the state that his affairs have come to, needs very much indeed to keep what he can of what remains naturally wild in a world full of people. I think that man needs to hang on to and to cherish the remnants of what is naturally wild more than he does to make room for and to afford means of subsistence for more people.

*

That the great values of our natural out-of-doors may be recreational is something I am willing to concede for the time being, from man-centered criteria and up to a point. I do not concede that recreational values must be primarily something to hunt or fish or even to visit at first hand. There are other matters of definition that I am not willing to concede, either; and I do not want to be pinned down too closely concerning some things that I know by feel more than by reasoned analyses.

My view has been—and still is—that civilized man should exploit only game species that are well enough situated to withstand a reasonable amount of exploitation. When I was young, waterfowl and prairie grouse were so abundant where I lived, so secure in their excellent habitats, and so little hunted by man, that gun pressure did not constitute the problem in their management that it now does. Today, in addition to the hoofed game that may be in many places far too abundant for its own good, the introduced ring-necked pheasant occurs by the millions where living conditions favor it in the agricultural United States. In fact, numerous wild species are now available for orderly harvesting on a scale that would have been unimaginable during my youth; and I see nothing wrong about our taking advantage of these thriving or even overabundant wild species to the extent that exploitation of them is properly conducted.

*

Up to a certain point, unselfish motivations in conservation may hardly be dissociated from the selfish. I do not know when I became more concerned about what natural values posterity would have left than about what remained for me during my lifetime. But I do want posterity to have, and to continue having, opportunities for wholesome outdoor enjoyments such as I had when I was young.

As a conservationist, I have been disappointed in the losses of outdoor values that have occurred since my youth. The peace of mind that the out-of-doors has meant for me has often been offset by the wastage of woodlands, wetlands, and grasslands. I may wonder if mankind's overrunning and despoliation of the earth will stop short of ruin of the values that go so far in making life worth living for people who now and then need solitude or natural wildness to remind them of something other than man. For there are those who maintain that the earth will ultimately be so full of people that they will have to use everything for subsistence.

There are even those who maintain that such is not only inevitable but desirable. There are certainly people to whom loss of outdoor values is no loss that they feel at all. National parks have lumber or other exploitable features that someone wants, and, in almost unlimited variety, someone is always seeking economic gain at the expense of what is left in the natural out-of-doors.

When I have something like this to brood about, I may doubt that the interests that grew to be such a big part of my life since boyhood are anything to recommend for others. Then, the mood passes, and I know that modern civilization is not exclusively money-making and gadgetry. An increasing number of articulate and determined people, like the late Bernard DeVoto, have been seeing something very wrong indeed about having to drive a hundred miles or more from home to reach a "reasonably neglected natural area." As has happened many times in recent years, it is heartening to have demonstrated that influential groups of people can, in the words of Ernest Swift, "refuse to swap a clear-running stream, a National Monument, public rights or a wilderness area for a fast and slippery buck." There is more behind the growing power of conservation movements than the nostalgias of an ex-trapper like myself.

My early outdoor life instilled in me an appreciation for the integrity of Nature. This feeling may be expressed otherwise as a love of Life—not Life in any narrow man-centered sense but Life in the sense of associations of plants and animals and physical environments that were age-tested long before man dominated the earth or even was on it. As a participant in living processes, modern man has his place; but my view over the years is that Life collectively is a greater thing than mankind collectively. I do not believe that man, with his most exceptional capabilities for dominance as a living form, should dominate ruthlessly and irresponsibly the other living forms that also belong on earth.

In questions of what living forms belong (and where and when and how much?), I know that I am still influenced in my late fifties by some of the wilderness ideals of my youth—though I am willing to make some concessions forced upon me by realities. We patently cannot have wilderness everywhere and have the civilization that we know today. Neither do

I think that, as responsible beings, we should consider ourselves entitled to obliterate wilderness everywhere. Recognizing that there have to be compromises, I should say that a civilized attitude would be to try to preserve a good deal of Nature in as natural condition as we can, if only for the sake of our own mental health. From our own selfish standpoints, the good life needs more than man and the man-made. To at least some civilized people, opportunities to enjoy and to reflect in the natural out-of-doors are as important as material comforts.

*

In considering my own sentiments toward wildernesses and their creatures, I cannot underrate the motivations and trophy value of memories. In my case, memories comprise a big part of what I feel that I got out of my early life as a hunter and trapper. To a considerable extent they remain a part of my day-to-day living. At any rate, the places that I like best wherever I may be include those reminding me of the places that I knew in my early years—that is, the wilderness and the wilder places of backwoods, prairie marshes and prairie streams, and the rugged country and great expanses of the high plains.

There is carryover from youth in my regrets that the larger wolves had to be extirpated over such a tremendous proportion—nearly all—of the range that they once held in those parts of the United States lying south of the Canadian border. There is carryover in my wanting to protect the remnant populations that persist in wilderness tracts where they neither do nor are likely to do much of anything detrimental to man.

The distinctive quality that wolves impart to the memories of my younger years leaves me with a special awareness of how superbly they represent wilderness.

It was easy for me to feel responsive to an article by R.J. Rutter on a winter outing in Ontario's Algonquin Provincial Park. The author's companion, upon seeing the tracks of a wolf pack of four animals, had exclaimed that there were more wolves than people—a thought that obviously had much appeal to both visitors. They would like to think that there would always be more wolves than people in the three thousand square miles of frozen wilderness. Perhaps the best illustration of what

I have in mind may come not from wolves and not in my own words at all but from Aldo Leopold's essay on the mountain Escudilla in *A Sand County Almanac*:

There was . . . only one place from which you did not see Escudilla on the skyline: that was the top of Escudilla itself. Up there you could not see the mountain, but you could feel it. The reason was the big bear.

Old Bigfoot was a robber-baron, and Escudilla was his castle. Each spring, when the warm winds had softened the shadows on the snow, the old grizzly crawled out of his hibernation den in the rock slides and, descending the mountain, bashed in the head of a cow. Eating his fill, he climbed back to his crags, and there summered peaceably on marmots, conies, berries, and roots. . . .

No one ever saw the old bear, but in the muddy springs about the base of the cliffs you saw his incredible tracks. Seeing them made the most hard-bitten cowboys aware of bear. Wherever they rode they saw the mountain, and when they saw the mountain they thought of bear. Campfire conversation ran to beef, bailes, and bear. Big Foot claimed for his own only a cow a year, and a few square miles of useless rocks, but his personality pervaded the county.

Those were the days when progress first came to the cow country. Progress had various emissaries. . . .

Since the beginning, time had gnawed at the basaltic hulk of Escudilla, wasting, waiting, and building. Time built three things on the old mountain, a venerable aspect, a community of minor animals and plants, and a grizzly.

The government trapper who took the grizzly knew he had made Escudilla safe for cows. He did not know he had toppled the spire off an edifice a-building since the morning stars sang together.

The bureau chief who sent the trapper was a biologist versed in the architecture of evolution, but he did not know that spires might be as important as cows. He did not foresee that within two decades the cow country would become tourist country, and as such have greater need of bears than of beef-steaks.

The congressmen who voted the money to clear the ranges of bears were the sons of pioneers. They acclaimed the superior virtues of the frontiersman, but they strove with might and main to make an end of the frontier.

We forest officers, who acquiesced in the extinguishment of the bear, knew a local rancher who had plowed up a dagger engraved with the name of one of Coronado's captains. We spoke harshly of the Spaniards who, in their zeal for gold and converts, had needlessly extinguished the native Indians. It did not occur to us that we, too, were the captains of an invasion too sure of its own righteousness.

Escudilla still hangs on the horizon, but when you see it you no longer think of bear. It's only a mountain now.

CHAPTER 10

Of Wilderness and Wolves and Scandinavia

Long before I first saw Sweden, I had surmised that the Swedes of northern Minnesota had been attracted to that area because it was like their
homeland. Except in the very southernmost tip of Denmark-like Scania,
and along the seacoast and in the high mountains, one may in Sweden
imagine himself in a northern Minnesota stretching northward and
southward for a thousand miles.

Mixed hardwood and coniferous forests, rocky outcrops and glacial
boulders, the cultivated flatlands and the hay lands, the lakes, all can look
somewhat the same—not quite—at one end of the country as at the
other. The relative lack of change with latitude in the visible nature of
the terrain seemed most remarkable to me the first time that I saw the
Swedish Arctic.

North of the Arctic Circle, a potato patch lay on one side of a trout
stream, and a commercially managed forest lay on the other side. Another
trout stream had a sawmill on the bank and a huge pile of sawdust spilled
over into the water. There were pine forests clean cut except for seed trees,
logs piled beside the roads for trucking, log rafts covering the surfaces
of hydroelectric impoundments, log chutes from impoundments over or
around the dams down into the flowing streams again, streams rigged to
guide logs through the main channels.

Because of a warm ocean current, Scandinavia does not have the fri-
gidity that one would expect of most places of similar latitude in North
America—although some Scandinavian places can be very cold. The
Torne River boundary between Sweden and Finland north of the Gulf
of Bothnia can have extremes of low temperature comparable to those of
northern Minnesota. Southern Sweden, with the latitude of Hudson Bay,
has more of the winter temperatures to be expected of central United

States. Scandinavia can have much snow and it can have strong winds, and its storms deserve to be called storms. But compared with the deadly ferocity of a real Dakota or Montana or Prairie Province blizzard the worst of the Scandinavian snowstorms of which I have read or heard seemed almost benign.

Scandinavia's northern latitudes are manifested by changes in daylight. One knows that it is north not only at times of the famous midnight sun but also when the sun creeps along the horizon at midday, even when the lakes and streams may have less ice than open water on their surfaces. Whether sunset colors show at midnight or at midday, one knows that it is north.

✶

In Scandinavia, the last Ice Age affords the main starting point for what is usually considered history. A book on natural resources or the story of some province or valley will often begin with an account of the withdrawal of the glacial ice and the emergence of the land in its modern features.

If one watches for glacial signs almost anywhere over the undisturbed landscape, he sees the striations and groovings on the softer bedrock surfaces where the debris-laden ice once planed or pushed whatever got in its way. The rocky islands of the Baltic archipelagoes show their scratched faces, and so do the sloping rocks of inland lakeshores and many of the boulders left heaped or scattered almost anywhere. The ponderous casualness with which the glacial ice gathered and carried and dumped its debris or remodeled the terrain with melt waters can still be appreciated if one does no more than look about. In its way, the Ice Age is still present and dominating or, at any rate, not so very far off.

I shall not attempt to say how long man has been in Scandinavia. Concerning this, the archeologists themselves do not seem to be in full agreement. There are views that man may have been present there throughout the last glaciation, perhaps hunting over the ice and adjoining un-glaciated parts. The most frequent estimates as to human antiquity in Scandinavia are of several thousands of years. The idea of an early hunting culture following the retreat of the ice seems to be generally accepted.

Undoubtedly, the Scandinavian ancients responded to what they found advantageous among the physical remains of the glaciation. I think of eskers, those strung-out deposits resulting from subglacial rivers. A long esker, resembling a road grade, winding between a couple of lakes in central Sweden, suggested how inviting such places must have been to primitive hunters while traveling and prowling and watching—and to the wolves that were then a part of the landscape.

Sweden now has very few free-living wild wolves to frequent eskers or any other place else.

*

As late as the early decades of the nineteenth century, the forests and open spaces all over Sweden had wolves. Even intensively farmed Scania's wolves were not so far back beyond the memory of living people. When I first saw farmsteads constructed to enclose completely within a square of buildings a central yard for poultry and livestock, I thought that they must have been so designed for protection against wolves. Upon inquiry, I learned that the enclosures more likely had been designed with a more prosaic intent: for protection against human thieves.

I could still find in wolf-less Scania places where wolves might have hunted a century and a half ago, in tracts of landscape that may not have changed much since then. In the forested estates about Sövdesjön and Snogeholmsjön there are trails and logging roads where one may walk in the winter twilight—and think of what wolves would look like as they slipped in and out of shadowy coverts or loped around a bend in a trail. One might get a little skin-prickling from imagining wolves in Scanian woods, but to imagine wolves there might require some working at it. It was easier to imagine how long a wolf would survive if it did appear in Scania.

I recognize that modern Scania is no proper place for free wolves. They simply could not be tolerated. (The only wild dogs that Scania could reasonably be expected to retain are the red foxes. It has a substantial population of foxes, which, though severely hunted, do quite well at taking care of themselves. The opportunities that I had to watch or read signs of hunting foxes in the course of a winter that I spent in Scania gave me some of the most intimate views of the old contest between hunters and hunted. An opportunity to peek out of the edge of a forest and watch a fox hunting was not in the same category of specialness that I should assign to an opportunity to watch a wolf hunting, but I was glad to settle for foxes. A fox working past in slough grass or over a snowy meadow, sniffing, listening, pouncing, demonstrated in its own way what canine aliveness and alertness could be.)

What is called Middle Sweden has extensive backwoods and, along both east and west sides, belts of at least passably wild country: On the west lie the mountains between Norway and Sweden and on the east the archipelagoes of the Baltic Sea and the Gulf of Bothnia.

The Swedish and Finnish archipelagoes have the lives and works of man and they have wilderness too. Much of the land is in a transition stage between the sea and the land, much retains the wildness of the sea.

The islands in the archipelagoes consist of everything from rocky islets that are bare except for lichens and a scattering of low ground plants up to islands of large size that are but extensions of the mainland forests. In between are islands of varying size and appearance—some with coniferous growths, some with deciduous, some with pools and small marshes and marshy bays.

They may have nesting colonies of gulls or other sea birds, including the eiders and other ducks that like to nest on islands. Outlying islands may have vipers and voles and a few black grouse. They may have weathered pellets left by the miscellaneous birds of prey that come in as winter guests. There may be seals in places, otters along the coast, foxes on the islands that the animals can get out to; and the Bothnia and Baltic archipelagoes have not been entirely unknown to wolves in the past when the sea iced over.

Between the archipelagoes and the mountains, Middle Sweden has a mottled pattern of farmlands and forests, lakes and waterways. Great areas of unproductive agricultural land are now being taken over for forestry or are more or less reverting to a wild state.

I have seen marten signs at timberline in the mountains to the west and in the deepest old forest of the eastern coast. Nothing about this was astonishing, but it was astonishing to learn that this same wilderness species not only picks the nearest equivalents of wilderness amid the coniferous plantations of thickly settled communities but likewise lives and breeds in cities, including Malmö, Sweden's third-largest. Free-living lynxes—more than just rare wandering strays—may live within the city limits of Stockholm, an even greater biological marvel than Malmö's martens. A wolverine may stray down into Värmland (Selma Lagerlöf's homeland), where state or private forests extend for miles to the sides of intensively cultivated valleys. Up toward the Norwegian border, Jämtland has bears and wolverines, and, the winter before my visit, three wolves had been reported from there.

Across the border from Middle Sweden into southern Norway, the sides of a river valley had one little farm after another cut out of the forest about wherever room for buildings or clearings could be found; but the headwaters came from Dovrefjell, the wildest and most grandly austere country that I remember from Norway.

In Dovrefjell, in a distant sloping valley in the midst of mountains and tundra that could have come out of prehistory, I saw my first herd of reindeer—genuine wild reindeer, digging and eating lichens out of the snow. The wild reindeer, totaling up to forty thousand animals in Norway, were different from the partly domesticated reindeer of the Lapps, so much more what must have been during the Ice Age. The wild reindeer, as mentioned earlier, were able to take care of themselves even against wolves.

The wolves are assured of perpetuation in Norway only in memory and folk stories. A type of hard winter is known as a wolf winter, a winter of game shortage and hunger that could be expected to bring wolves—when wolves were there to bring—down to the settlements.

I remember a winter day spent on a mountain side south of Trondheim Fjord. The snow was deep, and up above reached the bald whiteness of a plateau where ptarmigan and snowy owls and golden eagles lived. Below the timberline lived more ptarmigan and the woodland capercaillie and hazel grouse, the martens, weasels, foxes, and moose. Lower down were some roe deer that could not be said to belong there, but there they were, starving but trying to make out somehow. The hillside farms had sheep, which were sometimes preyed upon by lynxes. During the long ride up the mountain and back down again, the small party of us breathed the exhaust gases of the snow tractor that pulled our bobsled, but, over us, we had an old wolfskin robe.

*

Lapland, to the Swedes, is back of beyond. From a main highway, one may look off across the most sweeping panoramas of lakes, wooded islands and peninsulas, open bogs, swampy forests, wooded hilltops. Or one may follow the scene to timberline and higher, up to bare mountaintops and snowfields. Up there where no automobile roads lead, most of what Sweden can call wilderness extends north and south for about a third of the length of the country.

Most of this wilderness is partly tamed, if not by roads, by tourist trails, by hotels and cabins, by aircraft, and by the presence of indigenous people.

White cattle graze against backgrounds of lakes, forests, and mountains. The wildest areas within any sort of reach by road have their cut stumps, their fences, their clearings, their cabins and sheds. On the other side of a herd of loafing reindeer there might be a hill illustrating modern forestry practices, the cutting and plant-succession stages blocked off in straight-line patchwork across the hilltop.

It may be mining that dominates an Arctic area, as at Kiruna. There may be a newly built village or small city, everything so clean and fresh and painted and well planned, from the new service stations to the new cooperative stores and schools. Human settlement in northern Sweden is nothing new. Farm buildings along the Torne River between Sweden and Finland are utility buildings, and many of them have long been there, built and kept up according to the customs of the land.

The wide belts of power-line rights of way go over and through, and Sweden's hydroelectric dams are the subject of much controversy, some of it bitter. The proponents of the dams argue that the economic value of the power generated outweighs the values lost for salmon runs and other economic resources. That may be, but the dams still have their impacts on Scandinavian wildernesses. Throughout the northern parts of the peninsula, the dams have been built across nearly all water courses having gradients sufficient to make damming feasible. A visitor seeing one regulated river after another can do little more than imagine what the rivers once were.

The dams may themselves be well planned and well made, architecturally perfect, and beautiful—as works of man. Their impounded waters may afford fishing, boating, bathing, and entertainment for crowds. There may be public parks adjacent to the dams or impoundments. Concessions may sell the Scandinavian equivalents of hot dogs, postcards, reindeer horns, and other things that concessions sell and tourists buy. Maybe most of the visitors see what they want, but, if they by any chance drove up from Stockholm or Copenhagen or Paris to see northern wilderness, they will scarcely see it at the dams and the regulated waters.

Away from main rivers there may be some relatively un-tampered lesser streams or meanders, but it seemed to me that wherever there should have been natural rapids or falls worth looking at, there so often would be a dam or an artificial chute. I should not say that there would be any inevitable dam, but I doubt that anyone would challenge the assertion that hydroelectric power development dominates the river valleys in most of the wilder parts of the Scandinavian Peninsula.

The Swedes active in a nature-protection movement are trying to reserve a river in northern Sweden from hydroelectric development, one river to be kept in as natural condition as possible. The people who are carrying on this campaign are determined and able and aware of the urgency of the problem. In this and other aspects of nature protection, they feel that unless they can save the remaining, most nearly primitive wilderness in the next few years it cannot be saved at all.

In northwest Swedish Lapland, the adjacent Sarek and Stora Sjöfallet national parks together constitute the largest (over twelve hundred square miles) nature preserve in Europe. There are places in the interior where a person may wander for weeks without seeing other people.

Up high and deep within, the tundra and plateaus have their ptarmigan, relished by about whatever wilderness flesh-eaters are able to feed upon them. The willow ptarmigan changes its plumage, brown to white, as winter comes, and the willow in its name suggests the biotope in which it belongs and which is so extensive in the wilder parts of Scandinavia. Its close relative, the rock ptarmigan, is also a species that changes from brown to white and back again with the seasons and is a bird living on the rocky slopes and mountaintops, higher up than the willow ptarmigan. "Mountain ptarmigan" is what the rock ptarmigan's name means literally in Swedish.

Another Lapland dweller with mountain in its Swedish name is the mountain lemming that is so famous for its fluctuations in numbers. When abundant, the lemmings furnish food for all manner of predatory mammals and birds. During years of abundance-peaks, when the lemmings may fairly swarm in places, the hawks, owls, foxes, and weasels, the skuas and ravens thrive. The large predators too, the bears, wolverines, and wolves eat the Lapland lemmings when the lemmings are so available.

But, when the predator populations build up in response to the lemmings or other small rodent populations of mountain and tundra, and then the rodent populations collapse, Life can be hard for many of the creatures that must remain there to eat or be eaten. The more mobile of the predators may leave, and the appearance of snowy owls far south of their usual wintering grounds may be one of the manifestations of food shortage.

For birds that fly relatively short distances and for mammals that must travel on foot, there may not be any satisfactory answers, especially if they have no suitable places to go elsewhere. The resulting situations described in the literature are those not only of the famished predators preying upon whatever remnants of their customary prey they can get but also of predators preying upon each other. Hawks and foxes prey upon weasels, weasels upon weasels, hawks upon hawks, eagles upon foxes, and the weak and hungry upon the weak and hungry as they have opportunities. Add severe weather to this equation, and the result can be another wolf winter, still called that whether wolves contribute to it or not.

✳

The Lapps and their reindeer represent a way of life, a culture, and an adjustment to what can be at times a particularly harsh environment. The Lapps and their reindeer are almost traditionally inseparable over the sprawling areas—whether in Sweden, Norway, Finland, or Russia— where the reindeer herds must range and the Lapps must keep moving with them. In northern Norway, the Lapps winter with their reindeer in the fells, then take them to the coast when spring comes; but the general procedure for the Swedish Lapps is to herd their reindeer into the mountains in summer and into the forests lower down in winter. The lowlands of Swedish Lapland may also have sizeable herds living there all summer; these are called forest reindeer, and they may be attending to their business of living with or without any human beings in sight. One particular herd remains in my memory because it was wallowing in a large, charcoal-burning lot.

Now there are only the so-called tame reindeer in Sweden, totaling about three hundred thousand. The Lapps originally extirpated the Swedish wild reindeer and, since then, whenever wild reindeer came over into Sweden from the Norwegian population, the Lapps extirpated the newcomers. For their own reasons, the Lapps do not want wild reindeer around.

The Lapps do not want any wild animals around that could conceivably under any circumstances cause them trouble. They hate the lynx, the wolverine, the bear, and the wolf, and they carry on campaigns of extirpation against them all, wherever they have opportunities or can make opportunities.

Of the larger carnivores, the lynx, wolverine, and bear seldom do any really serious damage to the Lapp's reindeer and then usually under exceptional conditions. Only the wolf, when present, may be said to specialize on the Lapp's reindeer, and, toward the wolf, the Lapps may be said to specialize in hatred.

For all of Sweden, as of 1958–1959, the time of my stay in that country, the most authoritative estimates of the stocks of large carnivores were around a few hundred each of lynxes and bears, a considerably smaller number of wolverines, and perhaps twenty wolves. Swedish biologists felt that their wolf population was maintained to the extent that it was chiefly by animals coming in from Finland and Russia.

The Lapps, themselves, fit into the nature-protection scene in peculiar ways that make the problems they present in Sweden greater than the problems presented by ordinary Swedes living in the same region. In their nomadic culture, the Lapps are regarded by public agencies as part of the indigenous fauna, and one may read in tourist literature that they and their reindeer add colorful life to otherwise barren wastelands. On broad grounds there would seem to be nothing wrong with that, but, it should not be forgotten how ruinous the customs and privileges of the Lapps can be to some of the wilderness values that are so hard to retain. This is particularly true concerning the threatened forms of Life that the Lapps so intensely hate, the same animals that continue to have their best if not their last Swedish strongholds in Lapland.

One of the purposes of establishing the Sarek and Sjöfallet areas as national parks has been to preserve samples of wilderness in as undisturbed and primitive condition as possible. It has been to preserve samples of wilderness fauna as well as the plant life and the mountains, plateaus, wetlands, and valleys, as such. Among the animals that at least some Swedes have been so motivated to protect are living examples of the vanishing large predators, the genuinely predatory constituents of what a primitive fauna should be in such places.

According to the special official treatment accorded the Lapps as a rightful and picturesque part of the northern scene, these people are permitted to kill virtually anything predatory virtually anywhere whenever it may be killing or endangering their reindeer.

Even if it be conceded that the Lapps have a big problem in wolf predation, the lynx, the wolverine, and the bear are still species persecuted by the Lapps far beyond justification. Despite the fact that the Lapps are compensated by the government for damage done their herds by the predators, the Lapps can pay bounties out of their own funds on predatory species that are even protected by law from the rest of the Swedish public. They may enter the national parks and kill the very animals for the protection of which the parks were, in part, established.

It is true that, in the event of a flagrantly senseless killing, a Lapp as well as an ordinary Swedish citizen may be punished by law—I read about one such case during my stay in Sweden. Even so, it is not a comforting thought that precariously situated species in their best remaining range must still be persecuted by people who hate them so. To the Lapps, their reindeer are threatened as long as any possible reindeer-killers exist at all, anywhere within possible reach of reindeer.

The Lapps may attribute all manner of losses to predation. If a reindeer disappears or is found dead, one of the readiest of explanations to be offered is that some predator killed it. A dead reindeer eaten upon by a predator must, perforce, have been killed by that predator, be it wolf, bear, wolverine, lynx, even fox or eagle. Of course, the government reasonably expects a minimum of proof that a dead reindeer actually represents killed prey before it pays indemnity; it cannot subsidize the Lapps for all reindeer that they lose from weather, hunger, disease, old age, accident, and other causes of death.

I gained some concept of what may be the easy availability of reindeer flesh for predators and scavengers alike, from a total of about a month spent from Jämtland on up in the northern part of Sweden. Stray reindeer were to be seen along roadsides for almost the whole length of Swedish Lapland, and some of these were manifestly aged and ailing.

Kai Curry-Lindahl of Stockholm's Northern Museum referred to a loss of forty thousand reindeer from weather conditions, sickness, and poor care in one of the provinces adjacent to Lapland during 1934–1936. He suggested keeping this number in mind when considering the Lapps' perpetual complaint about the losses they suffer from predation. The actual losses suffered from predation obviously represent but a very small fraction of the annual reindeer losses. By late winter, the herds may be in poor condition, and, if the weather during calving time is bad, dead calves may lie all around. Also, between fifteen hundred and two thousand reindeer are annually killed in Sweden by railway trains and hundreds more by automobiles.

*

In considering attitudes of Scandinavians toward their native predators, the fact should not be lost sight of that neither may non-predatory game species themselves always escape public animosity. Local residents do not necessarily regard uniqueness or other special categories of interest as any valid reason for protection of even plant-eaters as long as the animals do or are capable of doing damage.

In the early 1940s, a small stock of wild pigs escaped from a park in southern Sweden and established itself as that country's sole population of the free-living species. Their damage in cultivated fields caused so much complaint that the government wiped them out through an intensive three-months campaign.

Sweden's remaining population of free-living red deer—totaling about a hundred and fifty as of the mid-1950s, and essentially restricted to Scania—does so much damage to forestry plantations that at least some people agitate for its extirpation. After spending most of a fall and winter in the midst of this red deer population, I can verify both the damage inflicted in the plantations and the responses of plantation owners thereto. As concerns the abundant roe deer (which is a favorite game species having at the same time very substantial potentialities for damage to orchards and coniferous plantings), sentiments may vary depending on how much personal interests are affected. Another favorite game species, the moose, may be hated by foresters, some of whom may be highly immoderate in their recommendations for solving the moose problem.

Perhaps it would not be quite fair to generalize that Scandinavians are casual in calling for extirpations but some can be. I have an impression, also, that Scandinavian resentment toward a wild creature doing damage or causing trouble in any way or trespassing upon what man claims as his own may be based upon a sense of outrage.

Any such sense of outrage attains its highest intensity whenever activities of flesh-eaters—the robber-animals—are involved. There is much here that may be said to represent ingrained tradition or carryover from the collective experience, folk tales, customs, and superstitions of centuries.

One day I visited an archipelago in company with local ornithologists. The two nests of sea eagles that we looked at showed evidence of human plundering. One of the ornithologists called them typical eagle nests—typically plundered. This same man for years had banded young sea eagles in the part of the archipelago nearest his home, and then on one visit he found on the ground under a nest tree the pile of bands representing his years of effort. The bands had thus been returned to him as an insulting reminder that nothing he tried with the eagles would do any good. The fact that Sweden has in all only between forty and fifty pairs of sea eagles makes no perceptible difference to the fishermen of the archipelagoes—so angry and so jealous are they of anything that the eagles might do.

Scandinavia's game-keeping is still largely of traditional types, in which strict repression of flesh-eaters is routine. Game-keepers still contend that the land cannot have both vermin and game—surely not very much game. Not even do legal restrictions always protect predators from the game-keepers. I found in one tract of beech woods a steel trap of a design outlawed in Sweden for decades because of its cruelty. Hawks of species as nearly harmless to game as predatory birds could be were still shot. This sort of thing, I was told, was nothing unusual where the old-time game-keepers operated.

When it comes to the harshness with which almost anything predatory can be treated by Scandinavians, Norwegians seem to me at times to have gone, if anything, to greater extremes than Swedes. A decade and a half ago, bounties were paid in Norway on practically everything that ate flesh, irrespective of rarity; and bounties are still paid on some of the same predatory species that now receive year-round legal protection in Sweden. Yet, as relates to the hated predators, it would be hard to surpass the example of one of the editors of a leading Swedish newspaper, who wrote that the existence of any bears outside of zoos in Sweden must be regarded as a disgrace to a rational society and that he and all civilized people with him awaited the day when the country became rid of its last free-living bear.

In my efforts to understand just what (besides the views of generations of game-keepers and other professional land-use specialists) might be responsible for the perpetuation of such extreme attitudes, I have wondered about the role of childhood teachings. Particularly, I have wondered how much the writings of Sweden's beloved Selma Lagerlöf might contribute to public misconceptions as to wilderness and wild creatures.

Gösta Berling's Saga may be prescribed reading in Swedish schools, and it could hardly help having some influence on impressionable young minds, whether they regarded it as only a story or not. It not only treats wilderness as a cruel and evil thing but it also gives flesh-eaters the worst sort of press.

The chapter on a fabulous bear begins with the forest darkness in which live creatures having ghastly shining teeth, sharp beaks, and sharp claws, long to cling tight to a blood-filled neck. The eagle owl is a ghost that can come out of the dusk and strike out one's eyes. The lynx—dangerous to mention by its right name—forces itself in through a small opening in a sheep shed and throws itself upon the sheep, hanging on their throats and drinking their blood and tearing and ceasing not in its wild death-dance until every sheep is dead. The wolves come in the night and pursue the countryman's sled until the mother throws her child to them to save her own life and her husband's. The bear attacks children in the forest. (The most dangerous and feared of bears, protected by evil powers, may be killed only with a silver bullet.) Forest birds can be witches; the cuckoo that calls so merrily in the spring becomes in autumn a hawk with grim eyes and frightful talons, and other birds sing troll songs and seize human hearts with iron hands. Full of evil is Nature, sly as a sleeping snake; and the unholy animals of the forest are possessed of the souls of blood-thirsty cheats.

Yet, the hero, Gösta, spared the life of the great bear. He did not regard the bear as evil, seeing him as he was, as a poor, persecuted animal. Although Gösta could be depressed because of the dark forest and snow and cold and solitude, he still longed for the forest's peace. The forest's peace may not in Gösta's case be wholly dissociated from a longing for the peace of death, but it is apparent from the author's wording that the forest was also a beloved part of the natural scene.

In a story, there can be inconsistencies and contradictions. It should not be surprising that the forest could be majestic, inspiring, soothing, and menacing, all together, that a great bear could be a scourge over the countryside yet a harassed creature that the hero would not harm. It should not be surprising that witches ride wolves and that wolves also respond to Divine command. It should not be surprising that *Gösta Berling's Saga* should have the fanciful and the realistic intermixed, much as the fanciful and the realistic can be intermixed in human thought.

Story that it is, it remains effective literature and as such has its impacts upon its readers, from emotional levels little complicated by subtleties way down into the devious undercurrents of subconsciousness. The forest emerges as something more good than evil and on the whole a cherished asset, but the creatures of the forest, the lives of which are linked with any spilling of blood, come off on the whole not well at all. Evil is not always bloodily predatory, but little of what is bloodily predatory escapes the markings of evil. Even the green-eyed forest woman, dressed in green silk, a heathen witch more beautiful than Christian women despite her possession of a tail, had small, pointed predator-teeth that gleamed back of her red lips.

As Selma Lagerlöf wrote for her Swedish readers, so presumably she wrote as one of them. Whatever may have been the extent that her own psychology reflected or molded the psychology of her readers, her popularity is proof that she wrote what they wanted—as one of them.

I can understand that. I have read *Gösta Berling's Saga* in the version that the Swedes read. Like one of them, I responded to the story that wanted to be told. The story that wanted to be told just about had to be read, also; and, from where I sat with a big dictionary for looking up obsolescent Swedish words, I could give witness to the Lagerlöf power.

To me, with the closing of the book, the myth creatures and the moody forests and the conflicts between good and evil in Nature became innocuous fancies. The wild flesh-eaters had no more evil left in them than had anything else that was natural and wild.

But what might be the effect of this reading on a child's formative psychology, in imputing evil to wild things according to human moral standards?

The blame cannot all be laid on Selma Lagerlöf, for the attitudes that she reflected can be traced back much farther than her time. She only built upon the common superstitions about trolls and witches and woodspirits and their alliances with grim predators, the widespread fears of sorcery and predatory evil. Naughty children had long been threatened with punishment via wolves and bears as well as chimney sweeps.

Worse, perhaps, may be the old schoolbooks in biology that continue to be in use, in which generations of school children are taught that predators ravage and murder—kill for the joy of killing—that cruelty shines from their eyes. A prominent Swede, who is very critical of these schoolbooks, referred to their contents regarding predators as "incredibly warped nonsense."

There is further question of how much the daily press may perpetuate extremes in the public's attitude toward predators. I could see for myself when in Sweden that a report of a lynx, bear, wolverine, or wolf could constitute first-class news and that such reports could be irresponsibly blown up to sensational dimensions. Since then, my Swedish correspondents have sent me additional examples, from which one could get the impression that almost every bear that anyone encounters must rear up on its hind legs and attack, that the appearance of a large predator in a locality must mean a bloodbath for defenseless prey animals. A newspaper item reported that large numbers of bears and lynxes wandered from a Swedish border province over into Norway where they killed over six hundred sheep—and that province is one in which bears occur only exceptionally and in which there are only a few lynxes.

*

Here and there among the Scandinavian public may be people or groups of people having broad viewpoints, notably those combining interests in hunting, fishing, photography, and nature-protection. Among the more influential people working to get away from the narrower of objectives relating to outdoor values may be mentioned a forester whose hobby is experimenting on the land to reduce the conflict between forestry and game management—and to encourage modern attitudes toward biology, land use, and conservation, generally. One well-informed and active local group has among its leaders a dentist, a farmer-hunter, and a graduate student. Other leaders include amateur ornithologists doing professional-grade work in their spare time, newspaper and radiomen, university and museum staff members, and enlightened and public-minded people wherever found, throughout all of the Scandinavian countries.

Some friends at Lund University had hunting rights and a weekend retreat beside a Scanian lake. They were enthusiastic hunters, but their hunting was kept in balanced perspective with other outdoor values. It was on their leased land that the only sizeable tract of heather that I ever saw in southern Sweden was being intentionally preserved in as natural condition as possible. The abundant foxes were moderately hunted for sport and trophies, not to get rid of them, though they were living almost entirely on rabbits, the chief shootable game. The rabbits, themselves, were heavily exploited by the human hunters without jealousy toward the wild hunters. The rabbits were, in fact, observed to be holding up sufficiently well under all of the exploitation centering upon them to be present by spring in wholly adequate numbers for a good breeding season, to remain fully as abundant as they should have been anyway in the strong biotope in which they lived.

The management of this hunting lease constituted an exception in the Scanian landscape, in that the emphasis in management was placed, so far as possible, upon retaining completeness in the fauna and flora that belonged there. It was not merely a one-sided production of forest products or game or songbirds. During the many times that I visited hunters on this lease, I heard nothing about their introducing foreign species, raising game in cages, and artificializing in this way or that. I remember a polecat—a species perhaps even rarer than the marten in the parts of Scania that I knew best—also living on the rabbits, living explicitly unmolested despite the heresy that such represented to the neighboring game-keepers.

At this point, it would be fair to state that I do not wish to berate the game-keepers unduly. At least some of the leading men among them were emphasizing environmental management for game, discouraging the promiscuous killing of predatory creatures. They claimed they wanted to see no species extirpated for the sake of game-keeping—merely kept within reasonable bounds. How much this moderation may trickle down to the operational levels of game-keeping may be another question, and the game-keepers must, after all, be responsible to the estate owners or organizations that employ them. Nevertheless, it is good to note that there are people of broader viewpoints in a profession that has long been notorious for its intolerances and upon which much blame must be placed for the impoverishment of some of the most interesting types of northern Europe's native wildlife.

In fairness also, I should say that the tone of the articles on predators and predation for Scandinavian periodicals has been moderating for years. Articles in *Svensk Jakt* (the monthly magazine of the Swedish hunters' association) reflect many viewpoints, including some on predators and predation with which I disagree; yet I think that its articles reveal substantial public responsibility for outdoor values that might be threatened by extremist attitudes.

As a hunters' magazine, *Svensk Jakt* contains articles on fox hunting, but the hunting emphasized is recreational hunting. Foxes are often pictured as interesting and attractive creatures, and unsportsmanlike practices in hunting them are discouraged. Protection of the rarer predatory birds such as eagles, ospreys, eagle owls, and gyrfalcons has the expressed approval of the hunters' association, which may also publicly agitate for increased protection of lynxes, bears, and wolverines at times when their numbers appear to be declining to unsafe levels.

That the lynx, bear, and wolverine may be regarded as prize game species does not detract from the fact that the hunters' association is trying to prevent a much-reduced part of the Swedish fauna from becoming lost from the country.

I do not recall ever having seen in *Svensk Jakt* or in other magazines of Scandinavian hunters any recommendation to protect the wolf—nor, when it comes to the opposite, do I recall having read any demands to complete the extirpation of the wolf in at least Sweden. Rather, the impression I have is that at least Swedish hunters greatly value the wolf as an object for sport-hunting and trophies.

One *Svensk Jakt* article gave a dramatic account of the occurrence of wolves in modern Europe. It was a good, informative article, without hatred in it, though the problem of wolf depredations in thickly settled communities was understandingly treated. It concluded with the statement that irrespective of how interesting and thrilling the thought of those wolves may be to hunters and naturalists, one cannot be justified in sparing or protecting wolves in places where they can do much damage to livestock. Human economic interests must be given precedence. As relates specifically to the protection of reindeer herds from wolves in the north, the author felt that hunters' guns should be until further notice the regulating factor. From the hunters' standpoint, he did not regard the killing of wolves from aircraft as a satisfying form of hunting.

Another article recounted sympathetically the story of a wolf that lived for a time in a mountainous setting in west-central Sweden. The wolf became fairly tame toward local mountain folk that made no effort to harm it (which incidentally shows that the attitude of the public does not invariably conform to a pattern of hatred toward all flesh-eaters, even toward a wolf). But the wolf proved not wholly unrealistic toward man: When the hunters came forth in pursuit, it retired to the more inaccessible mountains. Anyway, there was no hatred on anybody's part in the article—only some melancholy reflections because of man's jealous domination of the mountain wilderness and a realization that the wolf's sought-after skin would probably result in its death before the end of the winter. The author felt that the wolf alone had restored something of the former life of the mountains.

The Swedish *jägmästare* with whom I have discussed public attitudes toward predators at greatest length believes that the word "hate" may be somewhat too strong to represent the viewpoints of modern hunters in his country. Their general outlook is that predators should not be exterminated but rather kept within the reasonable bounds—a common expression in conversation between hunters. When it comes to specific instances, a hunter may not have to find many pheasants killed by goshawks, roe deer killed by lynxes, or other evidences of predation upon game to feel that the predator population is exceeding reasonable bounds; and it can easily happen that even moderate people can lose their heads and sense of proportions whenever predators are talked about. Nevertheless, he is convinced that there is a growing tendency toward moderation among Swedish hunters—much more than has formerly been the case.

This, I have also been informed, is true in Norway. Apparently a great change has taken place even during the few years since my visit there, early in 1959. I have seen reference to the extremists as a dwindling minority. It is due to the combined efforts of the Norwegian game biologists, district game administrators, and the people working for nature protection; and the hunters' association, itself, officially supports a policy "to follow the more advanced viewpoints in this matter."

There is indeed modern thought in Norway on conservation biology. The worst absurdities of the bounty system are being rapidly eliminated, parish after parish. There are responsible opinions that the remnant lynxes and bears, possibly the wolverines too, might some day be given the legal protection that they need before they are completely gone. These large carnivores, as well as the wolves, are very nearly gone now. The biggest obstacle to the preservation of any of them as free-living species in

Norway seems to be the political pressure from the owners of two million sheep and a hundred thousand goats.

The Norwegian public, it is said, would never agree to give wolves legal protection, and that very possibly is true and may always be true. Norway is—despite its scenic grandeur and wild expanses—a thickly settled country in terms of people making a living off the land. Except possibly in the Arctic, I am not sure that wolves could live in many places in Norway where they might still be a comfortable distance from man's vulnerable livestock.

Northern Sweden may still offer the best chance of anything like a sanctuary for the last few wolves in Scandinavia, if ever there is to be anything like that. If ever there are to be any effective measures in this respect, whatever is done must be done carefully and well and must make sense.

I cannot feel optimistic about the prospects of the wolf being saved as a free-living wild species in the Scandinavian Peninsula, as a biological monument for education or aesthetic purposes. Neither do I quite feel justified in going the whole way in pessimism, in giving up in complete hopelessness. The right kind of people having the right kind of interest could do a great deal, especially in insuring that national parks or similar nature preserves serve their highest, most nearly unique purposes.

Scandinavia does have plenty of informed leadership or potential leadership on local, national, and international levels; and, while in many ways that leadership may be just beginning to make itself felt as a force in conservation biology or nature protection, it is a healthy, growing thing.

*

At Lund University, two brothers told me that they knew of wolves in one Swedish wilderness. The brothers had been brought up in northern Sweden, though educated and making their livelihood elsewhere. They were real wilderness men and loved their homeland for the memories of their younger years and for the wildness and beauty that their north represented for them.

In the summer previous to our visit, one brother saw tracks of a pack of wolves in the snow high up on a mountain—a pack of eight, which had killed some reindeer, according to Lapp hunters. He actually watched

one of the wolves as it trotted across a slope among large boulders immediately below the place where he stood. A month later, or toward the end
of August, the brothers were together on the Sweden–Norway border.
While they were sitting before dawn at a cooking fire, a deep wolf howl
came from the distance on the Norwegian side, "expanded across the
valley where we sat, and then died away again." Shortly afterward, the
howl was answered from still farther away on the Swedish side. "It was a
strange, dreary sound, frightening and fascinating at the same time."

The following summer, in mid-July, I was heading with Volkswagen and
camping equipment for northern Sweden. I had much more to do than to
get up into the wolf country, but the wolf country was in my plans too.

When I got up there, I could understand how that place, if no other,
could have wolves. I could see in a road atlas that the motor road coming
nearest the wilderness on the east side was separated from the nearest
road on the west, on the Norwegian side, by a distance equal to about one
hundred American miles. I tried one route to get as close as possible driving the Volkswagen, then drove around, through valleys and forests and
along lake chains and rivers and between and over mountains, and tried to
approach the area from another direction; and the remoteness of the area
was as imposing when looked at from the second direction as from the
first. To the eye, both ways, it was a lot of country, from the rough and
wooded to the rough and barren, with some distant snowfields in sight
from the right view.

I heard a little more about Sweden's wolf country a few months after
returning home in 1959. A pack of eleven wolves dispersed a large herd
of reindeer right in the mountains, the tops of which I had gotten close
enough to see—right up there where wolves belong.

Undoubtedly, the thought of an eleven-wolf pack being alive anywhere
can be abhorrent to people who can hate lesser predators with a hatred
that surpasses hatred; and I do not expect the Lapps whose reindeer
were attacked to agree that the wolves belonged there. It is not that I am
unsympathetic toward the Lapps—it is merely that, in some things, there
can be public values greater than those of personal property.

As long as the few free-living wolves that remain in Sweden are almost
exclusively living in the high mountains of Lapland, it may be maintained

with some logic from a public-responsibility standpoint that they belong there. The Lapps have their rights as people, but surely some equitable way must exist so that a nation that does have a suitable wilderness for a remnant of such very special animals as wolves might retain the species other than in zoos.

CHAPTER 11

Of Modernity and Wolves and a Wolf Named Dagwood

Forty years after my trapping in the Big Bog, I walked again in northern Minnesota's winter woods. The wolves were probably somewhat overharvested for bounty at the time of my visit and so far as I could learn the intensiveness with which the wolves were hunted had no relation to any need for reducing the wolves. Numerous inquiries that I made brought out no evidence that these wolves were doing or threatening to do any material damage to livestock in or about the area nor were they exerting undue pressure upon game populations. Indeed, Milton Stenlund, my biologist companion, felt that the area might have benefitted had there been more wolves to prey upon overabundant deer. He had seen in spring many starved deer on the small spruce islands scattered throughout the willow bog—the deer had retreated to the spruce for cover, to die there, as many as three on an island.

The bounty hunting could be financially profitable for hunters having the equipment, the time, and the opportunities to kill bountied animals. Some of the more successful could thus get several thousands of dollars in bounty money during a single winter. Naturally they found fault with a governmental ban on use of private aircraft over those parts of the Quetico–Superior area in which wilderness features were especially protected. They could still go in and hunt wolves from the ground, but that was harder, slower, and much less profitable than hunting from the air.

It may be difficult to judge just how much hatred of wolves or bounty economics, or both, may actuate individual hunters. One bounty hunter regarded the whole bounty system as nonsensical, but, as long as he could sell dead wolves to the state for thirty-five dollars, why should he not do so? The bounty hunters working the Big Bog were said to have put on their almost annihilative campaign because they feared that the bounty would be discontinued.

But the bounty hunters seemed to be predominantly wolf-haters, and modernity seemed to be having little influence on either their psychology or the general public's psychology concerning the wolves.

The story was told that, when the Minnesota legislature was considering the possibility of discontinuing the bounty, the bounty hunters and wolf-haters brought a dead wolf to St. Paul and left it on exhibition in the capitol. As it lay there with lips pulled back to show its teeth (a similarly sinister effect may be obtained by displaying the teeth of almost any dog, including somebody's Old Bozo, that perhaps never so much as chased a cat), the lobbyists developed their theme: Who or what could be safe with such savagery loose in the land? Not only was the game in danger of extermination, but there was abundant testimony as to the menace these beasts could be to human life. The lobbying tactics seemed to have been successful, insofar as the legislature retained the bounty.

An old caretaker for a resort took in his winter's stack of magazines and paperbacks and settled down in the bunkhouse to let his beard grow. As a patrol plane would occasionally swing over the resort, all of the signs of human presence that the pilot ever saw were two paths in the snow, one path leading to a water hole at the lake and the other leading to the privy. When the caretaker, complete with beard, came out in the spring after fighting wolves all winter, the townspeople gathered around him to hear of his newest adventures.

Another old-timer reported a most harrowing ordeal to sympathetic listeners. He had been walking to his cabin when attacked by a pack of thirty wolves. In running for the cabin, he had fallen and then had crawled, beating off his attackers until he reached the cabin, and slammed the door in the snapping wolf jaws. In the morning, he went into town, to stay. He had had enough of that kind of life, as the townspeople could well understand. But somebody did not quite accept everything as the old-timer had told it and went out to see the record in the snow. The facts of the case were that the old-timer had been drinking, that he actually had fallen and crawled to the cabin, and that there had been wolves—three or four of them rather than a large pack—but the wolves had not approached nearer than a quarter of a mile to his crawling trail to the cabin. They had been running parallel to the old-timer's trail and probably had howled.

When it comes to the credence that the public puts in wolf tales, I no longer find myself surprised at much of anything. I do not need to be told what kinds of wolf tales get around the fastest and sink deepest in the public's collective awareness.

During the writing of this chapter, I glanced through a story published in a magazine of extensive circulation, in which wolves received their usual justice from rifle bullets. In the story, a trapper was outraged by the roughness of four snarling demons toward a moose valiantly defending itself in a hopeless battle. The trapper's rifle of course equalized the unequal; two of the wolves would sin no more.

*

At the time of my winter visit I spent a few days in the Basswood Lake area on the Canadian border of the Quetico–Superior. I had previously seen some of this country in summer on foot and from a canoe. The areas covered during both visits included those in which the Minnesota Department of Conservation had been carrying on a long-term study of wolves and deer.

The somewhat overharvested wolves were still sought for despite restrictions on the use of aircraft; times were hard, and unemployed people would do considerable work for thirty-five dollars a wolf, even when they had to travel on snowshoes. The deer, on the other hand, were withstanding well the hunting pressure of wolves and man, alike; but, as their basic food resources deteriorated as a result of natural changes in the forest, the deer also declined.

Only six to eight inches of snow lay on the ground and ice by late January 1961, when Stenlund led our small party of biologists into the bush through the islands and mainland timber and along the edges of lakes and streams. For the season and the place, this lack of snow was most remarkable. Still, as we followed the trails of browsing deer, we picked up deer droppings—light-colored droppings of irregular shapes and mostly of large sizes—that betrayed poor feeding conditions even with so little snow cover. Conditions did not look at all favorable for the deer, even at the rather low densities that were present. If the snows really came, these deer could starve. The cold was there already: 22 below zero by midmorning and 40 below the previous morning.

At the edge of a wilderness area, we visited a white cedar swamp in which deer had starved ten years before. Thereafter, the deer had largely stayed out of the swamp for years because of human activities near by. As we waded the snow-covered mossy hummocks and smelled the distinctive odor of cedar, we could see where the deer had waded and browsed, but the deer had not again reached excessive numbers. Not yet. Their droppings were dark, small, round, and even-sized, indicative of well-fed deer.

Following the almost deer-less period of overbrowsing, a new fern-like growth of cedars had taken form beneath the old browse line. One of the small stems having about a third the diameter of a lead pencil showed eight annual rings on a knife cut. Up above, the trunks and main foliage of the cedars looked about the same at the time of our visit as they may be presumed to have looked when the deer starved. The deer line gave the appearance of open doors between the trunks, despite the passage of a decade and the new growths coming in below.

In the course of the possibly fifteen miles of walking that we did near the Canadian border, we saw some moose tracks along with the numerous deer tracks, three widely separated, more-or-less-fresh wolf trails, and one coyote trail. The coyote had approached and turned back from an otter trail of about the same degree of freshness. One of the wolves had been hunting in the bush where the deer fed on poor and scanty food-plants; the others had run along and across streams.

We examined the remains of two wolf-killed deer on the lake ice. Remains of two other wolf-kills had been reported to us, but these were too far away to reach on foot unless we wanted to take a day for it.

I had hoped to learn something about the condition of the wolf victims and the circumstances of the killings, but the sign was too old. The blowing snow had left raised rings representing the bloody and trampled spots, and in these we could dig out little except deer hair and paunch contents. At one kill there were two leg bones with hoofs attached; the upper ends had been sheared off by the wolves. Ravens had cleaned up what they could, and red foxes had carried away the heavier bones.

(A fox was scavenging on the ice one sundown as we drove past in a car. It tamely ate garbage remnants from an ice-fisherman's lunch. Everything that it did was graceful, its big fluffy tail following it like a second animal.)

We walked up a meandering creek where a wolf had passed a beaver lodge and a fox had climbed on top. We walked across a peninsula that had an old browse line of deer and many weasel tracks around an island where the white cedars of the edge had been trimmed as high as deer could reach from the ice. Around the end of the deer-trimmed island and in a bay near the wharf of one of the few remaining private resorts, we found one of our wolf-kills; nothing remained except the characteristic rim of hardened snow and the paunch contents frozen partly into the lake ice. We passed another focus of weasel tracks as we walked among the resort buildings.

There were also weasel tracks in many other places; and it was good to see them again as part of a North Woods scene in numbers reminiscent of the Big Bog of my youth. It was good, for one who had lived away from the North Woods so long, to see the tracks of such commonplace animals as red squirrels and snowshoe hares, to look at runways of the hares and partly debarked shrubbery and an occasional ravaged young pine. It was good to see the bounding, sliding otter trails and ice-slicked holes of the otters leading through frosty surfaces and snowdrifts to flowing stream waters, to see beaver and muskrat lodges and mink and fox tracks. It was good to see ravens and Canada jays, the tame ruffed grouse, so tame that I could line up two of them in the viewing field of a camera as they sat barely out of reach, just as the wilderness grouse had sat for me in the Big Bog forty years before.

It was good to walk at night on the cold-creaking lake snow and to try lonesome-wail howls in the hope of reaching responsive wolves, even though no wolves answered.

*

Several times, we drove past the home of one of the wolf-haters who had a wolf hung up from a tree in his yard. Apparently it had been hanging there for months, a small wolf that looked rather like a coyote, as an example to somebody or something or perhaps as an invitation to get people to stop and talk. Wolf-haters seldom seem reluctant to talk.

*

But modernity does not mean exclusively the deadly ten-eighty poison or shooting from aircraft or other intensified persecution for the remaining populations of North American wolves. It can mean efforts directed toward a more discriminating treatment of wolves, as animals and as part of a wilderness fauna, this also through the use of aircraft and the gadgets that man shows so much ingenuity in devising.

In several places in North America, studies of wolves are underway to explore questions of behavior, predator-prey relationships, and various aspects of population dynamics involving wolves. Besides the very respectable older and some newer studies in the northern Lake States, western Canada, and Alaska, there are two investigations in east-central North America: at Isle Royale, Michigan, and Algonquin Provincial Park, Ontario.

At Isle Royale National Park, the site of a famous overpopulation of moose studied by Adolph Murie in the early 1930s, Purdue University has a most important study of wolves and wolf prey in progress. The latter began as the thesis research of David Mech, a graduate student of Durward Allen. It is concerned with a present-day moose population of about three per square mile—much more in balance with the habitat than the once-ruinous density of fourteen per square mile in the wolf-less time of Murie's study—and a total wolf population of nineteen (possibly twenty) for both of the two winters for which detailed work has been reported.

Winter investigations on Isle Royale are carried on largely by aircraft, to which the wolves have become accustomed. It has been possible to fly over the wolves by the hour, to observe their behavior and their success or lack of success in attacking moose almost as if the whole outdoor drama had been staged in a laboratory. The facts that the wolves and the moose are confined to the island, that the wolves are forced to subsist upon the very formidable moose, and that the numbers of wolves are somehow kept in check in natural ways, all contribute to the outstanding potentialities of the study. Data on the social order of the wolves and the psychological factors underlying the killing or escape of prey are among the scientific dividends to be expected as the work goes on. It should lead to a clearer understanding of what constitutes the local Balance of Nature, whether in a Malthusian or Darwinian sense or in the sense of something more subtle.

Algonquin Provincial Park is an irregularly blocked-off area that averages out at about fifty by sixty miles. It lies only about a hundred and twenty-five miles northeast of Toronto and less than a hundred west of Ottawa but it is northern wilderness in the midst of wilderness.

At one time, the park was managed more than it is now to attract the conventional tourist visitors. Now, the emphasis is upon the values of solitude and wild beauty. Canoe routes are accessible by road from only a few places, and camp and picnic grounds, public docks, concessions, and park-maintained buildings are localized along a paved highway that cuts through little more than a corner of the park.

Long ago the lumbermen took the big pines, and old tote roads and other reminders of human activities are still visible even in some of the remote parts of the park. The forester still works in places today, and fire lookout towers are situated about ten miles apart. But the park does include and is surrounded by great expanses of wilderness—wilderness properly designated as such even though it cannot rate as primeval wilderness. It has the creatures native to northern wildernesses, including wolves and wolf prey.

*

In early December 1960, I had an opportunity to spend a few days with Douglas Pimlott on the Ontario government's wolf-study area at Algonquin Provincial Park. His work was centered in but by no means confined to a wildlife research area of about two-thirds of a township, which extends northward from the highway in the southeast corner of the park.

During my first afternoon in the park, I was shown about half of its area by air, from a light plane that circled or dipped down for close views whenever there was anything of special interest to look at.

There was snow on ground and ice, and steam arose from the still-unfrozen waters of the deeper lakes and the swifter streams. Water welling up from cracks streaked the snow surfaces over the ice in intricate patterns. As far as one could see in any direction, it was like this, the ice, snow, water, rocky and wooded hills, swamps and bogs, meandering streams, islands and peninsulas, a few old farmsteads with clearings and crumbling buildings, the sites of a few old lumber camps with equally crumbling buildings.

Down below were beaver lodges in suitable places and many old beaver ponds and dams. Some dams extended across a whole creek valley; others blocked the top of a small gorge; sometimes, a series of dams might give the appearance, from the air, of rungs on a ladder. Otter trails, bounding and sliding, ran parallel to lakeshores or stretches of stream—about a dozen otter trails ran back and forth on the past night's new snow between one patch of open water and another. We saw two otters on the ice and a fisher on the snow at the edge of the forest. Like a black cat, the fisher slipped under overhanging green boughs as the plane passed.

We saw small groups of moose and so many deer that no one made any effort to count them. The deer were everywhere in the particular hardwood stands that should have had deer at that season, while the hardwood browse was still generally accessible before the deepening of the snow. We could look right on down through the bare tops and among the trunks of sugar and soft maples, the yellow birch and ironwood, the ash and beech; and the deer stood underneath or lay on the ground.

We saw a fresh trail of a pack of eight wolves heading across the ice and open meadow of a narrow creek valley, loping across from woods to woods.

That evening, we went out to howl to the wolves. The cold penetrated boots and mittens and parka while we sat still playing wolf howls on a tape recording and Pimlott howled by mouth. A howl came from far away, from the regular home range of a known pack. Sometimes, the wild ones answered enthusiastically; sometimes, they came close, even close enough to be seen. But the one faint answer was all for us for the evening until we returned to the research station's headquarters and gave the station's caged wolves their chance for a social howl with us. By the time that these were all howled out, we did not know if any wild, free wolves had joined in with us or not.

Late one afternoon, we parked the car and went on to visit on foot a loafing place of a wolf pack. It was in the sparse vegetation of a rocky hill face near an old beaver burrow that had been used as a family den during the pupping season. To reach it, we walked about a mile into the bush and through a bog, as the weather settled down to a slight blizzard.

On the way in, we crossed the usual fox and deer trails and followed a new fisher trail for some distance, all trails partly snowed over and losing some of their distinguishable outlines in the soft snow. The lesser tracks of snowshoe hares, red squirrels, weasels, grouse, and ravens took the form of indentations in the snow. Not until we reached the hillside did we find wolf sign.

There they were, the tracks of a pack, exactly where expected, the snow trampled where the wolves had been, perhaps fifteen minutes before us. Pimlott gave them a series of howls, but, because of the blowing of the wind, we could not be sure the wild ones answered. The Labrador Retriever dog we had with us acted somewhat uneasy. In all probability, the wolves were right in there close, giving us the proper inspection by means of our wind-carried scent or even looking at us through the snowstorm.

It was getting dark when we went back to the parked car. On the way, we jumped one of the abundant deer of the hardwoods; its fresh tracks stood out in contrast with the snow-filled tracks of the other deer, the foxes, the fisher, and our own earlier trail. . . . Streaking of snow in the headlights and obliteration of almost everything except darkness and lit-up snow. . . .

When we drove along the side road to the station headquarters, we saw a lone trail in the middle of the road, the partly snowed over trail of a big wolf, heading where we were heading. (A trail of what seemed to have been the same wolf had also been laid down the previous day at the same place; we had seen it as we had first neared the station headquarters.) The new prints showed hand-sized in the headlight glare; they fell in pairs, the prints of each pair about two and a half feet apart, then fifteen feet or so to the next pair of prints, and so on, until they either left the road or we could not make them out any longer.

The half foot of new snow in the morning showed tracks of a flying squirrel visiting a garbage can, tracks of a fisher and the usual foxes, some tracks of grouse and snowshoe hares, of early-morning ravens and red squirrels. I worked along the side road between the station headquarters and the highway and in a circle extending about a half mile into the bush, covering about all places where I thought that the wild wolf might have gone, but found nothing of its trail on the new snow.

✳

The purpose of the Ontario government's work on wolves in Algonquin Provincial Park and elsewhere is made plain over and over again in public relations: to acquire a sound factual basis for wolf management. Such management, when the factual basis exists, may call either for control of wolves or for protection of wolves, or measures in between, depending upon what the local and provincial situations may be.

If the Ontario public does not have a large proportion of wolf-haters, it has some vocal ones. They include trappers and veteran woodsmen who live in wolf country, tourist groups who think that extermination of wolves would be advantageous to their interests, people who exhort and make charges and draw up petitions and invoke scorn upon anyone who does not agree with them. Some of these people, when they ask about what the research program or the government at large is doing about wolves, want to know only what is being done to kill wolves.

Such attitudes may be self-perpetuating and put objective search for the truth under a tremendous handicap in dealing with public emotions. One report was spread by a wolf-hating old-timer that remains of sixty wolf-killed deer of the previous winter had been found during a two-week fishing trip along a particular stretch of stream; in contrast with this report, the wolf-study personnel, working the same stretch repeatedly, piece by piece, with helicopter and on foot, found only four deer carcasses in the course of the entire winter. The layman's contentions that deer do not starve, that the trouble is only a matter of wolves, may be made with the force of a religious conviction beside which tempered statements based upon biological findings seem of watery substance indeed.

The wolf studies go on, however. Experienced fieldmen plot the location of wolf groups by howling from different positions as well as by observations from the air and reading of sign on the ground; they catch wolves alive in non-choking snares, take measurements and other data on individuals, mark, and release them. They map the location of dead deer, those killed by wolves and those dying from other causes, taking advantage of the most modern methods and such old-fashioned tricks as watching ravens to learn the whereabouts of dead animals. They study distribution of the deer and follow their fortunes through the critical hunger months. They carry on much other work bearing on the role of northland wolves in human economics and wildlife management; they examine stomachs of wolves killed for bounty, wolf droppings, specimens of both wolves and wolf prey to obtain sex and age ratios, and so on.

Pimlott was understandably cautious in making generalizations about wolf-prey relationships on the basis of a few years of data, but, so far as the data went, they seemed to indicate that Algonquin Provincial Park needs its wolves. The park does have plenty of wolves and plenty of the game adapted to live there; and the relation between wolves and game in the park may not be far from the biologists' concept of a primitive Balance of Nature.

The white-tailed deer of Algonquin Provincial Park were at the edge of their range in that part of wilderness Ontario but still about as abundant as deer should be in relation to the parts suited to them. These deer could starve if the snow reached excessive depths or crusted over, but their spread-out distribution in innumerable little woodland pockets and deeryards suggested an essentially healthy situation. The wolves seldom bothered the moose or preyed much upon beavers or smaller game while they had an abundance of deer to prey upon. The wolves preferred the deer, and the deer fed them, and both seemed adjusted to each other, as if in accordance with testing over man-less millennia.

That, in brief, conforms to my idea of what a wilderness preserve in a man-crowded and man-tampered world should mean: a living, natural museum on an immense scale, dedicated to the perpetuation of the unique values that man can much more easily ruin than restore.

The Pimlott family raised a litter of five wolves during the summer preceding my visit, living together with them, children and all, on an island.
The wolves had the free run of the island, except for property that had
to be fenced in to protect it from puppy teeth—the tent ropes and clothing and instrument cases that could be damaged because of the chewing
impulses of puppyhood.

After transfer from the island to a big cage, one young wolf found an
electric extension cord left behind by a photographer, cut it up into short
sections, ate some of it, and died.

The four survivors included wolves differing greatly in temperament.
Two, Dagwood and Blondie, were happy extroverts, friendly toward everyone; and Blondie was taken away from the station to learn how much the
equivalent of a domestic dog might be made of her. Dagwood remained
at the station with two other litter members, both females: One, called
Lup (from *lupus*), was as friendly and happy but not such a positive character as Dagwood, and the other, called Kit, was very sensitive and shy of
strangers.

Pimlott took me into the cage with him on his return after an absence
of several days. He advised me to keep an arm up to my face, but I did
not fully realize what kind of welcome I, as a stranger, would get from
even the tamer wolves. The first thing that I knew, I had been nipped in
the face by both Dagwood and Lup, as they had leapt over my upraised
arm. Then, I got my arm up higher, and, after some more leaping, my
two welcomers quieted down and became merely a couple of dogs that
mouthed my mittened hands and wriggled and rubbed their heads against
me as I patted them.

Feeling the gentleness of those sharp teeth on my face (they did not
come anywhere near breaking skin) and the tooth points that came
through two thicknesses of heavy knitted mittens only to touch my hands,
I remembered Lois Crisler's reference to gentle grooming by the teeth of
her wolves.

Kit, the third wolf, never stopped watching me even while greeting
Pimlott, whom she trusted. Hoping to see her at ease, I would withdraw

Wolf and Fence, by Charles W. Schwartz. Charles W. Schwartz Collection, the State Historical Society of Missouri.

from the vicinity of the cages and sneak back to peek around tree trunks or thickets or the edges of buildings. No matter what I tried, any time that I could see her, she was looking at me. Once, Pimlott had been forced to seize her, and the experience had been so upsetting to her that it had taken weeks of patient handling to bring back her confidence in him. Her social attachments were toward Dagwood and Lup and the Labrador Retriever and toward the Pimlott children; and, when she was left alone in the cage, she howled and howled, howling the short "lonesome" howl, with a drop at the end.

In late afternoon of my first day at the research station, I had a chance to romp with Dagwood alone about the cages and down along a road and a lakeshore. He had gotten past his earlier cavorting mood and now ran and sniffed and ate snow in a matter-of-fact way, occasionally returning to the vicinity of the cages to greet everybody and be friends. As he came up to me, to rub against my parka, I would give his big head a shake and call him a mutt. When Pimlott wanted to put him back into the cage, he just reached down, gathered up an armful of docile, satisfied wolf and carried the limp animal over to the cage door. Not any trouble, not the least, all between the best of friends; and it was a happy Dagwood that we left in the cage.

Dagwood at seven months weighed about sixty pounds on a frame for about eighty to a hundred. His feet, spread out, left tracks nearly as large as my hand, spread out. His tracks were about the same size as the wild-wolf tracks that we had seen heading along the side road in the direction of the station.

Two times in two days, we took Dagwood and Lup for long walks along a trail leading through the bush. They ate snow, circled and explored, engaged in hiding and chasing games. Lois Crisler wrote that wolves did not run, they flowed; and Dagwood and Lup flowed over the trails, over and under windfalls, and through the balsams and deciduous brush. They were as close to the embodiment of grace as anything animate that I ever saw, and so joyous, so much at ease, and so friendly. There was no master-servant relationship between Pimlott and the wolves; they stayed with us or returned to us in response to howling because of their own will, as friends; and, when Pimlott picked each up to put it back in the cage at the end of the outing, each went trustingly limp.

On the second day that we took Dagwood and Lup for a long walk, we were out of contact with them for a couple of hours. We thought that the wild one of the big tracks and the long stride might have met our tame friends somewhere off in the bush, and we walked while Pimlott howled. Pimlott and I separated, so as to cover more ground, and, off by myself, I knew from lonesome Kit's continued howling back in the cage that it was as yet of no use for me to come in. Finally, the strays were howled in at the far end of the trail that we had first made, and they came back without any further nonsense. Everything was all right as each armful of wolf was gathered and dropped in through the cage door.

Pimlott was less worried about Dagwood in particular joining wild wolves than about his special pet getting lost before knowing enough about hunting and other facts of a normal wolf's life to take care of himself. Dagwood was much more than an expendable experimental animal. Pimlott wished to do right by this splendid creature; he wished to insure for Dagwood an optimum freedom that a wolf should have, with protection from people if it had free run of the park.

Dagwood did wander down to the highway on one occasion, and human friends who knew him found him there wholly by chance. The danger was not only that some wolf-hater might deliberately run him down with an automobile but also that some stranger on foot might be frightened at the sight of a big wolf running toward him the way that Dagwood runs—Dagwood, the hearty extrovert who trusts and likes everybody.

Nothing about this had easy answers, and it was not the first time that people who have been friends with wolves have had like problems.

I last saw Dagwood looking at me from the big cage of the tame wolves shortly after daybreak on a Sunday morning. He would have romped, I am sure, but Pimlott and I had other things on our minds. We were trying to start the third of three motor vehicles that would not start at 39 below zero, and I had a plane reservation for three o'clock that afternoon at the distant Toronto airport.

Afterward, I could think about Dagwood some more, about how much he might be a living answer to old questions as to where domestic dogs originally came from or, at the least, to questions as to the degree of tamability that a wolf could have. Whatever a wolf might need in the way of psychological undercurrents to be friendly toward man, Dagwood seemed to have them. He had been shown on TV. He had unselfconsciously howled on a lecture platform before a large audience in response to an invitation to howl. Life among people, as he knew it, had been good; and, so far as I could see, he accepted most things as they were.

There was not much of the obedient servant to be seen in Dagwood, little if anything more than what the tame wolves of prehistory may have shown the campfire men. He was no wolf to object to minor infringements of his liberties, as when picked up and deposited inside the cage door. That was a normal part of his life, with nothing disquieting about it, all consistent with his own experience and nature as an amiable, tolerant, and happy wolf. His restraint in using sharp teeth on friends was consistent with his nature as a wolf and did not represent any trained-dog type of responsibility.

Dagwood was still a wolf, certainly far from being an immediate predecessor of a lapdog or herdsman's dog or any other artificially bred-up form of domestic dog. He was the product of evolutionary refinement of a different sort. He was built for agility, endurance, and power, to rip through animal tissue in preying upon large game—although, as a seven-months pup, he had never killed his own food—and to fast or gorge if that was what was required of him as a wolf. His eating manners were those long sanctioned by his line of descent: A few snaps, a few gulps, and he had fed, wolfing food even when alone and unhurried. To this limited extent, man's traditional concept of wolfishness was not inconsistent with the reality of the wolf Dagwood.

Dagwood, in his basic wolfishness, remained in my estimation essentially unspoiled despite his close association with man. He was himself, in his sinuous body and expressive face, his alert intelligence, and in the curiosity, mischievousness, and friendliness that he so openly showed. Dagwood's behavior, along with that of the tame wolves of the centuries, might be construed as saying, "Take us as we are and we can be friends, but do not expect of us what we are not and have not."

I do not claim to be a dog man—that is, any owner or trainer of dogs. Possibly I have not really liked more than a couple of dozen individual dogs in my whole life; and fewer still are those I would have wanted to own.

I would not want Dagwood, either, as an animal to be owned, even if I had the time and means for taking care of him; for I do not think that ownership in the usual sense would be compatible with what is best and most interesting about him. I enjoyed him because he was his own wolf, notwithstanding his faculty for putting a strange human at ease.

CHAPTER 12

Of Man and Maturity

Man, like the wolf, is an animal doing what he does with what he has. Man's natural endowments differ from those of the wolf in degree; both man and wolf are highly gifted as living things go.

Among the non-human animals, the dog family may be rated as having exceptional intelligence, and, in this family, the wolf has one of the superior brains. Moreover, the behavior of the wolf does not differ so fundamentally from that of man at man's less advanced social levels. But the wolf brain would appear to have relatively little left in unrealized potentialities, and we may suspect that it never will be much better than it is now.

I keep thinking of how really adept wolves can become in staying alive and making a living despite human enmity. One does not need to think only of the great renegade wolves, such as old Three Toes of Harding County, South Dakota, which made man so conscious of their presence by the scale of their depredations upon his livestock. The renegades included extremely wary individual wolves, but, in my opinion, the wolves that live with minimal conspicuousness from man may represent still more advanced adaptation.

The most notable cases of adaptation with which I have had close-at-hand experience were furnished by coyotes rather than by the larger wolves, so my own illustrations shall be from coyotes.

Shortly after becoming an Iowa resident in the early 1930s, I studied the prey remains outside of a coyote den in a farming community in the northwestern part of the state and wondered if this family could keep out of trouble, living as it did in the roughest pasture and marshland and subsisting only on wild prey and carrion. The adults were obviously behaving with great respect toward inimical man, and, except for my scientific colleagues and me, I doubt if anyone suspected that there were coyotes in that part of the country at all—not until late summer when some members of the coyote family made their big mistake. My guess is that the young ones were those that advertised themselves by howling in response to train whistles.

Years later, in central Iowa, I discovered a coyote wintering within a few miles of the Iowa State University campus. For a time, I followed its food habits, hoping that no one else would notice those tracks and other sign in the ravine where a farmer had left a dead hog. The home range of the coyote, however, happened to coincide with that of a highly skillful hunter whose hobby was hunting foxes by stalking and trailing, and the hunter saw all that he needed to see while the snow lasted.

Another central Iowa animal about which I had a chance to learn something was a probable dog-coyote hybrid with predominantly coyote features that a game warden brought in for identification. This creature had been seen off and on for a couple of years in the rough land of the Des Moines River Valley, near Boone. I do not know that it ever did any harm, but, as soon as people knew it was there, they tried to shoot it. It out-ran, out-sneaked, out-hid, and eluded everybody and everything until the day that high-powered expanding bullet reached far out and caught it. When I skinned it for a specimen, I found numerous shotgun pellets imbedded in the hide and a perfectly trained-down canine body—massive running muscles and practically no visible fat anywhere. The stomach contained some muddy bones and bristles from a carrion pig carcass.

Northern Minnesota wolves have been adjusting to man during the last two decades by becoming increasingly wary of the aircraft to which they had once been so vulnerable. Stenlund observed that wolves avoided the ice of lakes as aircraft approached in the winter of 1948–1949, after large numbers had been shot from the air during the previous two winters. I have since heard of other northern Minnesota wolves detecting the approach of a plane before it came into human view, to run off to shore for the concealment of the woods until the plane had passed—then back on the ice to continue on their way. It has taken some painful learning, for many wolves had to be killed far out on the ice before enough survived to discover what this was all about and gradually pass on the lesson of their experience to their fellows.

In contrast with the Iowa coyotes and the Lake States timber wolves, which human persecution may be forcing to use their brains close to the limit of their capabilities, I think that man collectively might be doing better than he does with the brain that he has.

I have acquired great admiration for the quality of headwork often displayed by members of the general public—the humor, the astuteness, the clever improvisations of people very nearly everywhere. If manifestations of genius are not frequently to be perceived at almost any time throughout most strata of human society, there are certainly manifestations of a high grade of intelligence as we define it. This may all be said without implying commensurate admiration for the quality of thinking man too often does with his naturally excellent brain.

In so stating, I do not think that I am claiming perception and maturity that I myself do not have, for only within what happen to be my fields of competence do I feel especially qualified to examine the thinking of others. It is with respect to the overall fields of population ecology and dynamics, the so-called Balance of Nature, predators and predation, natural resources and outdoor values that I feel that I have the most to offer in the way of constructive opinion.

The farther I go outside of these areas of my own personal competence or experience the more I can expect to do so at my own risk. Nevertheless, one should be entitled to ask questions, and one question that recurs to me is: How much may public reactions to what is wild be symptomatic of immaturity?

Within the content implied by the title of this book—*Of Wilderness and Wolves*—many greater or smaller topics could be singled out to illustrate immaturities in human thinking. I shall simply express my misgivings concerning man's continued wastage of the natural values of which we have little left to waste, his continued misappraisals of biological relationships that should no longer be subject to so much misappraisal, his continued imputation of moral evil where moral evil does not exist, and his continued punishment of wild animals for being what they are, for being wild and for living in the only ways that they could be expected to live.

＊

Let us consider some of the exaggerations in mass attitudes toward wild creatures, especially toward predators and other wild species that may do damage under conditions favoring damage. Control of this or that wild species, intended on behalf of someone or something, has been notorious for the extremes to which it may lead. Down through the list of nearly everything that eats or digs or roosts or is suspected of doing something or of being something we have man's proscriptions, often without any semblance of balanced judgment.

I do not and never did maintain that we can always ignore economics in our philosophies concerning predators and predation. I am willing to reiterate as many times as need be that depredations of large wolves upon livestock can be serious, that I know that large wolves could not be tolerated in a part of the country where they could do so much damage as, say, in South Dakota. There may be economic aspects to predation even by the much less formidable coyotes that man may be entitled to do something about, though, in protecting his interests, I do not think that he is entitled to overdo his campaigning.

It does not have to be that man always overdoes, and very practical people can set some good examples. In addition to the realism I have admired on the part of ranchers who felt that they could have some coyotes around without having coyote damage if they took proper care of their livestock, I recall a fairly recent conversation with one of the neighbors near the old home farm, a man who lived at the edge of a hilly tract south of Lake Tetonkaha. He told me about a coyote den that he could watch from his own yard. He too felt confident in being able to take care of his stock without killing the coyotes, and he watched the coyote pups playing unmolested as long as they occupied the den site. He made a point of telling me all about it, with a certain exultation. What if the coyotes did kill some pheasants along with the jackrabbits and ground squirrels? There was plenty of game and plenty to spare, and it was not every day or every year that anyone could watch a family of coyotes growing up.

But, again, it seems that man's tendencies toward anything to be called reasonability or broad-mindedness or just governing his actions by facts can be less than they should be. The human capability for hatred without good reason is one of the things that may trouble me the most when I worry about whether man is mature enough for his position of dominance over the earth.

I recall, as a graduate student, one of my earlier conversations with Aldo Leopold: He advised me to discount a certain viewpoint in a controversy on the grounds that the holder of the viewpoint was known as a hater and that haters seldom got matters wholly straight. In most cases, it is not the actual persecution of wild animals by this or that faction that troubles me so much as it is the intensity of the hatred so often underlying such persecution—and the narrowness, willfulness, ignorance, and poor thinking that the hatred and persecution so much reflect. What makes sense in human motivation is one thing, but it is quite another thing when a psychological attitude can be paraphrased as:

It makes no difference what you say or do because we are going right ahead and do what we intend to do anyway!

It may be a private matter of someone resisting all reason for the sake of his prejudices. It may be a legislature passing a worse-than-useless bounty law. Whether demagoguery is triumphant or merely unreason on an individual scale, we may still ponder the socially frightening aspects that it has.

Apart from our attitudes toward wild animals, may we not ask if this is the kind of thinking that motivates and directs us in great economic and political trials and in the safeguarding of what we regard as the precious gains made by our civilization? I do not know but am afraid that it is. There can be no doubt that, in exaggerated forms, our psychological immaturities are reflected by many inclinations to use power irresponsibly, to throw weight around, to commit the outrages by which man can demean himself in any part of the world. At other extremes, we may only be naive.

What do we think of as civilization? More and more people and taller skyscrapers? Faster transportation? Universal gadgetry? Material comforts and leisure and entertainment? Fads and dogmas? Industrialization and the manners of holiday traffic, littering roadsides and scenic areas with trash? Or should it be progress toward understanding and reason?

Should not civilization mean better perspective, with neither arrogance nor self-abasement? Should it not mean evolution toward impartial regard for truth, toward what we know as good taste and decency and thought-fulness, toward the maturity that man now needs as he probably never has needed before?

*

It might be wholesome, if nothing more, for man to reflect critically upon his own relation to the modern world and upon his relations with the so-called lower animals, including some that he professes to despise. He might do well not to switch unthinkingly from one opposing viewpoint to another, but rather to try to winnow what makes sense from what does not. It is just possible that if man showed a more truly enlightened and objective attitude toward other kinds of Life, he might learn to show more toward his own.

By all means, we should strive toward realism—toward realism in actu-ality, not toward the travesties of realism that may have labels of realism placed upon them.

Realism calls for a scale of proportions. The either-or, good-or-bad, all-or-nothing oversimplifications in our reasoning may offer us easy thought patterns and catchy slogans; they also can lead to appalling falla-cies and to pogroms and wars along with lesser excesses.

Because the early settlers regarded wilderness as an enemy to conquer or something to exploit and because we cannot have wilderness every-where and still maintain agriculture and industry, it should not follow that we cannot have wilderness anywhere.

Wilderness values are priceless to some people, even if more or less indefinable. They have meant a great deal in my own life and, in my earlier years, possibly as much as anything else. I need not be told that my love of wilderness is not uniformly shared by the public, for such an attitude would not be expected; but, as wildernesses are increasingly encroached upon, more people show interest in preserving wilderness values.

Wilderness and what it stands for could mean still more in terms of human tranquility and reflection in an era of artificiality and unrest. There is much that could be written about the needs for mental health and solid, constructive interests during times when the problems of nuclear threats and power politics, increasing uncertainty and increasing leisure, beatnik cultism and juvenile gangs, and the whole array of man's social afflictions come as near to dominating our society as they do today. One need not be grasping for utopias to see the psychological illness manifested by our young hoods. I have seen the same dull faces in Europe as well as at home in the United States, spitting on sidewalks, bored with everything, going around looking for excitement, just any kind of diversion, and maybe making some. Delinquency is nothing new in human history, and my home neighborhood had its equivalent of hoods during my youth—reflecting then the same cynical escapism of the modern hoods, the parasitic philosophies, and the strong appeal of their own kinds of conformities.

I am thankful again that I liked to hunt and fish and trap and camp and do target shooting and go for long walks in the natural out-of-doors, that I had some companions who liked to do the same things (if not always to the extent that I did), and that enough of the natural out-of-doors existed close by so that we could do them. I am thankful that I liked to read, that I had access to what was worth reading, and that I could achieve at least a passable balance between indoor and outdoor pursuits. I am thankful for interests that could compete—as long as any competition could be said to have existed in my own case—with the diversions that only divert.

Without advancing any panaceas, I submit that what remains of our natural out-of-doors, of our wilderness and what belongs in it, is worth keeping. I shall not say that keeping it will be cheap or easy or without opposition or without the confusion of differing objectives.

*

There are always the questions of what retention of any natural wildness in a mechanized and crowded human society may cost, whether any possible gains in this respect would be worth the price, economically or otherwise.

Here too some of the most twisted reasoning may be advanced, perhaps honestly, perhaps with a sly profit motive concealed somewhere in the wording. I think especially of the agitation against nature preserves in or near great metropolitan areas on the grounds that their lonely trails and concealing vegetation may provide a setting for crime and that they are unsafe for people to visit—that they would serve society better if they were to be cleared and leveled and used for automobile parking lots or housing developments. Secluded wild places may in truth be scenes for holdups, rapes, and sadistic murders as criminals spill over into them from the slum districts. But what irony there is in the argument that, because of the evils of the slums, we must get rid of something that offers to at least some people who need it at least a partial relief from those evils.

We may be informed that a single human life is so precious as to outweigh any possible advantage of a wild area. I do not deny that human life can be precious, but the arguments leading to such open-and-shut conclusions can be farcical. The three central Iowa marshes that I know best have each been sites of at least one accidental human death during the years I have known them. National parks have their fatalities of both visitors and park personnel. What recreational waters may not over the years have tragedies or chances for tragedies? Yet, in terms of danger to human life, what really compares with our highways? What highways have ever been left un-built merely because of the possibility—the certainty—that people would in time be killed upon them?

The body of one of my family's best friends lies under avalanche debris in a great mountain wilderness on the other side of the world. He was in his mid-twenties, at the end of his graduate training, a young man of the finest character and promise. His death meant a great personal sorrow to me. A wilderness killed him, and, had it not been for his love of wilderness, he would not have been there to be killed. The mountaineering tragedy that took his life is no disproof of the pricelessness of mountains and wildernesses and the values they stand for to modern man. If anyone were to ask me if I would feel the same way if I had been the one to lose a son, I should say that I am sure that I would.

This is nothing that I like to contemplate, for I want no sorrow for anyone to result from wholesome outdoor interests; but it points up a homely fact that there have to be lines drawn somewhere in the consideration of different kinds and degrees of values. Even something as precious as human life has to be considered in reference to something else, to a sense of proportion, and to what may be meaningful among other values. There are still questions as to what values make life worth having.

There are still questions as to what we as a public are willing to risk and pay for outdoor values only in the prosaic terms of money, effort, and patience. We are willing to expend—according to the more liberal estimates—into the billions of dollars annually as well as vast effort to go on vacations into wild and scenic country. Our investment in equipment for hunting, fishing, camping, boating, skiing, and traveling, in accommodations and special licenses and guiding fees and transportation charges, may add up to impressive totals even for single individuals or families. No doubt about it—we can and will pay for the enjoyment of the out-of-doors when we are of a mind to. And we can work hard at extracting enjoyment from what we do in the out-of-doors.

What are we willing to invest in money, time, ingenuity, and un-dramatic purposeful endeavor to safeguard the essential features of what we are willing to spend so freely to find and enjoy in the out-of-doors? Are we willing to let our outdoor values be continually watered down or whittled down or lost by default while we travel farther and farther in search of them and hope that somewhere, someplace, there will always be something remaining of them that is worth having, seeing, or thinking about? Or do we just give up, talk about what we had or did when we were young or how we should have been born in the pioneering days or settle for having our out-of-doors brought inside for us via TV?

As concerns the preservation of wilderness or the essential features thereof, we can rather count on it costing money and having its troublesome aspects. Whether the necessary expenditures and efforts on behalf of wild land or wild creatures must be channeled into purchases, maintenance, indemnities for damage, educational campaigns, or something else, it all must cost. Outdoor values are unlikely to take care of themselves, with man's swarming increase and delusions as to what he calls Conquest of Nature.

When thinking of public indemnities as a part of the price for protection of outdoor values, I think of more than possible damage to livestock from any kind of predation. Hoofed game may also have expensive habits in relation to human property that gets in its way—all one needs to do is to inquire about wapiti herds where these are abundant in the American West. Waterfowl depredations on farm crops in concentration areas may be sufficient to arouse local agitation for exterminating our already overhunted and drained-out ducks and geese; as a general public, we have sufficient interest in the ducks and geese as prized game to resist any such nonsensical extremes but we still must be as fair as we can be toward other people who may have genuine grievances against the ducks and geese.

Besides the wapiti and the ducks and geese, moose and sandhill cranes and a considerable variety of other valuable and interesting non-predacious species may all be among those we cannot permit to be slaughtered off merely because of their sometimes very real damage to private property. When the damage by these species in which the public claims ownership cannot be prevented by feasible and bloodless means, one alternative may be for the public to pay compensation for the damages resulting.

In Sweden, hunters' organizations contribute funds for compensating private people not only for damages done by favorite game species but also by certain predators, including those that the Swedes are trying to safeguard from extermination in their country.

I propose, in substance, that the American public regard its own rare species of all kinds—whether predatory or not but especially the rare, large predators—as public charges. The public should assume responsibility to safeguard these species and to compensate private damages that must inevitably result now and then from free-living animals. This responsibility should embrace the grizzly and Alaskan brown and polar bears, the wolverine, the cougars, the Canada lynx, and the large wolves, all to the extent that their needs require treatment as public charges.

Surely, again, this would cost. I would not feel capable of calculating how much, but, if the cost be compared to the cost for a mile of newly paved highway or some tampering with a river or virtually any kind of pork-barrel measures, I am sure we could afford to pay.

Managing wolves according to what I should regard as enlightened criteria would call for appraisals and reappraisals of local, regional, national, and international situations. Balanced against each other should be the wolf's high reproductive potential, the wolf's potentialities for damage, and the excessive persecution to which the wolf is subject and the danger that at least certain forms may be totally lost.

Already, for North America, E.A. Goldman has listed five of twenty-three modern subspecies of true wolves, *Canis lupus*, as either extinct, probably extinct, or extremely rare, and four others as having greatly reduced ranges. These geographical casualties were all severe competitors for man's livestock. Irrespective of how much it may be reasoned that these wolves had to go, in every case where man has destroyed or doomed a subspecies, he has destroyed some evolution. It is or should be a solemn matter to obliterate a highly developed form of Life so finally. Civilized man should have sufficient regret in having done so to avoid repetitions through unnecessary heavy-handedness.

The wolves of some North American subspecies, having greatly reduced geographic ranges, may already be precariously reduced. But other wolves, including the eastern wolf or the one we usually call the timber wolf, may still be in no immediate danger of extinction.

The latter is probably true for most of the Canadian subspecies. Nevertheless, human pressure even upon wilderness forms can be intensive, through the use of aircraft and poison, and over vast areas of the northern parts of the northern hemisphere. Both the Canadians and the Russians may campaign against wilderness wolves with an effectiveness that leads one to question how racially secure some truly wilderness wolves may be. Remoteness from centers of human populations may afford a wolf population a tremendous advantage in its relations with man, but, except when the wolves have the further advantage of a protective terrain, remoteness may not necessarily insure their safety. Large predators in the Far North can be notably vulnerable to human persecution if man wants to lay it on, up there on the frozen landscape when food may be scarce and localized and the snow and ice fields and open tundra and tree-limit bush give little concealment from men in planes on days of good visibility.

Rational handling of the wolf problem may require campaigning against the wolves when and where they should be kept down, easing up on the campaigning or even protecting them when and where they need it, and trying at all times to keep them in the right balance as a resource of value as well as a pest. It is the sort of thing concerning which decisions and actions should be governed by the requirements of each particular situation, as of the particular time and place.

Apart from such generalizations that whatever is decided or done should be to the best interests of the wolves, the best interests of their prey, and the best interests of the wildernesses in which wolves and their prey belong, what I have in mind is nothing that fits together in convenient formulas. It is nothing that is covered too well by slogans or other substitutes for thinking. There is nothing cheap or easy about it at all.

Can it be said that many of the highest, best aims with respect to almost anything worth having are cheaply or easily attainable? How much in the way of solutions to any problems really stay put? The old sayings about eternal vigilance being the price we must pay for great values have very hard truths in them, as people have learned over and over. May we not just assume that extremely little about Life ever remains settled?

*

I am not forgetting that there are people who would gladly trade all of the wolves and all of the natural wildness left in the world for a mile of pavement or less. I know that there are people who would answer with derision any view of mine that the preservation of our national remnants of wolves in appropriate wilderness reservations should be a public responsibility, but the rights I claim in this respect are no more than those I am willing to grant to other citizens in the decent enjoyment of their own interests and pursuits.

I do not care especially for art galleries and formal parks, but other people do, and I respect their tastes and rights. I am quite willing to have a modest share of my taxes contribute to the support of art galleries, formal parks, and other wholesome things for someone else to enjoy. In turn, I should think it fair for persons who do not care especially for wilderness values to refrain from unnecessary destruction of them.

As one whose sympathies are with wilderness wolves, I would need something more than the prospect of a pelt, bounty payment, or sport to make me now want to shoot one. On the other hand, I am not opposed to their being hunted in moderation, even in our northern Lake States, where I regard our timber wolf remnant as being of outstanding value. A hunting toll that is restricted to the annual surplus or its equivalent can be borne by well-situated wolves as well as by other well-situated animals.

Moreover, I think that it would be a good thing if the public would come to regard wolves as game animals in the places where wolves belong—fair game themselves, within limits, and not just thought of or spoken of in outmoded clichés as enemies of game. That would not need to be contrary to good wildlife management, and it might substitute for some of the hysteria that wolves currently elicit.

As one who has killed for a livelihood, as I did in my trapping years, and as one who still likes to hunt, I confess that I do not care for the kind of sport-hunting or varmint-shooting that fails to utilize the animals killed. I do not, however, insist that mine is the only true faith in this respect. If sport-hunting were done honestly, humanely, and with a proper regard for the amount of hunting pressure that the hunted species could stand, I certainly would have less objection to it than I feel toward much that I know goes on.

Why cannot a hunter who has, through his own skill, bagged a wolf in a fair hunt be satisfied with the feat, with the pelt or trophy or the demonstration of his stamina or woodsmanship, with the recreation he may have gotten from the hunting? Why can he not consider that he has enjoyed a privilege, without pouring out words about ridding the land of a killer? And, if, for any reason, wolves or anything else be killed as a control measure, why cannot it be done without man, the killer, berating non-human creatures as being unfit to live?

*

To reiterate the thesis of this chapter: Man needs to do some growing up. This need is manifested, among other ways, by the emotional unreason he tends to show toward the behavior of wild creatures. The immoderations and inconsistencies in his attitude toward wolves or other predatory or competing species are particularly revealing of lack of maturity.

The bounds of knowledge should not be considered merely as something set by professional groups. Trained minds are not always free from biases, and training is only as good as the teachers and the receptivity of students make it. Knowledge must still be judged on the basis of whether a given person has the information necessary to justify conclusions, whether he has the ability and intention to follow evidence where it leads and whether he can distinguish between what he knows and what he does not know.

My own lack of confidence in the results of public thought on animal populations and related subjects does not mean that I would discourage public thought about such things. Very definitely, what I am trying to do is to encourage more and better thinking—not necessarily thinking that agrees with mine in all or even most respects, but thinking that takes realities into account. So far as I am concerned, anyone is entitled to a respectful hearing to the extent that he deserves it, but he will have to do better than to repeat old misconceptions and to attempt to speak authoritatively on topics outside of his fields of competence.

Man does desperately need to grow up. His claims to conquests of Nature are farcical in the perspective of the problems converging upon him. Modern refinements and gadgets notwithstanding, he is still much a savage who wants to impose his domination where he wishes and make it stick.

He certainly has gained physical power. As a species, he now can obliterate nearly anything that he can reach. He can build or destroy as no other inhabitants of this earth have done before. Within wide limits, he has, figuratively, attained a good share of the stature and thunderbolts of the Olympian Gods he thought up centuries ago. What is wrong is that his is still too much the psychology of the Olympian Gods whom he originally invested with pettiness and jealousies, primitive motivations, and whimsical concepts of justice.

And, there is man figuratively sitting on Olympus with his hands full of thunderbolts, draining marshes, damming rivers, flying supersonic planes, and inflicting his vengeance upon wolves for being wolves. There is man, whose social and ecological impacts have become increasingly out of proportion to his responsibility. There he is, far from being mature enough to toss thunderbolts in every direction; needing more than anything else to learn to live, with the intelligence, dignity, restraint, and goodness that he somewhere has in him.

Paul Errington, ca. 1955, courtesy of the Special Collections Department,
Iowa State University Library.

Going On from Some Reflections
about the Dog in the Manger

The case against the dog in the manger has a fine simplicity in the fable as we read it. Its patness leaves the reader nothing to fumble over. Only an ugly, unsociable mutt would persist in lying in the manger and not letting the ox eat, especially since the dog could not eat the hay, himself. This was selfishness of the worst kind, a selfishness that went beyond mere me-first or what-is-in-it-for-me or any kind of gainful selfishness. It was selfishness going to the point of not having a point. It was not the conduct to be expected of a nice, socially well-adjusted dog, nor the conduct that nice, socially well-adjusted people could be expected to approve.

Furthermore, the case against the dog and for the ox was most elementary, open and shut, in that only one value was accorded any standing: the food. The dog could not have eaten the straw but the ox could have, if the dog had permitted it to have done so.

There is a further supposition that the dog would not have found it disadvantageous to have withdrawn from the manger so that the ox could have eaten. Any possibility that the manger might have had special value to the dog is not developed in the fable.

I shall not attempt to prove that the poor dog might have been so much underfoot or driven about the premises, so distracted and perhaps even exhausted from serving its human master—perhaps serving as much in its own way as the ox had been serving in his—that it had to find relief for itself somewhere, even in the manger, where the ox wanted to eat. I admit that I do not know very much about the case except as the fable states it, subject to the biases of the teller. If there ever was any particular dog or manger or ox as the basis for the fable, I do not know why the dog picked out the manger for privacy, rather than the customary dog's retreat behind the stove or under the bed or behind or under or in or on top of something, somewhere else. I do not know whether the dog made a wise choice of the manger as anything to claim and defend as its own.

Maybe the dog does not have a defensible case. Maybe it just liked the feel of power, to make its presence felt, to take out spite on others, to be antisocial.

Maybe the moral of the fable is good enough as it stands, and maybe any further questions or comments or criticism would only represent straining.

But the fable is reminiscent of a complacent superficiality that is much too commonplace in discussions of values. The demonstrably practical or the consumer's goods almost always outweigh the subtler values when it comes to use of resources.

✻

According to the more literal versions of the land-use doctrine of the greatest good for the greatest number, wilderness values may be hard to justify, even when the need for outdoor recreation may be recognized. We may hear challenges as to how logical may be our grounds for reserving or hoping to reserve roadless areas in national forests or national parks for the mere dozens or perhaps hundreds of people who would be interested enough or hardy enough to go into them by foot paths or pack trails or canoe routes. These people are few compared with the thousands or millions who visit the national forests and parks with automobiles—and find their accommodations so congested and their highways so greatly in need of expansion. Frankly, we may be asked, are not the reach-primitive-Nature-under-your-own-power people just a bunch of cranks, anyway? Why should only the few have exclusive rights to the choicer views when so many more could also enjoy them if it were made convenient for them to drive there? Open up the backcountry and share what we have with everybody. That, we may be told, is the democratic, the American way.

✻

Sometimes, mass use may not be wholly incompatible with retention of at least a substantial part of the wilderness values of an area. The Quetico–Superior area of northeastern Minnesota and adjacent Ontario, visited by its thousands of canoeists annually, can have not only its roadless areas but can also be zoned against aircraft in order to preserve its wilderness privacy. The popularity of the area is surely the best safeguard for its perpetuation much as it now is. People incontestably like it, with no more commercialization and development than it already has. Large numbers of articulate voters would fight major incursions that might change its wilderness character. At the same time, the essential, more subtle values of the area hold up fairly well.

It is true that where people concentrate even there one can see the trash and the hacked trees and the usual unsightliness of human concentrations; but it does not take so very much effort for people in good health and normally capable of taking care of themselves to get off a few miles from the heavily used camp grounds and canoe routes. There, off to the side, it is still possible for one who seeks solitude to find it. One can get out of sight of other people, around some rocky or wooded neck of land, on the far side of bays or islands, among the irregularities of shore lines and hills and meandering waters. From a roadless area of a million acres and a primitive area of a third of a million more in the Superior National Forest, one can, if wishing to wander, go up into Canada to wander some more. Quetico–Superior seems to be a workable compromise between modern pressures and the salvation of something worth saving.

Nevertheless, Quetico–Superior stands as an exception in my experience. The voices that cry out in or on behalf of wildernesses may go unheard not because of lack of ears to hear them so much as because of the tumult of the expansionists. More often, mass use comes first in the criteria of values, and the less obtrusive natural values do not hold up in the competition, even when they may be those receiving the lip service.

And one does not need to look far in almost any community to find people to whom naturalness in plant-animal-soil relationships is distasteful, something to get rid of though the getting rid may involve work and expense.

There may be almost hereditary concepts of neatness. These may be manifested even by the straight lines and bare ground of old neatness cults still resisting modern methods of conserving soils in hill country. What looks best to someone's eyes may still be what determines the fate of the land, irrespective, in extreme cases, of whether ruin results. To some people, a marsh is always an eyesore, a woodlot has to be kept cleared of hollow or fallen trees or grape vines or briars. What is wild must never be allowed to look as if man did not have close control over it.

It is not always a matter of a community or people utilizing everything utilizable for the sake of subsistence. Cultural patterns of the poorest countries permit retaining flower gardens, shade trees, and lawns. They permit putting up bird boxes or hanging up a sheaf of grain for birds to eat. They permit non-utility decorations. They permit any number of little luxuries and an occasional rather big one. But, while these cultural patterns may even permit a substantial amount of thick brushy cover if it is put there and tended by the hand of man—especially if it consists of exotic shrubbery—anything native that is allowed to grow spontaneously may invite scorn and charges of shiftlessness, unless it is of the most obvious utility.

One tremendous obstacle in the preservation of natural values is that they must be defended chiefly on grounds of their cultural values to people who may seldom show awareness of wanting them or even appreciating what they are. When it comes to public appeal, wild and undisturbed Nature cannot compete with the bathing beaches and highways and the other manifestations of mass favor.

In part, a cultural pattern of this sort may be a carryover from old times when wilderness dominated the land. The role of wilderness as an enemy as well as raw material for conquest and exploitation may persist in the minds of many people who still dislike or fear being alone. Wilderness, to some, can still mean wasteland and desolation, if not personal menace; and its reassuring converse can still be people and what people do. Not long ago, I noted the response of a dinner guest—a cultivated lady and a very fine person—to pictures of a northern wilderness that I had selected for showing because of their exceptional beauty; to her, gregarious as she was, they were depressing.

(Fear of wild areas because of the dangers from lawless people should be distinguished from fear of wildness itself. Our American West had its peculiar threats for human life during the days of Indian warfare. Even up to recent times, some of the most magnificent wilderness in northern

Mexico remained unexploited by white men in part because of danger from the hostile Indians that held it. A Chinese friend—a naturalized American citizen—told me of the apprehension that he first felt when taking a vacation trip through some of the most beautiful country of our continent, for the reason that such places in his original homeland would have had bandits. After becoming reassured that the people of our wild lands were kindly and decent people, he could see the beauty of scenic wildernesses too. It is not the wilderness as wilderness that is at fault, when evil men use it for their purposes.)

✶

I know how hard it can be to make a living in a wilderness—or from land that is a long way from being in wilderness condition. It is no surprise to me that the people least appreciative of wilderness values include those who live in wildernesses—or in backwoods areas, or just out in the countryside somewhere. Granted, that people live in wilderness or backwoods or in rural communities by choice, because they like it there, I think that many—possibly most—live there because that is where they are, where they were born or raised or have relatives and friends or own property or know the essentials for getting along. Certainly, in my own wilderness and backwoods and rural experience, I have often enough heard expressed wishes to get out of this God-forsaken country or to bring in roads and industry and the rest of what some people call civilization and progress.

Indifference toward the not-so-easily-definable quality of natural wildness may be due either to people having no idea from any kind of experience that such a thing exists or to lack of personal responsiveness.

Aldo Leopold began the foreword of his celebrated book of essays, A Sand County Almanac, with a generalization that some people can live without wild things and some cannot. That is surely true. Among my own close friends and relatives are persons whose responsiveness to natural wildness must be minimal—I doubt if they ever wish to get farther away from a city than into a thoroughly tamed country estate, or a resort area, or a formal park. What matters to me is that they respect my interests in what is wild, as I respect theirs in what is not, so I have no trouble conceding that there should be a place for both of our kinds in a well-ordered world. As yet, we do not need to have conformity in all things.

I first discovered the wonder of wilderness through a few books in a public library. Although the concept I thus gained was not wholly realistic, it was motivation sufficient to make me want to go up north as a wilderness trapper. That is nothing that I am advocating for others, however. It only illustrates what may be tritely referred to as striking the responsive chord that is psychologically possible when a human being receives an impulse for which he is ready, either by his own psychological makeup, his previous conditioning, or both.

Many people do find themselves, sometimes gradually, sometimes suddenly—becoming converts of sorts as a result of moving experiences, of introductions to different ways of thinking. Once in a while, a brilliant and sincere leader such as Aldo Leopold can take much of the public with him in his efforts to make recreational development "a job, not of building roads into lovely country, but of building receptivity into the still unlovely human mind."

Aldo Leopold's own success as a leader in conservation thought could not have been possible without the minimum of receptivity on the part of the people that he influenced. He might not have been successful in the leadership that meant his greatness had he been born a couple of hundred or even a hundred years before his time, when in general, the American wildernesses were only for conquering and exploiting. He found people ready to listen to him in part because they were aware that something precious in outdoor values had been and was being lost, in part because he clarified their own deep feelings and put them in words.

I think of his descriptions of the love of wildness shown by people living in man-crowded parts of Europe, where spontaneous wildness has been so largely obliterated, where forests are planted in rows, streams flow through artificial channels, and where the game itself may be semidomesticated and managed somewhat as poultry or livestock. There, Nature conforms to human orderliness as much as man can make it. Where else would people who value spontaneous wildness look harder for it and be more delighted when they did find some of it?

This may be illustrated still more: According to my criteria of wildness, the wild lands along streams and the borders of fields and about the outskirts of my home city, Ames, Iowa, are fragmentary and overtamed; but, to a Dutch visitor on our Iowa State University campus, they held the greatest fascination. Recalling the impression I had of Holland as an almost continuous succession of immaculately kept towns and gardens on the one day that I drove through it, I could well appreciate the contrast. I could also appreciate his enthusiasm for some land in his own country in the process of being drained: It was remarkable as a very temporary weed patch. He had recorded in a series of pictures this unusual sight of plants growing as they would, without any human control. Holland is a beautiful country in its own way, but there is not much that is spontaneously wild about it.

On our North American side of the Atlantic, the diligent activities on behalf of the protection of Nature by individuals and organizations in eastern United States may be regarded as some indication of the interest that a considerable part of the public can show in lost and threatened natural values after it begins to realize close to home how far the attrition has gone. Even a century ago, movements dedicated to keeping some remaining parts of the state of New York "forever wild" and protected from human exploitation got substantial popular support; and there was other evidence that people saw and reacted against with positive measures of unrestricted human domination of the land.

Not so long ago, I read an article in a national magazine justifying a most shakily justifiable scheme of private interests to obtain control of some coveted public lands in the western states. The comment was made, with scornful overtones, that the people who lived in New York City rather than the westerners were the ones who obstructed efforts to put the public domain and national forests to more practical, money-making use. There seem always to be the terse, no-nonsense, handy rebuttals ready for throwing at anyone who gets in the way of an enterpriser making the well-known fast buck out of our remaining natural resources, especially as long as anything is defended on merely aesthetic grounds without mass backing of the voters.

Actually, why should a sensitive New Yorker who feels the lack of wild values at home not respond to threats against wild values in the still-beautiful, still-spacious west, where a local resident may still tire of looking at mountains and consider wide distances as only something to get through or over as quickly as possible with a motorcar or plane? Need the New Yorker have to know how tiresome it can become to be alternately frozen and roasted, dried out and soaked, year after year? Need he have to know in detail what a job it can be to pay bills and meet mortgages and send youngsters to school out of income from the home place, plus a rented tract up in the foothills or some grazing privileges in one of the national forests?

The New Yorker and the Washingtonian and the Bostonian and the other city people should still have decent rights and a share in the less tangible values that belong to their countrymen, all as citizens. Their right to safeguard what is theirs—and ours—as a public domain or national forest or anything else held in trust for the country as a whole should not be contingent upon economic advantage or mass support for their viewpoints. There remain, if nothing else, the ethical considerations of preserving what can be preserved of threatened outdoor values for posterity—the ethical considerations of thinking of posterity at all.

*

Frank Fraser Darling and I once had a conversation in which he elaborated on the thought that modern times and institutions were selecting for the types of people who could adapt well to crowding in suburbs and cities, whose tastes were conventional, and whose lives, in general, followed conformist patterns.

Recognition of the selection-force of such conformity and of the social and economic phenomena that lie back of it does not mean that it has to be endorsed as a good thing for everybody or as anything that dissenters must give in to.

As concern values that man tends to squeeze out by his crowding and exploitation, we can go back to the writings of antiquity and still find expressed something of the thoughts I am trying to express here. Even when human domination had made relatively slight impression upon most of the Earth's surface, people were aware of social consequences of crowding. In the Scriptures, wilderness is referred to as a place for wholesome meditation as well as a place having its dangers for bodies and souls. Certainly, there can be nothing evil, per se, about solitude when solitude is what is needed. Love of solitude and of wilderness values are not incompatible with good will toward man. A verse from Isaiah that has been widely quoted in support of wilderness preservation movements may be quoted once more: "Woe unto them that join house to house, that lay field to field, till there be no place, that they may be placed alone in the midst of the earth!"

The achievement of a fuller life, the good life, is not a new problem. I am sure that we can do better, however, if only by avoiding the more basic of mistakes. My emphasis in this book upon certain kinds of mistakes should not be construed as evidence of unawareness of other mistakes— or what I conceive to be other mistakes.

There has got to be a place left in our civilization for legitimate minority tastes, thinking, and efforts. I refer to nothing so shallow as someone wanting to be different just to be different, rejecting what is good just because other people like it. I am not defending the indiscriminate challenger, the posing intellectual. But, I think it important that people seeking the good life should have a fair chance for more than economic opportunity. A fair chance, in my estimation, implies right of choice and something to choose from, among values that are worth choosing.

Somewhere along the line, I think it must be recognized that majority rule in cultural matters does not necessarily represent democracy or the democratic process in a desirable sense. Maybe it can be stated without becoming too banal that, if there is to be leadership, it has to be more than giving the majority what it wants or thinks it wants. This may well take us up to unanswerable questions as to who should lead and how far and in what direction, but leadership, by its definition, must have its minority aspects. There must be a place for the exceptional in a society that is motivated by more than survival—and I believe that, in the long run, survival itself may require it.

Reconsideration of the thesis that the world's resources must be dedicated exclusively to subsistence could lead back to analogies with the cattle that have their psychological needs rather well satisfied by food and reproduction—though they still engage in a certain amount of fighting, play, and idle pursuits. We have places on earth where human populations also live with primary concern for food and reproduction, with or without the variants introduced by the fighting, the play, and the idle pursuits; and, whatever rating an unthinking plasticity may have in social survival, I still do not think that such is a satisfactory goal.

We can hope and work for something better than that.

Landforms of Iowa
Jean C. Prior

Of Men and Marshes
Paul L. Errington

Of Wilderness and Wolves
Paul L. Errington

Out Home
John Madson

*Prairies, Forests, and Wetlands: The Restoration of
Natural Landscape Communities in Iowa*
Janette R. Thompson

A Practical Guide to Prairie Reconstruction
Carl Kurtz

Prairie: A North American Guide
Suzanne Winckler

The Raptors of Iowa
Paintings by James F. Landenberger, Essays by Dean M. Roosa,
Jon W. Stravers, Bruce Ehresman, and Rich Patterson

*Restoring the Tallgrass Prairie: An Illustrated Manual for
Iowa and the Upper Midwest*
Shirley Shirley

Stories from under the Sky
John Madson

Take the Next Exit: New Views of the Iowa Landscape
Robert F. Sayre

Wildflowers and Other Plants of Iowa Wetlands
Sylvan T. Runkel and Dean M. Roosa

Wildflowers of the Tallgrass Prairie: The Upper Midwest
Sylvan T. Runkel and Dean M. Roosa